FINALLY . . .
ALL YOU NEED TO KNOW ABOUT SETTLING AN ESTATE

Discover the facts about:

*Pre-death Planning Techniques
*Probating the Estate
*Avoiding Fiduciary Liability
*Tangible Personal Property
*Government and Fringe Benefits
*Life Insurance
*Cash, Bank Accounts, and Listed Securities
*Real Estate
*Handling a Family Business
*Jointly Owned Property
*Trusts and Guardianships
*Debts and Expenses
*Inventorying the Assets
*State Death Taxes
*Gift-tax Returns
*Tax Elections
. . . and much, much more.

Complete with timetables and checklists, *How to Settle an Estate* is the only guide you will ever need!

CHARLES K. PLOTNICK, L.L.B., is an attorney in Montgomery County, Pennsylvania, and specializes in estate planning. He is professor of estate planning at Temple University in Philadelphia.

STEPHAN R. LEIMBERG, J.D., is professor of taxation and estate planning at the American College in Bryn Mawr, Pennsylvania.

HOW TO SETTLE AN ESTATE

A Manual for Executors and Trustees

Charles K. Plotnick, LL.B.
Stephan R. Leimberg, J.D.

A PLUME BOOK

PLUME
Published by the Penguin Group
Penguin Putnam Inc., 375 Hudson Street,
New York, New York 10014, U.S.A.
Penguin Books Ltd, 27 Wrights Lane,
London W8 5TZ, England
Penguin Books Australia Ltd, Ringwood,
Victoria, Australia
Penguin Books Canada Ltd, 10 Alcorn Avenue,
Toronto, Ontario, Canada M4V 3B2
Penguin Books (N.Z.) Ltd, 182–190 Wairau Road,
Auckland 10, New Zealand

Penguin Books Ltd, Registered Offices:
Harmondsworth, Middlesex, England

Published by Plume, an imprint of Dutton NAL,
a member of Penguin Putnam Inc.
Originally published in 1986 by Doubleday & Company, Inc.
A revised and updated edition was published in 1991 by
Consumers Union.

First Plume Printing, May, 1998
10   9   8   7   6   5   4

 REGISTERED TRADEMARK—MARCA REGISTRADA

Library of Congress Cataloging-in-Publication Data
  Plotnick, Charles.
    How to settle an estate : a manual for executors and trustees / Charles K. Plotnick,
  Stephan R. Leimberg.
      p.   cm.
    Previously published: Yonkers, N.Y. : Consumer Reports Books, 1991.
    Includes index.
    ISBN 0-452-27934-8
    1. Executors and administrators—United States.   2. Probate law and practice—
  United States.   3. Decedents' estates—United States.   I. Leimberg, Stephan R.
  II. Title.
  KF778.Z9P565   1998
  346.7305'2—dc21   97-32603
                                                                      CIP

Printed in the United States of America

PUBLISHER'S NOTE
This book is not intended to offer or be a substitute for professional or legal advice. If
legal or other professional advice or assistance is required, the services of a competent
professional person should be sought.

To my father, Benjamin Plotnick, who so thoroughly enjoyed being with us all for eighty years.

—Charles K. Plotnick

To my father, Edward Leimberg, who faithfully watered the money tree and fed the three-legged brown cow that gave chocolate milk.

—Stephan R. Leimberg

Contents

Preface

We wrote this book to tell you everything you need to know about how to settle an estate (or trust)—after the '97 Taxpayer Relief Act.

There are three reasons *How to Settle an Estate* is different than any other book on the subject:

First, this is a "no-holds-barred," honest look at the process you may not have obtained before. Rather than the "panic and panacea" approach ("terrible things will happen if you don't buy this book, rip out and fill out the forms, but all your problems will disappear in an instant with no thinking or outside help required if you do purchase this book"), you'll find a step-by-step, practical, objective consumers' view of the subject. Inside these covers you'll find out the truth about probate, taxes, and the psychological aspects of being an executor or administrator and what you need to do to protect yourself as an heir or beneficiary. You may even discover that the risks and responsibilities of being an executor outweigh the honor, and you may decide to decline. You may also decide that the person you've considered naming as your executor may not be capable of handling the tasks.

Second, rather than a quick "once over" treatment, this book will provide you with the detailed in-depth information to make considered, well-informed, intelligent decisions and ask the types of questions that will help you communicate more effectively (which often translates into less billable hours) with your attorney and other financial advisers. Unlike "fine print" books which are difficult to read and are written to impress rather than inform, or "picture" books which gloss over important details, this resource is both clear and comprehensive.

Third, rather than a "do-it-yourself" book, this is a " think-for-yourself" book. Rather than simplistic "ten-minute mentality" ("read this book and in ten minutes you'll know everything you need to know about settling an estate"), this book will give you the questions you need to ask to be an informed and pro-active executor, administrator, beneficiary, or heir.

How to Settle an Estate will help you save income, estate, generation-skipping, and other taxes at both the federal and state level. It is also a book that will give you many nontax techniques to protect yourself and those you love from both creditors and predators, and provide security and management protection for generations.

We suggest you read *How to Settle an Estate* slowly. Read the first five chapters in order. Then go through the table of contents and select the category that you are most interested in learning about or type of problem you'd like to solve. Use it constantly throughout the estate settlement process. We're sure you'll find this an invaluable and frequently used reference tool.

—Charles K. Plotnick, Esq.
Stephan R. Leimberg, Esq.

Introduction

The telephone rings. It's your Uncle Stanley's lawyer. Uncle Stanley has died and has named you the executor of his estate. The lawyer wants to meet with you as soon as possible to probate the estate and take care of certain details.

Of course, you are saddened by your uncle's death, but you are also flattered that Uncle Stanley has appointed you to this important position. After a short while, however, the realization begins to sink in that you have absolutely no idea what you are supposed to do.

You know generally that an executor is someone who handles the affairs of a deceased person, but you have no idea how to get the job done. In fact, not only are you unaware of the duties of an executor, you also do not know what your responsibilities will be to the other members of Uncle Stanley's family, to the creditors and other business associates, and to the state and federal government to which Uncle Stanley's estate may be responsible for death taxes.

The likelihood of being called on to act as executor, or personal representative, for a deceased friend or relative is quite high. When that time comes, we all hope that competent advisers will be available to help us. Nevertheless, the ultimate decisions and the responsibilities fall on the executors themselves.

This book provides specific information to help guide you

throughout your tenure in office. It is not written for the attorney, trust officer, accountant, or other adviser or professional executor (although in many instances it will be of considerable value to them), but rather to inform you, the lay executor, exactly what you are, or will be, required to do in order to handle the affairs of a deceased person properly. Because of the widespread interest today in revocable living trusts, we have included a chapter that explains the duties of a trustee in this situation.

Most important, the book discusses those intricate and potentially dangerous areas where the unwarned executor can become personally liable because of failure to act promptly and in the best interest of the estate and its beneficiaries. This means that courts can even require you to reach into your own pocket to pay for errors, omissions, or tardiness.

While the book covers almost every facet of handling an estate that you might encounter, it is not a substitute for competent advisers. In fact, we have devoted an entire chapter to the problem of how to select and when to use the other members of the estate settlement team (as well as how to negotiate fees with them *before* they begin working for the estate). Familiarize yourself with this chapter as quickly as possible so that you will know if and when an attorney, accountant, appraiser, real estate agent, stockbroker, or any other adviser may be warranted by the specific facts of the estate that you are handling. Nowhere is the adage "He who has himself for an attorney has a fool for a client" more true than in the case of the do-it-yourself executor.

We also discuss the matters of insurance, government benefits, and state and federal taxes. This information was accurate at the time the book was prepared and contains references to the major 1997 tax law changes, but tax laws and government interpretation of those laws change frequently. Therefore, before filing any tax returns or making any decisions based on tax laws, be certain that you are utilizing the very latest information.

After reading this book, you will be able to expedite the handling of an estate (or settle a revocable living trust). If you carry out our suggestions, you will perform the work involved more efficiently and with much greater benefit to the family, business associates, and other beneficiaries of the decedent (or grantor). If you follow our checklists in the Appendix, you will also minimize or eliminate the risk of becoming personally liable for mistakes in judgment or untimely filing of returns, for making improper investment decisions, or for failing to follow the accepted procedures in handling the specific assets of the estate (or trust). In short, this book should help you perform the duties of an executor as well as possible.

1 The Personal Representative: A Job Description

In most instances, when a person dies owning property of any real value, it is necessary to appoint someone to administer the estate. That person (it could be one or several persons, a bank or trust company, or both) who acts for, or "stands in the shoes of," the deceased is called the *personal representative*. The duties and responsibilities of the personal representative, and even the title of the personal representative, may change depending on the state laws and circumstances involved, but the need for such a person (or persons) is shared by all. Consider, for example, the following situation:

Tom and Irene Anderson were a married couple in their early forties with two children—Ted, age 21, and Sally, 19. Tom had a small consulting business, and Irene was a high school teacher. One night Tom was killed in an automobile accident.

As a result of his death, Tom's company did not open for work. Yet someone had to be available to handle or terminate the work in progress, pay the outstanding bills and salaries, collect the outstanding obligations, and make the larger decision about what ultimately would happen to the business.

Tom had other outstanding obligations apart from his business interests. Someone had to settle these accounts, as well as to collect any outstanding debts owed to Tom personally.

There can be other issues for the personal representative to handle aside from those involving financial considerations. For example, Tom might have had a child from a previous marriage for whom he was paying support. There could have been an outstanding agreement under which Tom, or Tom and Irene, was to purchase real estate, with the settlement or closing date after the date of Tom's death.

Even if Tom's affairs were precisely in order and there were no outstanding personal or business debts, a personal representative might have been necessary to distribute Tom's assets among Irene and the children. If Tom had any property in his name alone, in all likelihood a personal representative would have had to transfer the property from Tom to his wife and/or children. A bank account in Tom's name, for example, could not, in most circumstances, be closed out by anyone except the duly appointed personal representative of Tom's estate.

There are, in fact, few situations in which property of a decedent can be transferred at death without the appointment of a personal representative.

The Executor or Executrix

The title of the personal representative depends on the method by which he or she (or it, in the case of a bank or trust company) was selected or appointed. If a deceased specifically names a person or institution to act for him or her in his or her will, and if the will is accepted as valid, the named personal representative is known as the *executor* (male) or *executrix* (female). In cases when more than one individual or an individual and an institution are appointed to act, the joint designation is usually *executors*. Corporate entities (banks and trust companies) are also called executors.

(For the sake of simplicity, in most cases we have used *executor* interchangeably with *personal representative* to refer to a person of either sex.)

The Administrator or Administratrix

If the deceased left no valid will, and therefore has failed to designate his or her personal representative, a personal representative (called an *administrator*) is appointed by the Probate Office or the Register of Wills office having jurisdiction over the decedent's estate. This usually takes place in the state and county of the decedent's domicile. In most instances, state statutes stipulate the person who is entitled to be the administrator.

Usually, the order of preference is similar to the order in which an estate passes to the family of someone who dies without a will. In other words, the spouse or adult children are usually named administrator. It is possible, however, that a more distant family member could be named, or even creditors or other strangers to the estate and to the decedent. If the decedent failed to take advantage of his right to name a personal representative, and if no persons with close relationships are available, the court, in its discretion, might appoint someone unknown to the decedent and unfamiliar with his affairs. This is often the case when the court is concerned about possible conflicts of interest or the rights of creditors or other beneficiaries.

Suppose, for example, there is an obvious conflict between two brothers who are in line to be appointed administrators, or coadministrators (equal in right). Assume this conflict is brought to the attention of the court having jurisdiction over the appointment. The court, in order to avoid the potential conflict and the resultant complex problems, might appoint someone or some institution to handle the decedent's affairs in a manner that does not favor one brother over the other. The results of such an action, however, might not coincide with the wishes of the decedent.

Duties and Responsibilities

When a person dies, her property must be collected. After debts, taxes, and expenses are paid, the remaining assets are distributed to the decedent's beneficiaries. Distribution is determined by the person's will, or the *intestacy laws* (laws that govern the distribution of your estate if you die without a valid will) of the state in which the decedent was living at the time of death. It is the executor's or the administrator's responsibility to collect and distribute the assets and to pay the death taxes and expenses of the decedent.

While many executors and administrators perform these designated tasks in an expeditious and prudent manner, this is not always the case. Moreover, state law usually holds the personal representative to the standard of care of a "reasonable, prudent individual" under all circumstances. What is reasonable and prudent to the executor when performing his tasks, however, is not always so to the beneficiaries, especially retrospectively.

The various decisions to be made by the personal representative—for example, whether to sell or hold certain securities, what rate of return to seek on investments, and whether to carry on or sell the decedent's business—can often cause complaints by the beneficiaries. Sometimes complaints escalate into lawsuits against the executor(s).

If the court feels that the personal representative has not acted reasonably and in the best interests of the estate and beneficiaries, the executor or administrator can be *surcharged*, which means that the executor is personally liable for undue mistakes made in the administration of the decedent's estate.

Fees

A question often arises concerning the fees to which a personal representative is entitled for services rendered to the estate. The first place to check is the statutory law of the state where the estate is probated. Some states have standard fixed fees. There are also local county rules and customs that govern what the personal representative is entitled to charge.

Professional executors such as banking and trust institutions advertise fixed-fee schedules. However, with estates in excess of $1 million it may be possible to negotiate a lower fee. These negotiations occur between the prospective executor and the person making the initial designation (the individual desiring to name the institution as personal representative in her will). An attorney who specializes in estate administration may be helpful in negotiating a lower fee for a large estate.

In all cases, the executor or administrator is entitled to reasonable compensation for services. Fees should not be determined solely on the basis of the assets of the decedent; they should also take into account the nature of the work involved, the time spent, the complexity of the problems, the professional background and competence of the executor, and the ultimate results and benefits passed on to the heirs.

For example, two executors might be handling different estates, each having a value of $100,000. The first estate might have consisted of five certificates of deposit with a total value of $100,000. The principal duties of the executor would have been to contact the bank, have all the certificates of deposit placed in one estate account, pay the necessary taxes, and distribute the balance to the widow.

The asset in the estate of the second executor was, let's say, a retail shoe store owned by the decedent and valued at $100,000. It was necessary for the executor to decide whether to terminate the business immediately or keep it open so that it could be sold as a going concern. The executor had to review the insurance; watch the cash register; be present at the store to make sure that the estate received the full value from any sales; locate a purchaser and negotiate the terms of the purchase; then sell the business, allocate the proceeds among the beneficiaries, pay the taxes, and file an elaborate accounting with the court in order to be discharged formally from his duties.

In the first instance, the time spent as executor would have been minimal. In the second case, however, the executor might easily have spent hundreds of hours performing his duties. Remuneration for services should bear a reasonable relationship to the time spent as well as the quality of work and results achieved.

The personal representative should keep a detailed record of time spent, services performed, and expenses paid on behalf of the estate. Furthermore, the executor should make periodic written progress reports to the beneficiaries and, if the situation permits, submit periodic bills for services rendered.

In any event, *before* any work is begun, negotiate and settle (in writing) the issue of fees based on an estimate of complexity and other issues.

Psychologically, many beneficiaries have their shares "spent" before they receive them. The subsequent announcement that the personal representative expects to receive a significant portion of that amount for services performed doubtless will be met with some serious resistance. This is especially true if the beneficiaries were not periodically apprised of the work being performed and had no prior knowledge of the anticipated amount of the personal representative's fee. It is much easier to have a frank discussion of fees early on when the beneficiaries are aware of the complexities of the personal representative's duties and are anxious to have someone else take on this responsibility.

When the personal representative is an immediate member of the family, problems about fees are less likely to occur. For example, if the widow is the executrix and the sole beneficiary, it might be far more advantageous for her to receive the net proceeds of the estate as an inheritance rather than to charge an executor's fee that will ultimately come out of her own pocket. The executor's commissions or fees are taxable for income-tax purposes, and often at a higher rate than if the sole tax involved is the state inheritance tax—or even, in some instances, the federal estate tax (see Chapter 20).

Finally, there is the question of the division of the fee when two or more individuals are serving as coexecutors or coadministrators. When they are individuals, the fee usually is divided equally (although in a few states, such as New York, *each* executor could receive a full commission). But when a corporate executor is serving with an individual coexecutor, courts often award the corporate executor (bank or trust company) a higher percentage. For example, in Pennsylvania the bank would receive its usual fee and the individual executor would be awarded one half of the bank's fee.

Of course, if the decedent has specifically provided for the payment of fees in the will, the courts in most instances are guided by the decedent's wishes.

2 The Selection Process

Knowledge of financial matters is not necessarily the most important qualification of an executor. It is always possible for an executor, if lacking knowledge in certain areas, to learn more about the subject. Selection of a person (or persons) who can firmly adhere to sound values is also important. Likewise, personal integrity and devotion to duty should be valued attributes, although these are often difficult to measure objectively. That is why, in the final analysis, the human factor plays such an important part in the evaluation of the executor's functions.

For example, if two banks of comparable size are named executors for two estates, and the estates' assets are fairly similar, the reactions of the beneficiaries to the performance of the executor might be based solely on the beneficiaries' personal contacts with the individual or individuals at the bank administering the estate. The subjective perception of the amount of personal attention received by the beneficiaries, as well as the objective record of how the estates' assets had been handled, would certainly play a significant role in the beneficiaries' evaluations of the banks' performance.

No list of standards, therefore, can be complete unless due consideration is given to the personal image of the executor as an incorruptible and caring individual in regard to the psychological as well as financial needs of the beneficiaries.

Competence

Although it would seem obvious that an executor's "competence" must be paramount on any list of qualifications, this factor is often overlooked because of the sometimes emotional nature of the appointment.

Nancy, a dynamic and worldly business owner who ran an empire of interlocking businesses requiring the greatest amount of expertise, named her husband as her executor. Unfortunately, he could barely balance the family's checkbook. The results of Nancy's decision (based on emotions rather than logic) were disastrous. And the negative impact of her decision fell mainly on the spouse whom she had intended to protect.

Competence in a general sense is not necessarily measured by an awareness of all the decedent's personal affairs or the intricacy of the decedent's business. A competent executor is one who can analyze the affairs as quickly as possible under the circumstances, determine what facets of the estate can be handled within the bounds of her knowledge and capabilities, and then secure professional assistance in those areas in which it is needed.

The Best Interests of the Beneficiaries

One of the primary causes of friction between executor and beneficiaries is the failure on the part of the executor to appreciate the multifaceted aspects of the appointment and its corresponding obligations.

Executors who perform their duties in an objective vacuum, without giving due consideration to the interests of the beneficiaries, often find that they have put out the fire only after the building has been destroyed. While it is true that the executor must "stand in the shoes" of the decedent and attempt to perform his duties in a fashion similar to the manner in which the decedent would have performed them, the executor's ultimate responsibility is to handle the estate and preserve and transfer its assets in the most efficient manner possible under all attending circumstances.

To put the matter in its harshest light, few children ever think of suing their father because he does not give them the gifts or allowances to which they feel they are entitled. If the children are adults, however, and a stranger is handling their father's money, the protective aura of parenthood is no longer present. The executor who recognizes that she is dealing with individuals with their own opinions, concerns, and feelings is in a position to discharge the duties of the office with minimal likelihood of interference or hostility on the part of the beneficiaries.

Suppose a 19-year-old son of the decedent insists that the executor immediately release funds to enable him to buy a sports car because he must have transportation to college. If the executor determines that transportation is in fact essential, and that the respective share to which the son is entitled is enough to pay for adequate but not luxurious transportation, the recommendation of a modest automobile probably is the preferred solution. This is clearly in the best interest of the beneficiary and would be likely to receive the court's support should the issue be legally contested.

Many important decisions that an executor is called on to make can have lasting effects on the beneficiaries and can require more than merely financial knowledge. The decision whether or not to sell a business, for instance, can be greatly affected by the potential interest and active participation of the beneficiaries in the business. Whether to place securities in investments with guaranteed returns or with long-term growth potential is also dependent to some extent on the ages and needs of the beneficiaries. You must keep in mind that even though you were in essence hired by the decedent, you are in fact working on behalf of the estate's beneficiaries.

Knowledge of Beneficiaries' Needs and Subject Matter of Estate

Some personal knowledge of the subject matter of the estate and of the specific needs of the beneficiaries will be valuable to an executor. If one of the principal assets of the estate was a business owned by the decedent, and if the executor was also active in the business, the advantage to the estate of continuity and experience can be translated quickly into dollars and cents. A prior familiarity also is of considerable benefit if the decedent's assets were varied and located in different areas.

Prior knowledge of the needs of the beneficiaries is extremely helpful. They may be as specific as having money always available to purchase insulin for a diabetic child or to provide an elderly woman with cash for the daily necessities of life—expenses that may have been paid previously by the decedent.

Experience

You can read 20 books on how to ski, but until you actually come down the side of a mountain, you are not a skier. Experience is of similar value to the personal representative. The brightest 21-year-old son or daughter, or the most intelligent spouse, may lack experience in handling a decedent's affairs. Until they have to make decisions of major significance and have acquired the necessary experience, they lack a vital characteristic of a good executor. Therefore, the decedent who chooses an experienced executor has given his heirs a distinct edge.

Professional executors, banks, and trust companies are in the business of knowing how to collect the decedent's assets. They have separate departments to handle businesses and evaluate them, supervise and sell real estate, and analyze the relative merits and demerits of securities.

If the decedent has nominated as executor an accountant or stockbroker with expertise in all or some of these areas, a similar advantage often can be passed on to the estate.

But even though there is no substitute for experience, intelligent individuals who have the ability to obtain the necessary information and experience, as well as the time and inclination to administer the estate, can still do a credible and often outstanding job.

Familiarity with the Decedent's Business

There is no asset more difficult to administer than an active business. When the decedent has made plans for the disposition of the business, your task is greatly simplified. For example, assume the decedent had been in a two-person partnership and had signed a business buy/sell agreement. Suppose the agreement provided that on the death of either partner, the surviving partner would be obligated to buy— and the decedent's executor would be obligated to sell—the decedent's interest for a predetermined price. As executor you would only have to transfer the decedent's business interest to the survivor. In return you would collect the agreed-upon payment. If the surviving partner owned insurance on the life of the decedent, then the surviving partner could pay the proceeds of the policy to you in return for the decedent's business interest. You would then have cash, which could be handled easily as part of the estate.

If no such arrangements were made, as executor you would assume whatever role the decedent had in the business. Depending on the circumstances of the appointment and the nature of the business, you could either continue or terminate the business. If the decedent had a will specifically providing for the continuation of the business, you could perform her duties without the pressure of finding an immediate buyer. If, on the other hand, you were acting without a will, in most cases it would be advisable to secure the approval of the court before continuing to run the business.

Without knowledge of the details of the business, or without expertise in the area involved, you are obviously working under a considerable handicap. Even a professional executor, such as a bank or trust company, may not have the necessary expertise if the business is a specialized one.

Clearly, the executor who has an understanding of the inner workings of the decedent's business has a tremendous edge over the neophyte executor (see Chapter 16).

Management Experience

A person who chooses a bank or trust company to handle his affairs is opting for the financial experience of these large fiduciary institutions. They have the background and the personnel and have managed many similar estates.

In the same vein, someone who selects as executor a member of her family who operates a large business is trying to obtain management experience for her beneficiaries.

The president of the United States often selects, as members of his cabinet, individuals who have had management experience as chief executives of large corporations. Governors and senators running for office often stress their prior management experience. It stands to reason that someone with management experience would be in a better position to step in and take control of a decedent's affairs.

In most instances the executor controls the assets of the estate and works with the beneficiaries and various supporting personnel, such as lawyers, insurance agents, stockbrokers, and accountants. Therefore, the personal representative must be able to function as kingpin of an administrative management team.

Investment Knowledge

If an individual's estate comprises primarily investment-type securities, he would be well advised to select a personal representative with investment knowledge. Again, banks and trust companies figure prominently in this category, since they have entire departments geared specifically to following market conditions and advising their clients—both estates and others—regarding current market trends and investment possibilities.

Individuals who have had long and profitable relationships with stockbrokers and the like might want to include these advisers in their estate plan—perhaps as advisers to their designated executor.

An executor without extensive investment knowledge should secure the services of skilled advisers and investment personnel. When the estate consists of constantly fluctuating securities, lack of action can be just as serious as improper investments. The executor who retains a security in the estate for many years and watches its value decrease, or else ignores it, can be subject to personal liability despite the fact that she took no action in regard to that security.

Ability to Serve

Make no mistake about it: The duties and responsibilities of a personal representative can require considerable time and effort. (Most moderate estates take at least six to nine months to settle. Larger or more complex estates may take two or more years.) If the executor does not have adequate time, the heirs can suffer. If the executor has only limited time, a bank or trust company should be asked to serve as well.

Lack of Conflicts

Always consider the objectivity and impartiality of the party selected as executor. The decedent might have felt that an older child would be well qualified to manage his affairs. While this might very well be true, a conflict could arise between the personal interest of that older child and her younger siblings or their mother.

An estate owner might have chosen a business associate to act as a personal representative, without considering the effect that the associate's handling of the business might have on the apportionment of profits or proceeds between the associate and the family. It is therefore advisable to take steps in advance to prevent potential conflicts. If children are chosen as coexecutors, it might be advantageous to have a bank as the third executor, so that any tie votes could be broken by an independent third party. In the same vein, it might be more advantageous to have the third independent party act as sole executor, thus reducing the possibility of conflict.

Proximity to Estate and Beneficiaries

Another major consideration is the proximity of the proposed executor to the estate and to the beneficiaries. A close relative living thousands of miles away is sometimes appointed by the decedent in order to ensure that he will act in the best interests of the beneficiaries. In spite of its apparent merits, such an appointment fails to consider that the executor will be far removed physically from the beneficiaries and the assets of the estate. It would be better for the decedent to appoint a local executor—with the distant relative keeping in close touch with the estate and perhaps serving as an unofficial adviser. If young children were involved, and it was the decedent's intention to have them live with that distant relative, then the relative could be appointed "guardian of the person" of the children and therefore would have the right to keep close watch over the interests.

Added Insurance—the Lawyer

While few executors have all the attributes described, a good working relationship with an attorney experienced in estate matters and knowledgeable about the client's family and business can help in the performance of her duty. The services of such an attorney, and even her name, can be recommended to the executor in the will itself. This gives the decedent added assurance that the provisions of her will are likely to be carried out in a manner that is most advantageous for the beneficiaries.

A skilled and knowledgeable attorney who is familiar with the decedent's affairs and wishes can more than make up for an executor's lack of knowledge and experience. While in most states the executor makes the final decision in appointing an attorney for the estate (and, if he is uncomfortable with the attorney who drew the will, should exercise his right to select counsel), in most cases the executor should retain the attorney recommended in the decedent's will. Before the attorney begins the work, negotiate his legal fee and obtain a satisfactory written explanation of how the fee will be determined.

3 | What an Executor Must Know About the Psychological Aspects of Death and Dying

As executor your most difficult task may be dealing with the survivors; you may even be one yourself. Therefore, you must learn not only to face facts and figures, but also learn to face faces. A good executor should have the skill and sensitivity to work with people who are in shock, disorganized, and experiencing volatile emotions. These emotions may include guilt, loss, loneliness, and depression.

The Dying Person—Understanding the Grief of Survivors

If you understand how grief is experienced by a dying person, you will have a much better grasp of the way survivors handle that awesome experience.

Basically, a dying person experiences five stages of grief: (1) denial, (2) anger, (3) bargaining, (4) depression, and (5) acceptance.

Denial. This is a temporary defense. At almost any age, there is the "it can't happen to me" reaction to thoughts of death. Denial is the healthy route we use to sidestep our mortality. It is the means by which a dying person deals with the painful and uncomfortable fact of impending death.

Anger. This is the way a dying individual (and often close relatives, who can adopt the same emotions as the dying person) expresses powerful emotional trauma. This anger usually has little or nothing to do with what the individual's loved ones have done or not done—they just happen to be convenient targets.

"Why did you let me down?" "Why didn't you do more?" Anger is often directed—without reason—at doctors, friends, relatives, and estate-planning advisers. If such comments are directed toward you, it is important not to respond with your own hostility or just walk away. That will only tend to justify and magnify the anger. Patience and understanding of the incredible pain and loneliness of the dying person is the best course of action.

An executor should be particularly aware of the client who unreasonably takes out his anger on one or more family members and subsequently makes a vital estate-planning decision based on that anger. This may lead to reduced legacies or elimination of heirs—decisions totally inconsistent with the client's past desires. A sudden and last-minute change of beneficiary, executor, or trustee for no reason is an indication of this problem.

Bargaining. This is the "let me live one more year and I'll be good to my wife/husband/children" or "I'll donate money to my church/synagogue" plea. Bargaining is an attempt on an emotional level to postpone what is inevitable on the intellectual and physical levels.

Depression. This is a common response to the actual loss of health or use of part of the body. It is a preparatory measure to the impending loss of life.

Acceptance. This is the final stage. The dying person is devoid of feelings and usually expresses an increased desire and need for sleep.

Survivors often experience these same symptoms of grief while the person is dying and, almost always, directly afterward.

Effect of Death on the Survivors

A breadwinner's death results in drastic changes in the life of a family. These include loss of security and loss of the survivors' dependence on the decedent. Survivors are required to take over many of the decedent's roles and tasks, accept a strange new schedule, and shoulder what are sometimes actually (and almost always perceived as) harsh and awesome new responsibilities. This often means a sudden involvement in business and financial affairs.

In every substantial estate of a male decedent, the widow (if there is one) has major roles to perform. Yet in most situations she lacks previous exposure or training to function efficiently in handling legal, business, probate, and taxation problems. She has not learned how to do things that will certainly be her responsibility. Nor has she learned to avoid action that she should not even attempt.

Ironically, at the very time the widow is first involved in these matters, she is in the worst possible frame of mind. She is depressed, unhappy, and insecure, and her entire social life has changed. Friends, relatives, and close family are there to comfort her for a few days, but then they return to their normal lives. The widow is left—alone and lonely, confronted with strange and complex legal duties.

Less often it is the *man* who survives. Studies show that widowers face even more serious emotional problems: Men seldom have a support system to hold them up—and *keep* them up.

Survivors experience guilt for what they did or did not do in life to or for the deceased, or simply embarrassment or guilt for having lived while the deceased died. Survivors may feel guilty because the death of the deceased has relieved them from heavy burdens that were emotionally and financially draining. At the same time the bereaved may feel anger at being deserted and left to face life's problems alone.

Perhaps the most difficult of all emotions to overcome is a deep sense of loneliness and resentment at being left alone. There are 10 million widows in our country—one out of every six women over the age of 21. A study of more than 1,700 widows showed that loneliness is the single most serious problem of widowhood. The second most serious problem is the financial pressure of raising children alone.

So, besides their emotional problems, families are likely to have financial burdens, or at least concern about how they will pay current bills and continue to function. This in turn creates incredible psychological pressures.

The whirlwind shock of sudden change is a crisis with which many family members feel particularly unable to cope. Often a real (and almost always a perceived) imbalance exists between the difficulty and importance of the problems and the resources available to deal with them. Professional psychiatric and psychological help may be required.

What the Will and Probate Mean to the Survivors

The will and probate fulfill important functions in the process of emotional repair known as "mourning." The will is the last communication of the deceased. It has unique emotional implications because the decedent states in it many of his feelings about the bereaved. Of course, his thoughts are usually not implicit in the words used. But in terms of *who* receives property, *how* that property is to be received, and *when* it will be received, the testator has expressed approval (or disapproval), gratitude (or revenge), and confidence (or lack of it). Likewise, the terms of a will may emphasize that the testator recognized one child's need or another child's due. Or the testator may have favored a blood relative over someone who is loved but not related (or vice versa).

What the testator meant to say when she wrote the will may not be what is understood by the beneficiaries. For example, a devoted but less needy son who receives less than a proportionate part of his father's estate may resent the injustice of being slighted in favor of his more needy brother.

What Can—and Should—the Executor Do?

One of the positive results of the estate-planning process is to give survivors a feeling of control, a sense of usefulness, and the satisfaction of completing the decedent's (and their own) unfinished business. As executor you can increase the family members' dignity by empowering them with as much control as possible. It is not enough to give survivors a voice; you must also give them a listener. Only then can they be active participants in the decision-making process. Hopelessness and depression are precipitated and exacerbated when individuals can't (or perceive they can't) act.

Any steps you take to bring all family members into the decision-making process will relieve their feelings of helplessness. The death of a loved one will be experienced as less absurd, and may become more tolerable, if the family knows that the life of the deceased had meaning. So it is vital to do what you can to give the family a sense of pride in what the deceased accomplished.

Accumulating an estate, buying life insurance, and preparing the will and trust are like buying a car, filling it with gas, and expecting that a spouse or child who has never been in a car can get in and drive. We can't, of course, make survivors into mechanics, but the more you can do to explain what comes next and how the family can take charge, the better off they will be.

4 | How and When to Use the Other Members of the Estate Team

Decedent's Appointments

Coexecutors

In many instances people select more than one individual to serve as personal representatives under their wills. A husband can name his wife and his bank as coexecutors; a widow might appoint her two surviving children. If all the executors named in the will choose to serve, there is an obvious need for cooperation.

An executor named in a will is not required to accept the appointment. It is not unusual for one or more of several named executors (if there is more than one, each is a coexecutor) to decide for some reason that they wish to "renounce" their right to serve. This is usually done by filing a *renunciation*—a form setting forth their wish not to serve—with the local probate office. This might be done, for example, when a brother and sister are named coexecutors and the brother lives thousands of miles away. When there are close family ties and no possibility of conflicts, this could greatly expedite the handling of the estate and also reduce expenses. Some states, for example, require the out-of-state executor to post bond even if the will stipulates otherwise. Distance and travel always cause problems and delays in decision making that could be avoided with a local executor. Sometimes people name multiple executors so as not to exclude a member of a group, such as a child; if this is the only purpose, then renunciation might very well be in order.

In other cases coexecutors are chosen because each has something specific to offer. If, for example, a bank was appointed to serve as coexecutor with a spouse, two functions are fulfilled: The expertise of the bank is coupled with the spouse's knowledge of the family's situation, and in this instance there is no need for a renunciation. Usually the bank or other selected professional will perform most of the detail work, and the family member serves as consultant with regard to any important decisions. The family member is thereby relieved of the day-to-day tasks.

Major decisions involving the estate should always be made jointly by all the executors serving as such, because errors in judgment or other problems involving the estate will be the ultimate responsibility of all the executors. It is therefore essential for the executors to be in agreement on all major issues. Individuals who anticipate possible conflicts among their executors might make provision for this in the will. People have named individuals and banks as executors, and then given one or the other precedence in case of disagreement. Likewise, people have appointed either one or three persons to serve as executors, so that there can be a unanimous decision or at least a majority decision in every instance.

Consult with your coexecutor on any major decision, and make certain that each coexecutor is continually advised of the day-to-day handling of the estate. When one executor has an obvious field of expertise—for example, if an individual appoints his son and his own accountant to serve as coexecutors—then the expertise obviously should be utilized to its fullest advantage. In this case the nonexpert needs to be fully aware of what is going on. If you are the nonexpert, remember that ignorance of the law is no excuse. If you accept the appointment, an obligation goes along with it. Having a coexecutor can relieve the burden of handling all of the estate's affairs yourself—but the responsibility always remains on your shoulders.

Trustee

A trust is an arrangement through which the title to property is held by one party, the trustee, who is required to use that property for one or more other parties, the beneficiaries.

A testator might select a trustee to manage the property of one or more beneficiaries of his estate. Trustees are often appointed to handle funds for minor children or incompetent persons. Trustees are also appointed in order to take advantage of tax-saving devices such as a marital-deduction trust or a qualified terminable-interest trust.

Trustees are often chosen because they are equipped to handle the property in question. This is true in situations where the decedent has named a bank, a trust company, or a competent family member or other professional to act as trustee. In most situations the decedent will have advised the trustee in advance of the appointment. Trusts that are created in a will are called *testamentary trusts* and do not take effect until death. However, the decedent might have set up a trust during her lifetime, in which case it would be called a *living trust* or *inter vivos trust*. If there is a living trust, some of the assets from the estate often "pour over" from the will into the trust that is already established. For example, a testator might leave all his personal property (furniture, jewelry, automobiles, and so on) at his death to his wife. He might then provide in his will that the residue of his estate (the rest of his property) is payable to the trust that he had established with the XYZ Bank during his lifetime. Thus, property passing under his will is poured over into the living trust.

In cases when estate moneys are to be paid to trusts for

beneficiaries, the money or property must first be administered by the executor. It is your duty and responsibility to administer the estate, and to turn the assets of the estate over to the trustee only after the administration has been completed (see chapters 29 and 30). Therefore, in most instances trustees require a formal accounting from the executor so that they will know exactly what property they are receiving. The trustees will also know the exact amount of the administrative costs taken out of the share to which the beneficiary of the trust would otherwise have been entitled. Since this is the case, be sure to keep accurate records in order to prepare a proper accounting for the trustee, and keep in frequent touch with the trustee in regard to the progress of the estate. While calling on the trustee's services usually is not required during the administration of the estate, there often are situations when this should be considered.

An individual might select her spouse to act as executor but choose a bank or trust company to handle the property in the residue of the estate for the spouse and children. In these cases, especially when important business or investment decisions are to be made, it can be beneficial to all concerned if you consult with the trustee and utilize the trustee's services for investment advice, evaluation of the decedent's business, or other matters that are beyond your personal knowledge or expertise.

Guardian of the Person

Two types of guardians can be appointed under a will—a guardian of the person and a guardian of the property (see Chapter 18). The *guardian of the person* is an individual (or individuals) chosen to take personal care of the decedent's children. Since a surviving parent in most instances is the natural guardian of the children, the right to appoint a guardian of the person usually belongs solely to a surviving parent. In the typical situation, the children live with the guardian of the person, either in their home or in the guardian's home. In these cases the executor has to be someone other than the surviving spouse, and unless the same person is chosen as both guardian of the person of the children and executor of the estate, it is necessary for the executor to keep in constant touch with the individual or individuals caring for the children.

Make certain that the needs of the minor beneficiaries are being met, to the greatest extent possible, from the assets of the estate. This means that benefits to which the children are entitled—such as Social Security and veterans' or civil service or work-related benefits (see Chapter 11)—must be applied for on behalf of the children, and the estate funds in your hands must be invested in such a way that the children are being "properly provided for." What "properly provided for" means depends, of course, on the individual circumstances of the estate. Evaluate the standard of living of the children during the decedent's lifetime and the availability of funds in the estate against the future needs of the children. For example, $100,000 might seem sufficient to care for a five-year-old child, but when prorated over the life of the child, and with education costs included in the equation, that amount will not go far. Be aware of the needs of the beneficiaries and at the same time administer the estate as economically as possible. The guardian of the person usually serves until the minor attains the age of majority, from 18 to 21 years, depending on the laws of the state where the minor resides.

Guardian of the Property

A *guardian of the property* may have been selected by the decedent to handle funds or other property of the beneficiary when the latter is unable to handle them because of age or for some other reason, such as incompetence, and when the decedent has not appointed a trustee to manage the funds. In other words, when there is a need for a person or an institution to manage property for someone else, the testator has the choice of setting up a trust to be managed by a trustee or having the property managed for the beneficiary by the guardian of the property, although in some cases there can be both trustee and guardian. A guardian of the property, however, has much less flexibility in handling the funds for the minor or incompetent person.

If a guardianship is established because there is a minor child, the guardianship terminates when the minor attains his majority, regardless of the minor's ability to handle money at that time and regardless of the size of the estate to which the minor is then entitled. As executor, your relationship with the guardian does not differ greatly from your relationship with a trustee. It is your responsibility to deliver to the guardian of the property the assets to which the beneficiary is entitled under the will or under the intestacy laws.

In either event, advise the guardian of the property about the assets available to the beneficiary. Keep in touch periodically with the guardian. In all instances, you must be able to account in detail to the guardian for all the funds you administered for the child or other beneficiary, and present a complete accounting when you close the estate and deliver the property of the minor or incompetent to the guardian.

Attorney

If the decedent died *intestate* (without a will), you have absolute freedom to select an attorney to help administer the estate. If the decedent died *testate* (with a valid will), you typically have the same flexibility, even if the testator specifically mentioned in the will that she wanted you to employ a particular attorney; this, under the law of most states, usually is considered merely a suggestion and is not binding. Since the attorney is an essential part of the estate administrative team, many executors prefer to have an individual with whom they can work effectively. Whether the attorney is the one selected by the decedent or one selected by you, his services are vital to the successful handling of many estates.

Regardless of the asset structure of the estate, in almost every case there are legal as well as tax matters that must be handled properly. The Executor's Checklist (see Appendix) spells out in detail many of the "deadlines" that must be met. Most attorneys familiar with estate work have appropriate procedures for ensuring the timely preparation and filing of the tax forms and other information.

One of the major causes of lawsuits against executors is their improper handling of the decedent's business. Do you in fact have the right to manage and continue operating the business? How far can you go in making changes in the business? These questions require the attention of a skilled attorney. The question of "who gets what" is another major problem area. If the decedent left stock in the Mighty Oak Tree Company to a daughter, and you want to sell the stock or take advantage of an option available to that company's stockholders, what should you do? If the decedent owned a farm, should you value the farm on the basis of its present use as a farm or base valuation on the amount that a developer just offered for the property?

The attorney should be your sounding board for all but routine decisions. If for any reason you feel that you are not getting proper attention or advice, seek other counsel. There are cases in which executors who relied on their lawyers' advice were still held responsible by the court for improperly administering a decedent's estate.

One word of caution, which applies particularly to the estate's attorney but also to every party you hire to assist you in probating the estate: Be sure—*before they begin to work*—that an hourly or other reasonable fee has been agreed upon. *Demand that the fee structure be in writing and signed by the professional* (reasonable fees vary from city to city and according to the expertise of the professional). Before you sign *anything*, talk to at least two or three attorneys. (Keep in mind, however, that they sell time and knowledge and deserve to be compensated for the time you take to "shop around.") Read the fee structure carefully *before* you sign it. Do *not* be embarrassed to ask "what if" questions. When retaining an attorney for the estate, you are in charge, and it is a buyer's market.

Don't select an attorney merely because her fees are lower than another attorney's fees; the knowledgeable attorney who works in the field of estate planning and administration will not have to spend hours researching issues and can save the estate thousands of dollars by avoiding mistakes and seizing tax-planning opportunities.

Consider attorneys who belong to an estate-planning council. You can obtain a free list of the members of your county's estate-planning council by contacting the trust department of your commercial bank, calling your local bar association, or checking your local telephone directory.

Insurance Representative

Often, one of the real heroes on the estate administration team is the life insurance representative. Most insurance agents have had a great deal of experience with the financial problems associated with death. A call to the insurance agent who sold the policies should bring fast, *no-cost* help. Give the agent the following documents: (1) a death certificate, (2) the policy itself (photocopy the entire policy before letting it out of your hands), and (3) a claim form for the proceeds (the agent will provide you with this form). Alternatively, present these documents at the office of the local agency for the insurance company or mail them (return receipt requested, registered mail) to the company's claims department (the home office address is usually on the first page of the policy). Utilize the services of the insurance agent and the agent's company to assist you in such matters as selection of the appropriate settlement option, proper investment of the proceeds, optimal use of the vast resources of the insurance company for the benefit of the estate, and a review of the existing casualty and property insurance covering the assets of the estate. The insurance representative can also suggest new insurance needs.

If you can't locate or don't want to use the decedent's insurance agent, find an agent who is a CLU (chartered life underwriter). This designation means that the agent has passed a series of examinations in financial security and should be more helpful than the typical agent. (A good alternative is a ChFC—a chartered financial consultant.)

How can insurance proceeds be used to pay estate expenses and debts? As executor you may be able to borrow cash from the parties who received the insurance or sell estate assets to them in exchange for the cash. Before you execute such transactions, however, discuss them with the estate's attorney.

Cash proceeds (especially since they usually are not subject to income tax) are always a welcome addition to any estate. In most instances, insurance that has been set up properly will not be paid directly to the estate; therefore, technically it will not become your responsibility to administer. (You are legally responsible for obtaining the proceeds if the estate has been named beneficiary, or if you have been named beneficiary, or if the beneficiary named in the policy predeceased the decedent and no contingent beneficiary was named.) So, although you may help the beneficiaries obtain the proceeds, legally that money is not payable to you as executor, and you are not responsible for its disposition. That's advantageous, because proceeds that do not officially come into the estate are treated more favorably in many states' inheritance-tax laws. Furthermore, insurance proceeds payable to beneficiaries other than the estate will not become subject to creditors or other claims against the estate.

Stockbroker

Another individual with whom the decedent might have had a close relationship, and who can provide you with a wealth of knowledge in regard to the decedent, the decedent's investments, and the decedent's investment goals, is his stockbroker (see Chapter 15). If you are impressed with the stockbroker and the broker's performance on behalf of the decedent, you can continue with her services in handling and investing the decedent's assets.

There is no obligation on the part of the stockbroker to reinvest or change the structure of the decedent's investments. That responsibility belongs to you. If, for example, a corporation in which the decedent invested makes a limited offering available to its stockholders, and you, through neglect, fail to take advantage of this opportunity, to the detriment of the beneficiaries, you can be held personally liable for your failure to take action. Therefore, obtain all the information possible from the stockbroker concerning the decedent's investments and investment goals, obtain the broker's advice on the proper present approach to the investments, and make certain that the stockbroker was, and is now, acting in the best interests of the decedent and the estate. Brokerage firms today have the latest computerized equipment and permit customers to take full advantage of their multifaceted services.

Accountant

Although the services of an accountant may not be required in uncomplicated estates, an accountant usually is an extremely valuable member of the estate administration team. When the decedent had an ownership interest in a business, and when valuation and business decisions have to be made, an accountant is a must. In placing a value on the decedent's business, a review of tax returns, comparisons with other businesses, and a review of present business operations are essential. First consult with the decedent's accountant, and, if satisfied, continue those services. If there was no regular accountant, or if you feel that another accountant would better serve the interests of the estate, then obtain such services. The preparation of federal estate and state death-tax returns is a specialized area, and if the estate is large or complex, the use of a CPA with experience in filing fiduciary returns may save thousands of dollars for the heirs. You are responsible for death-tax returns, state, and, in many instances, federal estate-tax returns, but there also is the area of gift-tax returns to be reviewed—and always income taxes.

Professional Appraisers

When a decedent's assets consist of real estate, a professional appraiser may be needed (see Chapter 14). Many tax authorities of the state and federal governments require that appraisals for real estate be included on tax returns. Since the value of the property involved can vary considerably, obtain a professional appraiser, not just another real estate agent. As with all good tax returns, the more credible information you furnish to the authorities, the more favorably they look on your conclusions. A competent appraisal by a respected appraiser usually is well worth the cost.

Appraisals for business interests are also a must. While the value of the stock of a company listed on the New York Stock Exchange can be found in a few minutes, the value of a family-owned corporation is far from certain and requires painstaking evaluation to be given proper credence. A careful and accurate appraisal of the business interest is important not only for tax reasons but also for setting the value of the business as a going concern in the event of a possible sale and to fix the value at which the beneficiaries receive their interest.

Another area in which appraisals are necessary is that of

collectibles. If the decedent had a stamp collection, coin collection, antiques, art, or any other type of valuables, these should be appraised by an expert.

Real Estate Agents

If the estate contains real estate that must be sold, obtain the services of a real estate agent. The real estate office should be one that serves the area in which the property is located, it should specialize in the particular type of property (residential, commercial, or industrial), and it should charge a commission that is fair in the circumstances and commensurate with commissions being charged by similar offices in the area. In almost every instance, informally discuss the real estate involved with at least three different real estate offices before signing an exclusive listing for the property.

Bank or Trust Company

Although the decedent might not have named a bank or trust company as executor or trustee, bank services designed to assist in the handling of estates are also available to executors. These services may be obtained on a *fee for service* basis—in other words, you can hire a trust company or bank to assist you. You can also permit trust companies to handle and invest the estate's assets in a *custodial* account, in which the bank is acting only as custodian of the estate's funds. If you don't want to undertake the investment responsibility of the estate, this is an alternative. (Warning! The track records of banks vary considerably. Demand evidence of investment performance from at least two or three companies before deciding which one to use. Local newspapers often do these comparisons in an annual review of trust-company performance. Banks also provide, on request, the overall portfolio rate earned on common trust funds. Remember, even though you may delegate investment decisions to a bank or other financial adviser, as executor you remain responsible.)

Court Appointments

Guardian of the Property

In cases when the decedent died intestate and property is to pass to minor beneficiaries, the court must appoint a guardian of the property of the minor. This is also true when the beneficiary of the estate is incompetent.

Never deliver property to a minor or incompetent. When the decedent appointed a guardian or trustee, this problem does not arise. But if the will did not make provisions for minors or incompetents, or if there is no will, then someone—possibly a parent or close relative of the minor or incompetent—must petition the court having jurisdiction to appoint a guardian. If there is no such person to petition the court, you must take that action as executor.

If the property in question is small, the court, in some instances, may appoint a parent or close relative as guardian, with the limitation that the funds be placed in an insured bank account and not be removed until the minor attains majority. In cases when considerable funds are involved, the courts often prefer to appoint a corporate guardian (a bank or trust company) to handle the funds.

Guardians and Trustees **Ad Litem**

It may happen in the administration of the estate that someone has to be appointed to look after the interests of an individual or class of individuals. For example, the provisions of a will might be interpreted in more than one way. Assume that, under one interpretation, a nephew of the decedent would receive a share of the estate while under another interpretation the nephew would receive nothing. If the nephew is a minor, someone should be appointed to represent him in presenting his position to the court. The court, upon the petition of the executor, the administrator, another interested party, or by the court's own volition, will appoint counsel to look after the interests of the minors or other class of beneficiaries. These court-appointed persons are often called *guardians ad litem* or *trustees ad litem*. They are appointed solely to represent the interests of the beneficiaries in a particular situation, and they serve as such until a determination has been made by the court.

5 | Avoiding Fiduciary Liability

Fiduciary liability is like quicksand. The problem is not always readily apparent, and a liability can entrap you before you realize it.

Beneficiaries are not content to sit back and let things happen. If you leave questions unanswered, or beneficiaries neglected, you may find that attorneys have been retained and litigation is under way. *Surcharge* will become an all-too-meaningful word to you. Even the problems that do not end up in court and are resolved through settlement may adversely affect your relationship with the beneficiaries.

Duties of the Fiduciary

Your fundamental duty as an executor is loyalty. The relationship between you and the beneficiaries arises out of the very nature of your duties.

Every action you take must be for the benefit of those individuals. Confidentiality is inherent in the duty of loyalty. Never disclose information about the estate or its affairs to unauthorized persons.

Another important duty related to loyalty is avoiding conflicts of interest. You must never put yourself in a position that might favor your interest over the interests of the beneficiaries you are representing or favor one beneficiary over another. Furthermore, aside from a fee for the services you are rendering (assuming the will does not prohibit such a fee, and assuming you have not agreed to serve without a fee), you must not derive any personal advantage from, or realize a profit in, dealing with the estate.

As a fiduciary you have a duty to exercise care, diligence, and prudence in handling the estate's property. But what is meant by exercising "care, diligence, and prudence"? Your conduct will be considered reasonable if you act with the care and skill that a prudent man or woman would exercise in his or her own affairs. (Corporate and other professional fiduciaries are deemed to have special skills or superior expertise and typically are held by courts to a higher standard.)

As a fiduciary you must preserve and protect the assets in your custody. This is particularly important in the case of real estate, household furniture, furnishings, and coin, stamp, art, and other collections. Obviously, you'll have to provide adequate security and protection for such items. One of your first roles as executor is to have an insurance agent review all of the estate's assets and immediately obtain sufficient insurance coverage. You may be held personally accountable for any loss that occurs to uninsured or under-insured assets.

With respect to investing, your first duty is to protect capital. But you are also obliged to use reasonable care and skill to make property productive, within the guidelines of the will and the provisions in it (as well as state law restrictions). You must consider both inflation and the cost of undue risk. Obviously, if you invest estate money in speculative ventures, you are risking personal liability in the event a loss is sustained (unless that investment is specifically authorized by the terms of the will). The bottom line is that you must exercise prudence, discretion, and intelligence to safeguard the estate's principal, but at the same time generate as much income and growth as possible.

Fortunately, it is your conduct, rather than the investment performance, that is judged by the courts. You are personally liable only when losses result from imprudent conduct, not when investment performance has not been as good as possible. You may retain non-income-producing assets, but only if the will specifically authorizes you to hold those assets, or if there is some other good reason for keeping them.

Maintaining accurate records is another important duty. Account periodically to the beneficiaries (keeping them informed is an extremely good way to avoid litigation). Maintaining accurate records greatly reduces the possibility of your violating the duty of loyalty. Conversely, if you do not maintain good records, you will be held liable if there is a loss or expense that can be traced to your failure to do so.

You cannot delegate your fiduciary responsibility. This duty "not to delegate" is derived from the very nature of your position as executor. Obviously, you are entitled to employ lawyers, accountants, and others to help you, but you have a duty to the beneficiaries of the estate to supervise the people you hire. As stated in various cases, it is the executor who is responsible for filing an estate tax return even though an attorney was employed to do so. These cases have held the executor personally liable for the interest and penalty charges the estate had to pay, even though the attorney was the one who was late in filing the return.

If you are one of several coexecutors, each of you is under a duty to the beneficiaries to participate in the administration of the estate and to use reasonable care to prevent other coexecutors from breaching fiduciary responsibilities.

What Happens If?

What happens if you do breach one of your duties? If you violate (or fail to perform) any duty that you owe to the beneficiaries of the estate, and if that breach is intentional or negligent, you are liable for resulting damages. In other words, a beneficiary can recover those values that she would have enjoyed had there been no breach.

Here are some examples:

- If you sell an asset without authority to do so and the beneficiaries lose their interest in that asset because of your action, you may be liable for the full present value of the asset. In fact, if a beneficiary can show willful misconduct on your part, a court may grant punitive damages as well.

  Of course, if the loss would have occurred even in the absence of your breach of fiduciary duties, you may not be chargeable with the loss.

- If you unnecessarily spend estate money, courts may consider your actions negligent. Likewise, any action (or omission) that results in a loss can be considered "waste," and you can be held liable. Obviously, you must avoid speculation, since your primary duty is to preserve and protect the estate's assets. In this regard, undue delay in accomplishing your duties may be considered negligent. Ascertain as quickly as possible the amount of cash required to administer the estate. Estimate how much money you will need and which assets have to be sold to pay taxes and other estate administration expenses. If estate assets depreciate in value while you have unduly delayed selling them, you may be held liable. In one estate the beneficiary sought to surcharge the executor for negligence because too much time was allowed to elapse and the value of the corporate stock held by the estate had fallen precipitously. The executor had sold only a few shares of stock to cover cash needs. Fortunately, the executor had been given absolute discretion by the will to hold property and refrain from immediately diversifying a large block of stock received at the decedent's death. But a lack of attention in administering the estate and failure to notice a drop in stock values could cause you to be surcharged.

Litigation can often be avoided by combining prompt action with constant information and consultation with the beneficiaries. Make a reasonable, conscious effort to exercise judgment in arriving at investment decisions. If you do—and can prove it—the courts generally will look beyond the performance of any stocks, bonds, or other investments.

- When there is a clear conflict of interest or self-dealing, you will be held liable. For example, in one famous case three art dealers, executors of the estate of a famous artist, were engaged in self-dealing. They sold his paintings substantially below their fair market value. The court not only awarded the beneficiaries the actual value of the paintings but also added an award for "appreciation" damages. The executors' liability exceeded $9 million.

  When there is *any* question of a conflict of interest, instruct your attorney to seek court approval ahead of time before you sell any estate assets.

- At times you will have to hire experts to advise or assist you. You may delegate only *ministerial acts*—acts that are administrative and do not involve major decisions requiring judgment and discretion. Certain decisions, such as whether or not to make certain tax elections, may be made only by you. Here again, the advice of counsel is essential.

- You are liable not only for your own acts but also for the acts of your coexecutors. You have a duty to carry out your own responsibilities in a prudent manner, as well as to be certain that your coexecutors also act prudently. If you approve a breach of fiduciary duty on the part of another coexecutor, you are as responsible as if you had committed the breach yourself. If you are taking over the duties of a prior executor, have counsel thoroughly review all the acts of the previous executor before you accept the appointment. If your predecessor committed a breach of duty, and if you do not take appropriate action on behalf of the beneficiaries, you are guilty of your "own malfeasance." In other words, if you don't force a previous executor to make the beneficiaries "whole," you are permitting a known breach to continue and you yourself can be held guilty of a breach of duty.

Investing Estate Assets

In many cases courts have surcharged (imposed costs and/or penalties on) executors because estate assets have been depleted. Your most important job is to document meticulously what investment decisions you are making and why you are making them. If you can show the courts (and beneficiaries) why you made these particular decisions, and also that you periodically reviewed your investment decisions, you significantly reduce the potential for a successful lawsuit against you.

You must be more concerned with safety of principal than "making a fortune." This means that all the estate assets should not be in one investment. Diversification is the key to safety in this area. Is there a provision in the will relieving you from the obligation of diversifying assets? Even with this special language, maintain records to show why you did not diversify. Many states impose a duty to diversify, and if you ignore that rule, you may be held liable for any loss that occurs.

If you are going to make any investment changes, timeliness is the key. Implement your plans as quickly as possible after prudent decisions have been made.

Filing Tax Returns

An astonishing number of cases involve an executor's failure to file tax returns in a timely manner. In many of these cases individuals have relied on the advice of an attorney or accountant about when the return should be filed. It is your duty to know the appropriate filing dates and to be sure a return has been filed. Unless you have reasonable cause for not complying with the time requirement, you will be held personally liable if the tax is late or not paid.

You must also show that you have given consideration to tax planning. You can make a number of elections. Use Chapter 25 as a checklist to document (in the form of a written memo) the fact that you have considered each one of those elections and your reasons for accepting or rejecting them.

Communicating with Beneficiaries

Perhaps the key reason executors are sued is that they have failed to give personal attention to the beneficiaries. As stressed earlier, regardless of whether you are a corporate or individual executor, a solid relationship with the beneficiary—fostered by constant, thorough, and humanistic communication—serves as a natural deterrent to conflict and minimizes the possibility of liability. By discussing estate transactions, you invite compromise and agreement rather than litigation.

Keep beneficiaries informed by telephone (and keep written memos of your conversation) and, whenever possible, in person.

Before you take action, contact and consult with the estate's attorney, accountant, and other professionals.

Taking Time and Being Timely

Every beneficiary wants her share of an estate—yesterday. Certainly, you cannot make immediate distributions of all estate assets without incurring great personal risk in the form of liability to creditors and taxing authorities. (You may be able to make partial distributions, but do not do so without consulting the estate's attorney.)

You are, however, responsible for acting in a decisive, organized, and timely manner. Promptly return the phone calls of beneficiaries and professionals retained to work with you. "Tough" decisions also need to be made without undue delay.

Unfortunately, the very nature of probate and administration is time-consuming. The federal estate-tax return, for example, normally is not filed until at least nine months have passed. But beneficiaries should be informed when certain things can be expected to occur, and it is your job to ensure that the process is not extended beyond its built-in time delays.

Protecting Yourself by Agreements

There is no such thing as a "model" estate. Every estate has its unique problems and difficult decisions. There are several ways you can protect yourself legitimately for the actions you must take.

1. Obtain a receipt for any assets you distribute to a beneficiary. That receipt should describe the assets in detail so that you can prove what has been distributed, to whom, and when. It also shows that the beneficiary has accepted the asset from the estate; if he has signed a *receipt in full* for his share, the burden is shifted to him to prove that he has *not* received everything to which he is entitled.

2. Obtain the written consent of all beneficiaries who are of legal age if you are in the process of changing investments. If a competent adult beneficiary consents in writing to a new investment, assuming she was under no inducement to act, that beneficiary cannot later

hold you liable for losses arising out of the change in investment. Of course, if that consent is withdrawn before you purchase the new asset, you are not protected by the original written consent. Although you do not have to obtain consent to make investments allowed by the terms of the will, it is still a good idea.

If there are several beneficiaries, they must all consent to an act you are about to take. A beneficiary who does not consent is not bound by consents given by the others. For instance, a consent you obtain from an income beneficiary (one entitled to income, rents, or dividends produced by the property) does not protect you from remaindermen (beneficiaries entitled to principal at a later date) who question your actions.

3. Obtain a release. The *release* is a document that discharges you from liability for actions (or omissions) of the past. A *consent* is a written document exonerating you for what you are about to do. A release is what you obtain if you have not gotten a consent. But a release is not effective unless the beneficiary had knowledge of all relevant facts and you have not used any improper conduct to influence the beneficiary to consent to a transaction that has already taken place.

4. Obtain a court order from probate court. A court order authorizing a particular action protects you from future liability. For instance, in most states an "accounting" (see Chapter 29) is required before you can be released from your duties. You must account for what came in, what went out, and to whom it went. You must show that you have properly carried out the terms of the will. If the court accepts that accounting (after the beneficiaries have been given proper notice and the opportunity to be heard), you are protected from future liability for the acts you have disclosed in the accounting. In many cases the will may not be clear. It is extremely important for you to petition the court for direction so as to avoid (or

settle) disagreement among the beneficiaries (or among your coexecutors). If you do not petition the court before taking action, you expose yourself to liability.

5. The most expeditious way to limit your liability is to enter into a settlement agreement with all the beneficiaries. If there is conflict between you and the beneficiaries, a private, out-of-court settlement may be the most appropriate way to minimize conflict and deter liability.

6 | Pre-death Planning Techniques

If you are facing the difficult task of dealing with a dying friend or relative, consider and implement the appropriate devices and techniques to (1) ease administration, (2) increase the size of the estate going to beneficiaries, (3) reduce transfer costs, (4) decrease income taxes, (5) provide cash to pay taxes and other expenses, and (6) defer the payment of transfer taxes. The right steps taken in the weeks, days, or even hours before death can simplify the job of the executor and increase the financial security of the beneficiaries by thousands of dollars.

Easing Administration

Prepare a durable power of attorney. The first step in easing administration is to have the friend or relative sign a *durable power of attorney*. This is a legal document giving you or some other specified person the right to act on behalf of the dying person. The power can be drawn broadly so that as *attorney in fact* (you don't have to be a licensed lawyer), you can sign tax returns, make gifts, or take other tax-saving actions on behalf of the person who executed the power. The power should be "durable"—it should specifically state that it is to continue in the event of disability or incompetence of its maker (see Appendix).

Inventory and centralize documents. Locating and listing all important documents is your second priority. These documents—including bank accounts; life, health, fire, liability, and other insurance policies; real estate deeds; wills and trusts; stocks, bonds, and other securities; birth certificates, marriage licenses, and marital agreements; military service records; and Social Security information—should be placed in a safe-deposit box with an inventory of its contents. (Check with your bank to see if the box will be "sealed" on your death. Laws vary from state to state, but many states allow the surviving spouse access to the box almost immediately.)

List advisers. The names, addresses, and phone numbers of bankers, insurance agents, brokers, accountants, attorneys, and other advisers should be placed in the safe-deposit box.

Remove others' assets. Other persons' property should be removed from the box.

Update key dispositive documents. Review and change all wills, life insurance policies, and employee-benefit beneficiary designations if appropriate and necessary. Check to make sure that all life insurance and disability premiums have been paid (and receipts or checks indicating payment have been retained).

Consider a revocable trust. A revocable trust is one that can be altered, amended, revoked, or terminated at any time until the death of its creator. Placing property into a revocable trust can provide for property management both during and after the lifetime of the dying individual. A revocable trust allows a smooth transition and may also eliminate some of the cost, delay, and uncertainty encompassed in the probate process. The estate owner may be both the primary trustee and primary beneficiary, and he can also designate another person to take over at his death or incapacity as a secondary or "step up" trustee.

Consider a living will. If an individual desires that extraordinary means of life support be used or not be used to prolong life, that desire should be expressed formally in a *living will*. Almost all states have already enacted laws making it easier for doctors or family members to honor such wishes. In other states a living will has no legal effect (see Appendix).

Consider anatomical gifts. Forms for anatomical gifts, if desired, should be signed and the appropriate hospitals or other potential recipients should be notified. Individuals who feel strongly that no gift should be made of any part of their body should so state clearly in the will as well as in a *letter of instructions* (see below).

Write a letter of instructions. A letter of instructions is a private, informal, nonlegal document, usually left with immediate relatives, explaining one's wishes with respect to highly personal matters that should not be stated publicly in the will or that need to be handled immediately after death (such as funeral arrangements). This letter should contain a list of names and phone numbers of financial advisers, such as insurance agents, attorneys, accountants, stockbrokers, and others who can be relied on for advice and assistance.

Arrange for successor management/sale of business. If a business is involved, arrange for successor management and/or sale of the business. You can often do these things more easily and profitably while the estate owner is alive than at a time when you are more likely to be emotionally distraught.

Establish domicile. Establish domicile to avoid death taxation by more than one state. If the decedent lived in two or more houses in the course of one year, more than one state may attempt to tax her property unless the primary residence is clear.

To establish domicile, the individual should take the following steps: (1) register to vote in the desired state; (2) apply for a certificate of domicile if the state (such as Florida) issues one; (3) transfer all bank accounts to the desired state; (4) purchase all securities in that state and have them located in the broker's local office or in a safe-deposit box; (5) address credit card correspondence to the appropriate office in the desired state; (6) apply for a driver's license in the desired state; (7) affiliate with a religious organization in the desired state; (8) have Social Security checks and other correspondence mailed to the house in the desired state; (9) file all tax returns from the desired state; (10) live in the house in the desired state for more than six months each year.

Increasing the Size of the Estate

There are several ways to increase the amounts that will go to the heirs.

Check policies for "waiver of premium." A *waiver of premium clause* requires the insurer (assuming the requirements specified in the insurance contract are met) to continue the policy in full force if the insured becomes disabled. The policy owner then is relieved of the burden of paying premiums. In fact, the insurer must also repay every dollar of premium paid after the insured became totally disabled. (Money that otherwise would have been used to pay premiums can be used for living expenses or given away.) The policy cash values and dividends build up while premiums are waived, just as if the policy owner had continued to pay the full premium.

Consider extended term insurance. If the policy does not contain a waiver-of-premium provision, or if for some reason it doesn't apply, check with the insurer about *extended-term insurance*. The insurance company takes the whole life policy and converts it to a term policy (at no charge or commission). This relieves the policy owner of the burden of making premium payments and continues the full amount of coverage for a limited period of time.

Increase employee benefits through salary. Some individuals continue to work until shortly before their deaths. Increasing their salaries may enlarge death benefits under certain fringe-benefit plans. If the estate owner controls the business, and if pension, group life insurance, or other employee benefits are based on a multiple of salary, an increase in salary may significantly increase the amount payable at death. For instance, if group-insurance payments are twice the salary for all covered employees, a $5,000 increase in salary results in a $10,000 increase in life insurance coverage.

Reducing Transfer Costs

The cost of transferring property from one individual to another can be greatly reduced by a few simple steps.

Update the will. Check the will of a married estate owner. Has it been updated since *September 13, 1981*? An important change of law on that date makes it possible to eliminate federal estate taxes entirely on the death of a spouse who leaves property to the surviving spouse. This incredible tax saving is possible through the federal estate-tax "marital deduction," which now provides an unlimited deduction for property passing outright (or in a manner tantamount to outright) to a surviving spouse who is a U.S. citizen. But if the will has *not* been changed since September 13, 1981, it may *not* qualify for this unlimited federal estate-tax marital deduction. If it does not, roughly half of the estate may be needlessly subjected to federal estate taxes. Check with legal counsel and review all wills and trusts signed before that date.

Check to be sure the *surviving spouse* is a U.S. citizen. If not, the federal estate-tax marital deduction may be denied. One solution is for the surviving spouse to apply for citizenship immediately and become a citizen before the decedent's estate-tax return is filed. A second solution is to set up what is called a QDT (qualified domestic trust) (see chapters 21 and 25).

Repay life insurance policy loans. Most states treat life insurance more favorably than any other property for death-tax purposes. For example, in Pennsylvania, if an individual left $100,000 in cash to a brother, the state death tax would amount to $15,000. If the same person left the same brother $100,000 in the form of life insurance, there would be no tax at all. The $15,000 difference is only part of the savings. None of the life insurance is subject to probate costs, legal fees, or other transfer expenses.

Be sure the estate is *not* the policy beneficiary. If you have named your estate as beneficiary of life insurance (or if the beneficiary named has predeceased you), change the beneficiary *immediately*. Otherwise, the insurance proceeds may be subjected needlessly to both state inheritance taxes and the claims of creditors.

Use the annual federal gift-tax exclusion. Each person may give up to $10,000 (this may be indexed for inflation after 1998), in cash or in the form of any type of property—entirely free of gift taxes—to anyone (whether or not related) every year. Once the gift is made, it is removed from the estate—even if the donor dies within a day of making the gift. All income and appreciation earned by the gifted property from the day of the gift is removed from the estate and escapes taxation and legal fees. So a dying individual with three single children could give three gifts (one to each child) and remove the whole $30,000 from her taxable estate. These gifts also avoid probate and typically are not subject to a will contest. A broadly drawn durable power of attorney enables the "attorney in fact" to make these gifts on behalf of the estate owner.

Maximize benefits under the new tax laws. Beginning in 1998 the $600,000 gift and estate tax exemption will increase in steps to $1,000,000 by 2006. Make certain that your assets are set up properly so that your family will receive the full benefit from these changes.

Decreasing Income Taxes

A reduction in income taxes translates into an increase in the amount that heirs will receive.

Consider immediate charitable gifts. Estate owners who plan to make gifts to charity in their wills should consider making those gifts before death. Often, the income-tax savings on the immediate gift outweighs the estate-tax deduction available at death. This is especially true for most married couples and individuals with small or modest estates. A lifetime charitable contribution is almost always preferable to one made after death. Furthermore, lifetime gifts remove the property from the possibility of an attack on the will and may save probate and legal costs as well.

Providing Cash and Deferring Payment of Taxes

Individuals who own closely held businesses have two unique opportunities: (1) Their executors can elect to exclude, up to $1–3 million, certain qualified family-owned business interests from their estate. (2) They can arrange for their businesses to pay their estate taxes through what is known as a *Section 303 stock redemption*; and (3) they may be able to delay the payment of federal estate taxes generated by the inclusion of a business interest and spread payments out over as many as fourteen years from the date of death under what is called a *Section 6166 installment payout*.

Qualified Family-owned Business Exclusion

The requirements for qualifying for the family-owned business exclusion under the 1997 Tax Relief Act are extremely complex and require the services of a skilled accountant and attorney. The act provides that qualifying estates may elect to exclude qualified family-owned business interests from the gross estate to the extent that the exclusion for such interests, plus the amount effectively exempted by the unified credit ($600,000 in 1997 increasing in steps to $1 million in 2006) does not exceed $1.3 million. This is called a Section 2033A election.

Consider a Section 303 stock redemption. As in the case of all tax-planning devices, consult the estate owner's attorney and accountant to ensure qualification for a Section 303 stock redemption. In a nutshell, if the value of the closely held business *exceeds* a specified proportion of the estate (35 percent of the gross estate after certain adjustments), the corporation can pay cash or other property to the estate in return for stock.

Arranged properly, the transaction permits a tax-free bailout of cash that would otherwise be taxed as a cash dividend from the corporation and provides cash to pay (1) federal estate taxes, (2) state death taxes, and (3) funeral and administrative expenses. Lifetime planning can help ensure that an individual's estate qualifies for this extremely favorable means of obtaining cash for estate liquidity needs.

Consider a Section 6166 installment payout of estate tax. Deferring the payment of federal estate taxes is possible with the approval of the IRS. It is also allowed to an estate under Section 6166 of the Internal Revenue Code if certain tests are met. One is basically identical to the Section 303 "more than 35 percent" test. In both cases, planning while the estate owner is alive makes it more likely that the estate will qualify. In some cases, gifts or sales of assets other than the business interest may enable an otherwise nonqualifying estate to utilize these two important provisions.

7 | Getting Organized

Search for Will and Related Documents

Whenever a property owner dies, someone somewhere must determine what will happen to the deceased's property. The first inquiry must be, Did the decedent make a valid, enforceable will during his lifetime?

This is not always a routine matter. In the case of the death of a husband or wife, there should be no problem if both had their wills prepared by the same attorney. At the other extreme, however, when the person lived alone, with no professional contacts, the search can be long, costly, and complicated.

Without examining in detail the laws of each particular state, logic tells us that the law will not treat kindly anyone who conceals or attempts to destroy the will of a deceased person. The law requires the possessor of the will to present it to the personal representative chosen in the document so that it can be duly admitted to probate.

There are many different names for the office that handles probate matters, such as Probate Office, Register of Wills, Registry of Probate, Probate Court, Circuit Court, Orphans Court, or Surrogate Court. For the exact name of the probate office in your area, call your county courthouse and ask for the office that handles probate matters.

In most states, a person known to have possession of a will can be compelled to produce it. Any party at interest can direct the Register of Wills to issue a citation directed to the person alleged to have the will to show cause why it should not be deposited with the Register of Wills. If a will was made but it cannot be discovered, the estate will be probated as an *intestacy* (i.e., the deceased person is assumed to have died without a valid will).

The statutory recipients of a decedent's property under state intestacy laws are often not the recipients under the will. Survivors (including family, friends, or professional advisers) therefore must make a thorough search of the decedent's residence and business, coupled with extensive inquiries, to ascertain specifically whether or not the deceased made a will. Inquiries can be directed to the decedent's attorneys and accountants, banks and safe-deposit companies with whom the decedent did business, and, of course, relatives and close friends.

Many states have no specific time period following death in which a valid will may be produced; therefore, if the estate is handled as intestate and a valid will is discovered later, the confusion and the necessary readjustments can easily result in a legal nightmare for everyone involved.

Formal requirements for a "valid will" vary from state to state (see Chapter 8). Any written documents that indicate in any way that they are disposing of the decedent's property at death should be brought to the attention of an attorney. There are myriad cases involving what is or is not a valid will, and many seemingly innocuous pieces of paper have been held by the courts to pass title to millions of dollars. *Never assume* that what you have found is not a valid will, even if it fails to comply with the formalities that you think necessary. Handwritten notes signed at the end of the decedent's life can in many instances pass title to the decedent's property, and all of these should be examined carefully by experts. In many states, copies of wills can be probated if it can be shown that the original was lost or destroyed without the testator's consent.

Anatomical Gifts

During her lifetime the decedent may have made provisions for a particular part, or all, of her body to be given to individuals needing transplants or to hospitals, medical schools, or other specified recipients (see Appendix). If this is the case, chances are that such provisions were made known to one or more close family members or are contained in a separate document, so that they can be acted on immediately after death. Because many vital organs must be transplanted within hours of death, obviously the appropriate steps should be taken without delay. In the event that the decedent made no provision for anatomical gifts, many state statutes provide that members of the decedent's family may make the decision.

In most cases the anatomical gift—if it was made in good faith—will not be affected even if the will is later contested, because obviously it is too late to do anything about it. This is an area in which time is of the essence, and the immediate family usually is in a better position to take any necessary action than an unrelated executor or attorney.

Funeral and Burial

In most cases the funeral and burial take place before the formal appointment of an executor or administrator. If the will contains specific directions about the funeral and/or burial, these directions should be complied with wherever possible and practical. In any event, according to the dictates of our society, typically the funeral and burial must take place within days of death.

The necessary arrangements for the funeral and burial

usually are the responsibility of the immediate family, although the executor, in the end, receives the bill and pays the costs from the assets of the estate. The types of funeral and burial arrangements again depend on the desires of the family and generally adhere to the religious practices of the decedent.

If the surviving family members or friends are to make the funeral arrangements, the only practical guideline is to select a reputable funeral director. Detailed arrangements should be made by the next of kin, but an unemotionally involved person should accompany the family to the funeral home. When a surviving spouse or children make funeral arrangements, they often tend to pay more than they reasonably should because of their emotional involvement.

If the decedent and his family had previously arranged for a family cemetery plot, the cemetery deed should be located immediately. Many individuals are now making their own funeral arrangements in advance. This, of course, relieves family members of having to make difficult decisions under the pressure of time and can result in lower expenditures.

Analyzing the Will

Following death, after immediate matters such as funeral, burial, and anatomical gifts, if any, have been taken care of, the formal probate process takes place (see Chapter 8). If the decedent had a valid will in force at death, then what some states call *letters testamentary* (evidence of authority to act on behalf of the estate) are issued to the executor. If the decedent left no will, then the administrator has no guidelines to use in administering the estate and must rely on her own knowledge of the situation, coupled with the advice of the other members of the estate administration team (see Chapter 4).

If the decedent did have a will, you should first review the will in order to "capture the decedent's thinking" in regard to the handling of the estate. For example, suppose the decedent wanted to make certain that a daughter would be financially secure throughout her life. Let's assume the decedent had established a trust to make periodic payments of income and had named a corporate trustee to protect and invest the daughter's principal. These facts should put you on notice that the decedent was concerned that the daughter might not be fully capable or desirous of managing and investing the property that had been left for her. Another example is a decedent who was a partner in a business and whose will specifically stated that you should comply with the terms of the buy/sell agreement in effect at death. In this case you are put on notice that your handling of the business is limited to compliance with the lifetime agreement between the decedent and his partner.

Also review specific references about investment limitations. For example, the testator may have been opposed to investments in arms-manufacturing firms.

In many cases the testator will want her business sold as quickly as possible after death, while in others the desire will be to continue the business no matter what. Obviously, you must be guided by the provisions in the will. Make certain the property of the decedent goes to the persons specifically indicated in the will. When specific assets are bequeathed, they must not be disposed of in any other way. In general, you should have a thorough understanding of where the decedent wished assets to go and the manner in which they were to be given to the respective beneficiaries. If the will is unclear, if the property specified cannot be found, or if the intended beneficiary died before the testator, consult an attorney before proceeding.

8 | The Formal Appointment: Probating the Estate

Probate, in the formal and most narrow sense, is the legal process of proving the validity of the will and the competence of the testator to make that will. It is also the procedure by which a personal representative is appointed to handle the affairs of the deceased. Most of the formalities involved in appointing the personal representative are in many respects similar throughout the country. But in many states individual counties have their own regulations that must be followed.

Is Probate Always Necessary?

The answer is no. Probate is not necessary if all of a person's assets will pass automatically under the terms of joint ownership. One of your most important functions is to pass title from the decedent to the beneficiary. If title to property is transferred immediately at death (as is the case with jointly held property), there is no need for probate. For example, if the decedent was married, and his only assets of value when he died were owned jointly with his wife, there might be no necessity for probate. This is a common situation. Say the decedent and his spouse owned a home and a bank account. If both the home and the bank account were titled in joint names with the *right of survivorship*, in most states title passes immediately and automatically to the spouse at his death without probate. There will be no *probate assets*, and there is no need to appoint a personal representative to pass title.

Probate also may not be necessary if the only asset of value is life insurance payable to a beneficiary (other than the insured person's estate). Title to the insurance proceeds passes automatically to the party named as beneficiary in the policy.

The same principle applies to IRAs and employee benefits such as pension or profit-sharing proceeds payable to a named beneficiary (other than the estate). If there are no other assets of significance, probate may not be necessary, since the retirement plan money goes automatically to the beneficiary. There is no need to have a person appointed merely to pass title.

Many states have *small estate* exemptions from probate that apply to estates consisting solely of particular classes of assets. An example of an asset that might not require probate, if it was the only asset in the decedent's name, is unpaid salary or a work-related fringe benefit such as vacation pay and sick leave. In estates of very modest size, an executor is well advised to talk to the decedent's employer and then call the Register of Wills or Probate Office in the county in which the decedent lived to see if probate can be avoided.

Assets placed in trust during the decedent's lifetime typically do not have to be probated. *Beneficial title* or interest in the property in that trust passes automatically at death according to the terms of the trust. While this procedure may save certain probate costs, transfer taxes may still be imposed by the state or federal government. This depends on the form of the trust and the size of the assets involved. Therefore, if you find yourself administering a rather large estate in which it appears that no probate will be necessary because all the assets will be held in trust, consult an estate attorney before deciding to bypass the probate procedure. The amount of the assets involved certainly warrants the expenditure of a consultation fee.

Settling Small Estates

Many states have laws to enable a decedent's family to bypass the probate process. These laws apply to estates that lack valuable assets or whose assets are limited to certain classifications, such as unpaid wages, salaries, employee benefits, motor vehicles, or even bank accounts with balances of, for example, less than $1,000.

In some states, title to real estate passes automatically and immediately to the decedent's heirs or beneficiaries, so there is no need for a personal representative to be appointed in order to pass title. Not all states have these laws, however, and there is a wide discrepancy in the provisions of the laws of the various states. Before deciding whether the normal probate process can be bypassed, check the applicable provisions of the law of the state in which the decedent was domiciled. To help you make that decision, confer with an attorney who practices in the county of domicile.

Complexity of Assets

It is not the size of an estate that determines whether or not you must probate the estate; a $9 million estate consisting of $3 million in joint property, $3 million in life insurance, and $3 million in pension benefits may not (theoretically, at least) have to be probated.

There is no direct correlation between the necessity of paying state death taxes and the need to probate an estate. So, although your state may impose a death tax, a surviving spouse or other beneficiary may be able to pay that tax without going to the expense and trouble of probate. A good rule for determining whether or not to probate an estate is to decide whether the decedent will have, at the time of death, property in her name that will require the appointment of a personal representative to pass title to the surviving beneficiaries.

Should You Have a Lawyer?

Retaining the services of a lawyer may not be necessary if, after reviewing the assets of the estate, you can determine either that no probate is necessary or that your duties and responsibilities will be of such a routine and minor nature that you can handle them without complications. If, however, you have *any* question concerning the administration of the estate—even though you feel that you are competent to handle most of the important duties yourself—consult an attorney knowledgeable in estate matters at an early point. Hiring an attorney helps to avoid costly mistakes.

Moreover, an attorney who works in this field will see things or know things that you don't know. Let's use insurance as an example. In one case a man was hospitalized for several months before his death. His widow was advised by her attorney that the husband's insurance at work and his Blue Cross/Blue Shield insurance provided duplicate coverage. That meant the widow was entitled to an additional $25,000 in cash from one of the carriers, since the other carrier had paid the hospital bill directly. The widow was pleasantly surprised, since all of the family's income had been used up during her husband's prolonged last illness. In this situation the $25,000 uncovered by the attorney far exceeded the modest fee he charged.

How to Find the Right Attorney

The complexities of handling an estate are such that it is impossible for every lawyer to have in-depth knowledge of this specialty. Therefore, select an attorney skilled in the areas of estate planning and administration.

As the personal representative of the estate, you assume the difficult decisions and burdensome responsibilities of that office and therefore have the right to select an attorney of your choice. In most cases you are not bound by law to use the decedent's attorney, or even the attorney who prepared the will.

Various organizations, such as an estate-planning council, deal specifically with estate planning. Ask if the attorney you are considering is a member. Request a free copy of the council's directory of members.

If you have a good working relationship with an attorney who does not specialize in this area, he should be pleased to recommend an expert to you. Also, the estate-planning or trust officer of your bank or trust company can refer you to qualified specialists. Ask the trust officer for a list of four or five people and check on their qualifications. Your accountant or your insurance adviser may be able to recommend an estate-planning specialist with whom she has worked. At the first meeting with the attorney, ask questions. Get an idea of the attorney's background, have the attorney give you an idea of the work he will perform, make sure that this is an individual you would feel comfortable working with over the long term, and don't be afraid to talk fees.

How to Keep the Fees as Low as Possible

Attack the fee problem from the standpoint of one professional fiduciary engaging the services of another. Your duty to the estate and its beneficiaries is to provide them with the highest degree of service, and to do this you must, in most instances, retain a qualified attorney. The work of the attorney necessarily reflects on your performance. But as a fiduciary of the estate, you also have an obligation not to burden the estate with excessive costs and fees. Beware of the attorney who quotes the fee before discussing the services to be performed. The attorney should be fairly and adequately compensated according to the time involved; the nature of the work; her background, experience, and professional qualifications; and, when indicated, the beneficial results achieved for the estate and the heirs.

If you do not already know an attorney who can satisfy the above criteria, contact the indicated sources, meet with at least two attorneys suggested, and make your decision on the basis of your discussions of the work to be performed and the fees to be charged. Consider, too, your "gut reaction" to an association with that person. Before the attorney begins to work, ask for a written statement of the hourly fee and a rough estimate of how many hours it will take to do the job. Request a written "cap" on the total cost. But keep in mind that a more knowledgeable and experienced attorney who charges a higher fee may prove far more beneficial (and less expensive in the long run) than an attorney who takes longer to do the job, makes mistakes or omissions, or fails to seize tax-saving opportunities.

Where to Probate (the Question of Domicile)

Domicile is defined as an individual's permanent home. Your domicile is the place to which, regardless of where you are currently living, you intend to return to live permanently.

It is essential to determine the domicile of the decedent because the state of domicile will impose inheritance or estate taxes on the decedent's property. That state also will determine (and interpret) the rules and regulations governing the distribution of the assets of the estate.

In most cases, when there is no question about the decedent's permanent residence, domicile will not be a significant issue. However, because of increased mobility and because many people own homes in more than one state, the question of domicile can present serious problems.

Take Jerry Smith, who owns a home in suburban Philadelphia and a condominium in Florida. Jerry has just retired; he plans to spend May through October in Philadelphia and November through April in Florida. If Jerry was to die while in Philadelphia, there would be a question of where his estate would be probated.

Since Florida has more liberal tax laws, Jerry should redraft his will to indicate that he is a resident of the state of Florida, sign it, and have it notarized in Florida. He should use his Florida address for voting and his main address on income tax returns; he should register his automobile in Florida and use the Florida address on his driver's license. All of these constitute evidence of Jerry's intent to make Florida his permanent home.

It is your duty to analyze the relevant criteria for a determination of domicile (see Chapter 6) so that you are in a position to support that decision in the event of an attack by the other state.

In most instances the will will be probated, or the administrator will apply for letters of administration, in the county of the state in which the decedent was domiciled.

Ancillary Probate

Not every asset owned at the time of death is probate property. This means that probate may not be needed to pass title to the survivor at the decedent's death (see chapters 8, 12, and 17).

The local probate office or court does not have jurisdiction over real estate the decedent owned in another state. In such cases, a second personal representative must be appointed in the state in which the property is located. This procedure is called *ancillary probate*, and an ancillary administration is necessary for such property.

In the above example, even though Jerry was domiciled in Florida, an ancillary administration in Pennsylvania was still necessary because of the real estate Jerry owned there. Letters of administration had to be applied for in Pennsylvania (and the petition asking the court for ancillary letters had to be prepared by a second attorney, located in that state), and state inheritance taxes had to be paid on the Pennsylvania real estate.

Procedure Varying with Locality

Although most procedures are relevant to the probate process regardless of where the probate takes place, you must be familiar with the laws of the state in which the will or the estate is probated and the particular rules and regulations of the county probate office. You can obtain copies of the latest death-tax laws and procedure requirements of your state, as well as the regulations of the local probate office, at the office itself.

Probate When There Is No Valid Will—Intestacy

No one dies without a will. Either you prepare a will for yourself or the state in which you are domiciled at your death "makes a will" for you. This so-called will that the state makes for you is the *intestacy law* of the state.

The intestacy laws govern the distribution of assets. Provision is made first for a spouse. Children, grandchildren, parents, brothers and sisters, and nieces and nephews follow (depending on the particular state intestacy law).

Where either a husband or a wife dies, survived by one or

more children, state law might provide for a specified share to be paid to the spouse, with the children's share to be divided equally among them. The percentages allocated to the spouse and children often are determined by the number of surviving children. For example, if a woman was to be survived by a husband and one child, state law might provide for the estate to be divided equally between father and child; if the woman had two or more children, the husband might be limited to one-third, with the children equally sharing two-thirds.

Some states provide for the spouse to receive a specific amount plus a percentage of the excess, with the remainder for the children. For example, the surviving spouse might be entitled to the first $20,000, with a given percentage of the balance divided between the spouse and the children. Check with your attorney before making any decision based on intestacy laws, since state laws change frequently.

In relatively uncomplicated situations when the decedent failed to make a will (or the will is for some reason held to be invalid) and was survived by a spouse and children, letters of administration could be granted to the spouse. The only formal requirements are that the spouse obtain a death certificate and provide the probate official with other relevant data, just as in the probate of a will.

Intestacy is an unfortunate occurrence in most cases because the decedent has forfeited the right to specify (1) *who* gets her property (state law decides this); (2) *how much* each beneficiary receives (regardless of how much each person needs or how much the decedent would have wanted each person to get; (3) *when* they get the property (money or other property cannot be distributed to minor children); and (4) *how* each person receives the property (it passes outright upon the beneficiary's majority regardless of how well that person can manage or invest the property).

ꞏꞏꞏ Is Entitled to Act as Personal Representative or Administrator

If there is no valid will, most states establish a priority list of potential administrators, starting with the decedent's spouse. If there is no spouse, or if for some reason he does not serve as administrator, then children, parents, brothers or sisters, or other close relatives have the right to serve. Individuals who have priority but do not desire to serve can renounce their right in favor of others further down on the list.

In the event that no relatives are available or willing to serve, and the decedent has a creditor anxious to have claims paid from the assets of the estate, the creditor can petition the court to be appointed administrator. Legal proceedings then take place. Relatives of the decedent are given notice of the creditor's action. Unless a relative is willing to act as administrator or has a sufficient legal basis to dispute the creditor's right to act as such, the court can appoint the creditor as administrator.

How to Qualify as Executor or Administrator

Almost anyone over the legal age in the state where the decedent was domiciled can qualify to act as a personal representative. In order to qualify formally if you have been named executor in the will (or administrator of the estate of someone who has died without a will), go to the local probate office, file the necessary petition, and have *letters of testamentary* or *letters of administration* issued. These letters, or documents, are legal proof that you are qualified to act as the decedent's personal representative.

Executor's Right to Renounce

A person who makes a will, appoints an executor in the will, and fails to notify the executor of this fact is committing a great disservice—not only to the executor but also to the beneficiaries of the estate. Thrusting this responsibility on an unwilling recipient can precipitate disaster (see Chapter 6).

If, for whatever reason, you do not wish to act as executor, in most cases you have the right to "renounce" and be released from your responsibilities. This usually can be accomplished by filing a renunciation form in the probate office that has jurisdiction over the estate. File this form before you perform any duties or take any actions on behalf of the estate.

Renunciation makes sense if the estate could be handled much more efficiently by a lesser number of executors. For example, if a brother and sister were named coexecutors, there was little likelihood of any conflict between them, and if the sister lived 2,000 miles away, it might be easier for all concerned if the brother acted as the sole executor.

Renunciation should also be considered when the situations of the parties have changed considerably since the will was prepared and the designation of executor was not changed. In such cases logic would suggest (but not demand) that you no longer act as such. For example, you might be a former spouse, a former business associate, or a former close friend who has since moved to a different country.

Mechanics of Probate: Petition; Letters Testamentary; Letters of Administration; Bond

The mechanics of probating an estate are, in the vast majority of cases, simple. Probate itself is relatively inexpensive in most cases.

1. Go to the local county office responsible for the probate of wills. The precise name of the office varies with the state and sometimes with the county of domicile. It may be called the Register or Registry of Wills, Probate

Office, Probate Court, Orphans Court, or Surrogates Court.

2. Present evidence of death. This requirement usually is satisfied by giving the clerk a duly issued and sealed death certificate.
3. A petition is either prepared at the probate office or prepared beforehand by the personal representative and attorney and presented at the probate office for review, approval, and signatures.
4. If the decedent had a will, present the *original* of the will (copies are not accepted by most state laws except under very limited circumstances). The witnesses to the will, if available, should be present. Fortunately, many states allow what are called "self-proving" wills. These wills are notarized when signed by all the parties, so after the testator's death the witnesses do not need to appear or even sign any documents. These wills streamline the probate process.

The appropriate official reviews the death certificate, verifies the information on the petition, questions the witnesses about the validity of the decedent's signature, and determines whether or not you must post bond before taking charge of the estate.

A bond (insurance to protect the heirs in case the personal representative steals or misappropriates estate assets) is often required by probate authorities to protect the estate's beneficiaries and creditors. Most lawyers include a provision in wills that exempts the executor from this requirement. In some instances courts may direct that a bond be posted even when the will states that no bond is necessary, but this occurs only if the court feels security is needed (for example, if the personal representative is not a resident of the state where the probate takes place).

A bond usually can be obtained without much difficulty through a bonding or surety company representative. You can get the names, addresses, and phone numbers of several of them from the clerks at your local probate office. (Be sure to "shop around," as you would with any other insurance.) If you have hired counsel, that attorney usually can obtain the bond, and you need not appear in person at the bonding office.

As soon as the probate official has been satisfied that your petition to be named the personal representative is in order, and when the bond, if required, has been posted, the probate office issues letters testamentary to you. These letters (in the case of intestacy, letters of administration) are official evidence that you have been appointed executor (or administrator) of the estate.

Since you need to furnish proof of your appointment in order to perform many of the required duties, the probate officials issue shortened versions—in effect, summaries—of the letters testamentary or letters of administration. These *short certificates* (sometimes called "shorts" by clerks) indicate the formal appointment, the date of death of the decedent, and the date of your appointment by the court. Ask for at least six copies, as they will be necessary to transfer assets from the decedent's name into the estate's name.

Will Contests—Why Courts Invalidate Wills

Regardless of the intentions of the deceased when she prepared a will, and regardless of the skill and draftsmanship of the lawyer who prepared it, there is always the possibility that someone will *contest* the will.

As a practical matter, in most instances the reason for a will contest is that the contesting person(s) did not receive the property they had expected. Will contests, therefore, generally are brought by disinherited children, by close friends of either sex who were misled into believing they would be "remembered," or by someone who was more closely related to the decedent than the beneficiaries named in the will.

A will cannot be set aside merely because someone is not happy with it. There must be "grounds" for contesting a will. The law of each state specifies certain formal requirements that must be met for a will to be valid. If one or more of these key tests are not met, the will can be disregarded by the court, and an intestacy results. Check with an attorney for the requirements in your state.

Among the reasons frequently given by potential heirs who seek to have a will invalidated are the following: (1) the decedent lacked *testamentary capacity* (legal ability to make a valid will) because of weakened intellect; (2) the decedent was the victim of "fraud" (the decedent signed what he thought was a document other than a will or was deceived into thinking a beneficiary was dead who really wasn't); (3) *undue influence* (persuasion strong enough to overcome the decedent's freedom of choice); (4) the signature or the will itself was a forgery; and (5) the will did not comply with the statutory formalities required in the state of domicile (for instance, it was not signed by the decedent at the appropriate place or was not properly witnessed).

In most states, the contestants of the will bear a heavy burden. Obviously, courts want to encourage people to prepare wills. Therefore, as a general rule, wills are not invalidated unless the court is convinced by strong evidence that the will does not represent the wishes of the decedent.

If the will is held invalid by the court, a question arises about who then is entitled to the proceeds of the estate. The law of the probating state again governs the court's decision. Typically, the court has two alternatives: (1) The estate can be distributed in accordance with the intestacy laws if the court finds that no valid will was in effect at the decedent's death; or (2) if the decedent had a prior will that was revoked by the will found by the court to be invalid, the court can hold the prior will is entitled to be probated. (This is a good example of why [sometimes] an old will should not be destroyed when a new will is executed.)

Executor's Role in Will Contests

If you have been formally appointed as executor, and the will under which your appointment was made is being contested, immediately determine the extent of your duties and obligations for the duration of the will contest. In most cases you are expected to continue to perform your regular functions, with the expectation of being compensated for the time you spend on behalf of the estate (unless the will provides that you are to serve without fee or unless you elect to forgo that fee). Neglecting to perform these duties because of the will contest might result in financial losses to the estate. Therefore, if there is any question at all about what services you are to perform during the hiatus caused by the will contest, obtain written directions either from counsel or from the court.

9 | After Probate

Bank Accounts—Checking, Savings, or Combination

In the administration of an estate, setting up the proper checking and savings accounts holds a high priority. This is an area of estate administration in which banks are especially helpful.

One of your most important duties is record keeping. As personal representative of an estate, you are required to account to three separate and distinct entities or groups of people: (1) the beneficiaries; (2) the respective taxing authorities—local, state, and federal; and (3) the courts, if and when you must give a formal accounting of what money and other property came in and what went out to various creditors, taxing authorities, as well as agents, representatives, and employees of the estate.

Your initial record-keeping tool is the estate checking account. Funnel all moneys, regardless of the source, through this one central account to establish a permanent record that can be verified by the bank's records. It will always show exactly how much cash you have received, when you disbursed it, and to whom. Do not tie up a considerable amount of the property in a non-interest-bearing checking account. Keep just enough in the account to meet bills as they fall due.

Most banks establish a special account for an estate. A bank officer provides you with a separate checkbook that clearly identifies you as the personal representative. That makes it easier for you to administer the cash that flows through the account and put the payee of any check on notice of the origin of the payment. With the advent of interest-paying checking accounts, the availability of insured money-market funds, and the entry into the market of savings institutions with checking accounts, you have a wide diversity of options available.

Before you set up an account, talk to at least three different bankers to determine the type and the cost of accounts and services available. All bank accounts definitely should be insured. Other factors to consider include the advisability, in some circumstances, of using the same bank in which the decedent had the bulk of his accounts, the advisability of using a bank with which you have done business previously, and the suggestions of the estate's attorney. Obviously, an attorney who specializes in estate administration and who has considerable practical experience with local banks can help you select the right bank and the proper type of account.

A Caution About Estate Accounting

When the administration of an estate is completed, you must account to the beneficiaries (see Chapter 29). Unless you keep accurate records of every transaction involving the estate, it is impossible to prepare an accounting that will balance out to the penny. The hints that follow can save you many hours of trying to reconstruct the estate's past transactions.

- Describe the background of each deposit. Was the bank account closed out? If so, get the details. Was a stock sold? Keep the broker's receipt. Was this a stock dividend? What happened to the other dividends? A deposit without an explanation is a problem without a solution.

- Itemize in detail the reasons for each check you write.
- Keep a separate record to trace the history of each asset. For example, if you closed out a checking account in bank A and used the proceeds to buy a certificate of deposit in bank A, this transaction will not be reflected in the estate checking account in bank B.
- In addition to the checking account, keep a separate file containing documentation for each item of deposit or withdrawal. Examples of this documentation are the following:
    1. Bills for funeral, medical, or other expenses
    2. Bank withdrawal slips
    3. Evidence from brokers for sales of securities
- If the deposit represents a gain or loss on the sale of an asset, make a note of the profit or loss on the sale.

Safe-Deposit Boxes

A valuable source of information about the decedent's assets, as well as a potential depository of some of these particular assets, is the safe-deposit box. Quite often personal papers of value are essential in handling affairs. They can include deeds, mortgages, insurance policies, stock certificates, and business agreements. Cash and jewelry sometimes are kept in safe-deposit boxes, together with other valuables of limited size, such as coin or stamp collections.

If the family has no knowledge of a safe-deposit box, and if circumstances suggest that the effort is warranted, ascertain whether the decedent did in fact have a safe-deposit box. At the very least, inquire at the banking institutions with which the decedent did business, and, where appropriate, address written inquiries to other banks in the area in which the decedent lived or conducted business.

State laws vary widely in regard to accessibility to safe-deposit boxes. Some states permit the surviving spouse access to the contents of a box in joint names at any time, with no qualifications, following the death of the other spouse. If the decedent was an officer in a corporation, and the box was in the corporation's name, other corporate officers could gain access to it following death without undue formality. In many states, however, the state or local taxing authorities require that the box be sealed by the bank at the date of death and entered only in the presence of a representative of the state or local government. The purpose of the limitation on entry is to prevent possible tax evasion—i.e., the accumulation of unreported cash or other valuables by the decedent. Most states and the banks permit access to an otherwise locked safe-deposit box in order to see if it contains a will or to withdraw from it a burial lot deed or insurance policies. On such occasions a representative of the bank usually is present so that nothing is removed without a record being made.

When the access is limited, you usually must schedule an appointment with the bank and with the appropriate government official in order to gain entrance to the box. In addition, if you are not in possession of a key to the box, the bank must also obtain the services of someone to "drill" the box open. This requires coordinating the schedules of everyone involved.

If there is any question about your right of entry, consult an attorney before attempting to gain access. For example, suppose a box was in the joint names of a mother and her daughter. The mother died and state law prohibited the daughter from entering the box following the death. If she entered the box within hours or even days following her mother's death, the bank might very well not have noticed and would not have barred her entrance. The daughter's

..., however, would have violated state law, in which case she would be subject to civil or even criminal prosecution. She would also become a prime suspect in the event that any articles that might have been expected to be in the box could not be located. Survivors should familiarize themselves with the laws of their state before attempting to gain access to a safe-deposit box.

Notice and Advertising

One of your first duties as an executor is to ascertain that everyone who had contact with the decedent during his lifetime is notified of his death. Also be certain that you are kept fully apprised of all matters relevant to the decedent.

In order to put the world on notice of the death, and to inform the public that you now act for the decedent, notify the post office to direct the decedent's mail to you. You should also be in contact with any individuals with whom the decedent had business interests, and naturally all creditors as well as debtors.

Most states have laws governing the procedures to advertise that you have been granted letters testamentary or (when there is no will) letters of administration to act for the decedent. The laws stipulate when and where the advertisements should be placed. Many states do not permit you to be formally discharged from your duties until these advertisements have been properly placed.

One purpose of the advertisements is to give formal notice of the decedent's death to any possible creditors and to anyone with whom the decedent had a business relationship. The court, therefore, will not authorize payment to beneficiaries without first ascertaining that all creditors have been notified of the death and without giving them the opportunity to present any outstanding claims. The sooner you meet these statutory requirements the better, since the statute of limitations for creditors does not begin to run until you have duly advertised your appointment. After a specified period of time, if the creditors have not notified you of the decedent's debt to them and received payment, they lose the right to make claims against the estate. The statute of limitations typically runs from six months to a year. (Check with the county Register of Wills office about this law.)

Notice is also important to make certain that there are no long-lost potential beneficiaries of the estate (such as children of a deceased relative).

Determining the Estate's Claims

Before you can prepare an inventory of assets, you must determine whether the decedent had any outstanding claims at death and whether these claims can be reduced to cash for the estate and the beneficiaries. Legally, these claims can be classified under the general heading of *causes of action*. A cause of action is a legal, enforceable claim of the decedent at death. For example, suppose the decedent owned a retail store and sold a pair of shoes on credit prior to death. The outstanding bill for the shoes is an asset of the estate, under the general heading of "accounts payable" to the business. Personal loans or other fixed obligations owed to the decedent at death also come under this category. It should not be difficult for you to determine what accounts are outstanding and owed to the estate. Check through all of the decedent's records to make certain that no such claim is overlooked.

More difficult are the claims that are not so easily translated into dollars and cents. For instance, the decedent might have had an automobile accident several months before death. She might have intended to file a lawsuit because of injuries or other losses sustained, but formal procedures might not have been set in motion. Or a tenant in a building owned by the decedent might have moved out several months before the latter's death, leaving unpaid rent due on the lease.

Before preparing a formal inventory, you must know the precise extent of your duty in making a formal claim on behalf of the estate for all potential assets.

1. Conduct as extensive a review of the decedent's books and records as possible under the circumstances.
2. Make a list of all potential claims of the estate.
3. Determine whether or not these claims can be reduced to cash. Don't assume the responsibility of deciding the value of a claim or the practicality of collecting it. If it involves a potential lawsuit, secure the opinion of an attorney (and, if you decide not to follow through with the case, be sure you can prove that you discussed the merits of the case with the attorney and can document good reasons for not going to court). If the claim involves a debt that you feel is not worth the time and expense to the estate to try to collect, have supporting documentation in your file.
4. Document your awareness of the potential asset and the steps taken to effect collection. Should a beneficiary later raise a question about the asset, you will be in a far stronger position if your records indicate your awareness of the problem, the actions taken by you on behalf of the estate, and the supporting documentation of the professional whose advice you obtained before deciding not to follow through with collection.

Inventorying the Assets

At this point you should have a fairly clear picture of the assets that make up the estate. Since you almost always must prepare an inventory, even though it does not have to be formally filed and approved in every case, prepare a first draft.

You will then be aware of the size and extent of the estate, can determine how to go about collecting and securing all property listed in the inventory, and—more important at this point—can decide which matters should have priority (see Appendix).

It is essential at the same time that you understand what legally does or does not constitute an asset of the estate. If title to property was in the decedent's name alone, that property undoubtedly constitutes an asset of the estate, and one that you must administer. In many cases property in joint names, such as property owned by husband and wife, passes to the spouse at death by survivorship, and this property becomes the spouse's asset controlled by her, not an asset of the estate administered by you. Obviously, therefore, you must determine ownership in order to establish who has the right to the property and to its administration (see Chapter 17).

Determining Priorities

First attend to those matters in which time is a factor in preserving or creating property for the estate. Priority matters can vary considerably. Some situations obviously require prompt attention: If the decedent owned a business dealing in perishable items, such as fruit, it is essential to dispose of the property before it becomes worthless. Then there is the not-so-obvious situation in which you must renew the fire insurance on the decedent's home or risk being held personally accountable should a fire occur and the insurance not be in force. Another matter that requires prompt attention is the investment decision in which a time factor is involved. A six-month certificate of deposit might be maturing, and without timely reinvestment the estate could lose considerable interest. Stock options might have to be exercised by a given date. There could be outstanding contractual relationships that must be fulfilled or changed by reason of the decedent's death within a prescribed time. These decisions cannot be made without a knowledge of all the matters in which the decedent was involved at the time of death, and failure to act responsibly in these instances often can lead to serious problems.

Although estate priorities and timetables can vary, certain specific duties must be performed within stated time periods (see Appendix).

Meeting with and Assisting the Beneficiaries

If you are a close friend or relative of the decedent, you are most likely familiar with the needs of the beneficiaries. Otherwise, as soon as conveniently possible, meet with the primary beneficiaries. It is of the utmost importance that the beneficiaries be provided for during the administration of the estate. Make certain that the surviving spouse and children, for example, have sufficient income to carry them over the period of adjustment, which may be as long as a year. Determine whether there are sufficient funds on hand to meet their immediate expenses and, if necessary, arrange for the sale of assets in order to provide these funds. Next, obtain as much information as possible from the beneficiaries to facilitate the handling of the estate. The family may be able to tell you of any uncompleted business transactions, the names of the decedent's broker and insurance agent, and the whereabouts of assets that have not come to your attention.

Advise the beneficiaries of the various steps in the administration process. The beneficiaries' awareness of your timetable forestalls frequent and unnecessary contacts on their part to find out when they will receive their share of the estate. A logical and informative discussion of the process not only provides the beneficiaries with information to which they are entitled but also gives them confidence in, and respect for, your work and responsibilities.

The Family's Rights

The surviving family members have certain specific rights. Which of them has such rights and exactly what any survivor is entitled to are determined by the law of the state in which the decedent was domiciled.

Most states specify that a certain minimum amount of property that goes to the spouse alone, or to the spouse and children, is exempt from both taxation and the claims of creditors. This family exemption may apply to a specific amount of money or to a particular property, such as the family home.

State laws often give the surviving spouse a "nonforfeitable" interest in the deceased spouse's estate. This can take the form of election by the surviving spouse to take his statutory share of the estate, or, under some state laws, the right of the surviving spouse to interests in the decedent's property that are comparable to or in lieu of "dower" or "curtesy." The term *dower* refers to the centuries-old English law providing for a widow's support and the support of her children out of the lands or property of her husband. *Curtesy* refers to the assets to which a man would be entitled on the death of his wife under English common law. Some states still use these technical terms, while others define the rights of surviving spouses as their *right of election*, their right to *take against* the will of their deceased spouse (to take a share specified by state statutes *regardless* of what the will provides).

In some states, for example, a surviving spouse could have a right of election equivalent to one-third of the estate. If, say, a deceased husband had a net estate of $100,000 and left it all to his girlfriend, his widow would have a right to elect to receive a minimum of one-third, or $33,333. To qualify for this election, the widow might have to exercise her right to it within a certain period of time—six months, for example—and also be willing to relinquish any other property she might have received from her husband (her half of the family house, for example). In some states certain rights are also given to children who have not otherwise been provided for in the will.

If there is any indication that the will did not provide for a spouse or child, be extremely careful in regard to the practical, ethical, and perhaps legal question involved—namely, the question of your duty to advise the spouse or child who has been "cut off" from her rights. If the spouse is relying on you for guidance and you are not aware of the six-month grace period from the date of death during which the right of election may be exercised, the spouse might hold you personally responsible for failure to so advise her. On the other hand, if you do offer this advice, have you acted equitably toward the other beneficiaries of the estate, toward whom you also have a fiduciary duty?

There also may be qualifications to the rights given by state law to the surviving spouse or children. A wife, for example, might lose her right of election if she deserted her husband and was absent from the family home for more than one year before his death.

If, therefore, you have any indication whatsoever of a potential problem, obtain legal counsel.

10 Tangible Personal Property

Keep It Safe

One of your most time-consuming and least productive tasks is handling *tangible* personal property. By tangible personal property is meant specific items that we can touch and see, such as automobiles, jewelry, and furniture. (*Intangibles,* on the other hand, is a category in which the only assets represent the value of an article: for example, certificates of stock, savings certificates, and insurance policies—which, of course, do not have value in themselves but represent the monetary interest that stands behind them.)

In situations involving close family members, your duties can be limited to inventorying and appraising the property in question. If you represent the estate of a husband who died leaving all his personal property to his wife, it is your duty to appraise the property, determine whether it was owned individually by the decedent or jointly with his wife, and have appraisals made where indicated. However, if the decedent lived alone, and especially if valuable personal property is involved, it is your duty to secure (and in some cases seal) the premises and take every precaution to make certain that the tangible personal property remains intact. For example, if the decedent was a single woman living alone and her closest beneficiaries were relatives who lived several thousand miles away, and if the decedent kept valuable works of art in her apartment, you should take immediate precautions—in some instances, even before being formally appointed—to ensure the safety of the paintings.

In all cases, take a prompt inventory, change locks where circumstances warrant it, and check insurance policies to make certain that valuables are properly and adequately covered. If the estate contains items that could harm others in the wrong hands (such as a gun collection or drugs possessed by a doctor), contact an estate attorney immediately for advice on compliance with federal and state procedures.

Jewelry and Collectibles

If the decedent left valuable jewelry, or other valuable collectible items such as coins or stamps, place them in an estate safe-deposit box as quickly as possible.

Appraisals

In almost every instance you need to obtain an appraisal of the tangible property involved prior to distributing it according to the terms of the will or selling it. The appraisal can, according to the circumstances, be relatively brief, as in the case of household articles or furnishings that have no particular value. For example, a list of household articles indicating their approximate value is sufficient in most cases. On the other hand, the value of a stamp or coin collection, a Doug Mellor photograph, or antique crystal should be determined by an appraiser.

Automobiles

In the case of automobiles titled in joint names with right of survivorship, the surviving joint owner usually can obtain title from an appropriate agency, such as an automobile club or a notary public that specializes in this area. If the automobile was titled in the decedent's name alone, you have to transfer the title. In some states it is possible to avoid probating an estate if the only asset that would require probate is the decedent's automobile; therefore, review the rules and regulations of the Department of Motor Vehicles in that state. In all other instances, possession and disposition of the automobile are treated in the same way as other tangible assets of the estate.

Selling Tangible Property

When the decedent specifically leaves an article of tangible personal property to a beneficiary ("my diamond bracelet to my daughter, Mary"), make certain that the article in question is distributed to the named beneficiary after being inventoried and appraised. If tangible property has not been specifically bequeathed, or if the estate is in need of funds to pay taxes and other expenses and the items of personal property must be sold to produce these needed funds, then proceed to have the property sold.

If a sale of tangible property seems to be in order, set the wheels in motion for the sale as quickly as possible. This will prevent potential loss of the property itself or depreciation in its value. Give written notice of the sale (preferably by certified mail—return receipt requested) to the beneficiaries so that you cannot later be accused of permitting articles of sentimental value to leave the estate without giving family members the opportunity to purchase them at their fair value. Unfortunately, there usually is no real market for used and outdated furniture, clothing, and the like, and you must decide whether to dispose of it by public auction or private sale. An alternative is to donate such articles to charity, which should result in a valuable income-tax deduction for the estate.

If there is any likelihood of conflict with the beneficiaries over the manner of disposal of the tangible personal property, at the very least review your plans with the beneficiaries. Where possible obtain their written consent. In all events, make a careful inventory of all the property before the sale takes place.

One other word of caution: Where there is any possibility of conflict of interest on your part, refrain from purchasing or otherwise retaining any tangible asset of the estate. Self-dealing is treated harshly by courts.

11 | Government and Fringe Benefits

Social Security, Railroad Retirement, and Civil-Service Benefits

Government and work-related fringe benefits are not always treated as assets of the estate, so technically the collection of these benefits may not be your legal responsibility. Social Security benefits, benefits payable under the Railroad Retirement Act, and benefits payable to the spouse and dependent children of government employees covered by civil service are paid directly to named beneficiaries, not to the estate. In many instances, however, the amounts payable to beneficiaries from these sources can be greater than those passing through probate, and it is your responsibility to make the beneficiaries aware of the potential benefits to which they are entitled. If the benefits are paid to the estate, then their collection will be your responsibility. If paid directly to named beneficiaries, the latter must still be fully informed by you of the nature and size of the benefits and the name of each recipient.

Veterans' Benefits

If the decedent was a veteran, the estate may be entitled to a burial allowance and the beneficiaries to a pension, depending on the service or disability status of the deceased and the income of the beneficiaries. Since families may be entitled to both service- and nonservice-connected benefits, as well as to other death-related benefits and benefits often provided by local governmental agencies, pursue these in the case of any decedent who served in the armed forces, regardless of whether or not the individual was in the military service at the time of death. Contact the Veterans Administration or a veterans' service organization to make sure that all benefits to which the survivors are entitled have been applied for, and also ascertain whether the Veterans Administration life insurance was in force at death.

Making Direct Contact

In dealing with the family of a deceased, personal contact produces the most efficient results. Since every working American usually is covered under one or more of the above-mentioned programs, at the very least make certain that the beneficiaries apply to the respective governmental agency for death benefits or for continuing pension benefits. Whenever you have assumed full responsibility for all of a decedent's affairs, make direct contact with the agency in question, submit the necessary documentation, fill out the required forms, and follow through until payments have been received.

Work-Related Benefits

Work-related fringe benefits might be available to beneficiaries or to the estate if the decedent was ever employed. Since there are often time limitations and possibly loss of interest if these benefits are not applied for in time, advise and, where applicable, assist the beneficiaries in obtaining these benefits.

In most cases benefits are payable to beneficiaries and are not the responsibility of the executor. If, however, the named beneficiaries are deceased, or if the decedent failed to name a beneficiary, the proceeds are often payable to the estate and thus are your direct responsibility. Make sure that all available benefits are collected.

Group Life Insurance

Heading the list of work-related fringe benefits is group life insurance. Since many companies insure employees for a multiple of earnings, group life insurance benefits are often high, and they constitute one of the largest assets the beneficiaries will receive. When the proceeds are paid to adult beneficiaries, your duties may be limited to advising or assisting the beneficiaries in making their claims. However, when the assets of the estate exceed the minimum requirements for filing a federal estate-tax return, you have to obtain IRS Form 712 from the insurance company. This form, which states the amount and exact disposition of the proceeds, is required when filing IRS Form 706, the Federal Estate Tax Return (see Chapter 21), and it is therefore your responsibility to make certain that there is a Form 712 for every policy in which the decedent owned any interest at death.

You must also provide a Form 712 for any policy on the decedent's life owned by someone else (such as a spouse, child, corporation, or trust). If no beneficiary is named, or the named beneficiary has died and no contingent beneficiary is listed, the proceeds are paid to the estate to be administered by you. There are options available to the beneficiaries for how the proceeds should be paid, and you can assist in selecting the proper settlement option (see page 103).

Pension and Profit-Sharing Plans

Pension and profit-sharing plans can be significant. Here again, be aware of the amount and nature of the benefits and, in particular, determine whether a beneficiary has been selected by the decedent. List the exact amount and nature of the benefits—and benefits taxed, where applicable—on the appropriate state inheritance-tax return and on IRS Form 706, the Federal Estate Tax Return. Qualified pension and profit-sharing plans usually contain settlement options available to the beneficiary, with varying income-tax consequences; therefore, take care that the beneficiaries are informed of these tax consequences before selecting the appropriate option. If you are not knowledgeable in this area, advise the beneficiaries to consult tax counsel or an accountant before reaching a decision on how to receive benefits from these plans.

Other plans in which tax considerations are essential—and to which named beneficiaries or a decedent's estate might be entitled—include savings plans, employee stock-option plans, and other employee-benefit plans.

Retirement plan benefits are taxable for federal estate tax purposes, and by some states for inheritance tax. They generally pass through a beneficiary designation, the same as life insurance.

Retirement plan benefits are subject to income taxes as well as federal and state death taxes. The result of combining income taxes with estate taxes and inheritance taxes is to make the taxation of retirement plan benefits extremely complex. It is therefore very important that the beneficiary consult a tax adviser before retitling assets or making withdrawals. The failure to withdraw assets from retirement plans according to IRS regulations can also result in the loss of certain planning opportunities. It is essential that the executor, especially if she is the beneficiary, or is advising the beneficiary, understands the tax consequences, and acts in a timely fashion when dealing with retirement plan assets.

Type of Retirement Plan

The first step is to identify the category of retirement plan. Is it a pension plan, profit-sharing plan, Individual Retirement Account (IRA), or other plan? While the same general rules

are applied to each type of plan, there may be par
issues related to a specific plan. The plan adminis
should be contacted to furnish a written summary of the
available options and the income tax consequences of each.
While the discussion below will apply in general terms to all
retirement plans, it focuses on the rules relating to IRAs.

Age of Decedent. Generally, assets must start to be withdrawn from a plan before the beneficiary's "required beginning date," which is April 1 of the year after the decedent
reaches age 70½. The beneficiary's options may be affected
depending upon whether the decedent had reached this age.

Age and Identity of Beneficiaries. There are many options
available depending upon the age and identity of the beneficiary. There are four categories of potential beneficiaries.

Spouse as Beneficiary. In general, the surviving spouse can
select any of the following distribution options:

1. Delay taking distributions until the decedent would
   have reached age 70½
2. Withdraw the balance of the plan no later than December
   31 of the fifth year following the decedent's death
3. Withdraw all of the money from the retirement plan
   and roll the money into a new IRA owned by the surviving spouse

Beneficiary Other Than Surviving Spouse. If the decedent
dies before the required beginning date, the beneficiary can
either withdraw all of the money by December 31 of the fifth
calendar year after the decedent's death, or withdraw the
assets over the beneficiary's remaining life expectancy. If the
decedent dies after reaching the required beginning date
(April 1 of the year after reaching age 70½), the beneficiary
must withdraw the assets over a period of time no longer
than that in which the decedent could have during the decedent's lifetime.

Decedent's Estate as Beneficiary. If the decedent dies before reaching his required beginning date, the executor of the estate must withdraw the assets before December 31 of the fifth calendar year after the decedent's death. If the estate is no longer being administered, the beneficiaries of the estate must withdraw the assets within this time frame. If the decedent had reached his required beginning date before dying, the assets must generally be withdrawn over the decedent's remaining life expectancy.

For example, if the decedent had a three-year life expectancy immediately before death, the beneficiaries must withdraw the assets over three years.

Trust as Beneficiary. A trust will generally be treated the same as if the estate were named the beneficiary. In certain limited situations, a trust can be named as a beneficiary and the distribution rules will be applied as if the beneficiary of the trust were the direct beneficiary of the plan. This allows the beneficiary similar options to those indicated above for spouses and persons other than spouses.

Because of the many overlapping tax consequences, this is one area in which it is absolutely essential to receive expert advice.

Be Certain You Have It All

Conduct an extensive search of the decedent's personal papers and belongings. Most large companies issue periodic statements identifying the benefits to which an employee is entitled upon disability, death, or other termination of employment. Group insurance certificates should be available, and payroll slips often indicate deductions for various company plans. As executor, write to the last employer of the decedent, and all prior employers, to be informed about every work-related benefit to which the estate or beneficiaries are entitled. Also request written information on any accumulated vacation or sick-pay benefits to which the decedent was entitled. (Keep copies of all correspondence and extensive notes on any telephone conversations.)

Medical Insurance

If the decedent had a prolonged illness, there could be large outstanding hospital and doctor bills. Make certain that all available medical coverage is utilized. In some cases the estate might be entitled to double coverage—for example, if the decedent was covered at work as well as by private medical insurance. Death may also have been caused by circumstances that bring into play other types of payments. For example, if death was caused by an automobile accident in a state where no-fault insurance is in effect, the estate might be entitled to payment of the decedent's medical bills by his own hospitalization carrier and by the insurance company that insured the decedent's car (through no-fault personal injury protection payments). The estate or beneficiaries might also be entitled to damages from the party responsible for the accident that caused the death.

If death was work-related, the estate or beneficiaries may be entitled to benefits under the state workers' compensation law. Therefore, when there is any question about the cause of death, investigate the possibility of third-party payments to the estate and to other beneficiaries. Failure to do so could be considered negligence.

If there is any doubt at all about potential recovery of medical bills and costs, or damages under workers' compensation, or a negligence or *tort claim*—where another party could be held responsible for injuries or death to the decedent—consult with an attorney and document the advice given to you. Many death-related claims must be brought within a limited time following death.

12 | Life Insurance

While the collection of life insurance proceeds payable to a named beneficiary is not technically your responsibility (since the moneys paid do not constitute an asset of the estate), for tax and cash flow and control reasons, be aware of all insurance policies on the life of the decedent. If the beneficiaries are relying on you to handle all of the decedent's affairs, including the collection of nonprobate assets, take an active role in helping them collect the proceeds.

Life Insurance Payable to the Estate

If life insurance is payable to the estate, or if the proceeds are payable to a named beneficiary who predeceased the decedent and no contingent or substitute beneficiary was named, then the proceeds are paid to the estate. It is your responsibility to collect the proceeds of insurance.

In addition to handling insurance proceeds payable to the estate, you must have insurance information available for preparation of the federal estate-tax return (and state inheritance-tax returns where applicable). Insurance companies furnish Form 712 (at no cost) to the beneficiaries, as well as directly to the executor, but only when requested in writing to do so. Form 712 contains all the relevant data concerning the amount of the proceeds payable, the amount of any outstanding loan, dividends, and specific information about the ownership of the policy.

Collecting the Proceeds

The actual collection of the life insurance proceeds usually is not an involved or time-consuming process. To facilitate collection, contact the agent or local office of the life insurance company that issued the policy, find out exactly what documentation is required, and ask the company to send you a claim form. The insurance company immediately establishes a file. It also requests a duly certified death certificate and the policy itself (if it has been lost, the insurer will still pay the claim so long as the policy was in force at the time of death of the insured) or other relevant information. (See additional information on page 102.) Life insurance policies are written with contestable periods, usually one to two years. This means, with rare exceptions (e.g., in case of obvious fraud), that most companies will not delay payment of the proceeds once the contestable period has elapsed. Insurance contracts also contain a limited period following purchase during which payment will not be made if the insured commits suicide. Aside from these two considerations, proceeds typically are payable within a few weeks of death.

Photocopy the entire policy—especially the application—before releasing it to the insurance agent or mailing it to the insurance company. The information may be vital evidence in the event of a dispute with the insurer or in certain tax matters. Use registered mail and request a receipt.

Accidental Death

Many life insurance policies contain added benefits, such as *double indemnity* (double the face amount of the policy), payable in cases of death from other than natural causes.

Therefore, check to see if this type of coverage was in force. The policy should be reviewed thoroughly—if necessary by an expert such as an attorney or a CLU (chartered life underwriter)—before it is surrendered to the insurer.

Review of Prior Records

Most life insurance policies contain *nonforfeiture* provisions. These indicate the value of the policy in the event that the policy owner decides to discontinue payment or otherwise change the status of the insurance. Nonforfeiture provisions in policies with cash value usually include the right to cash in the policy for a stated amount and the right to purchase a reduced paid-up policy commensurate with the premiums paid to date.

A third option—and often the option selected by the insurance company if a payment is stopped and no other option is selected—is the *extended-term option*. Under an extended-term option, the company continues the policy in force, in effect utilizing its cash value to purchase a term policy that will expire in a given amount of years and months. All of these nonforfeiture guarantees are clearly indicated on a chart within the policy. Therefore, it is entirely possible that death benefits are due to beneficiaries, or to the estate, from a policy for which no premiums have been paid for months or even years prior to death. Never throw out a policy without writing to the insurance company for confirmation of its status.

While you certainly cannot be expected to know everything the decedent did at any time, review her checkbooks and other records to see if there are any payments to or receipts from insurance companies for policies. If you are not able to determine whether the decedent owned an insurance policy in a particular company, or whether a policy once owned but discontinued still has any value, then in every instance request specific information on any particular policy from the insurance company involved and keep a documented record of the response for your permanent file.

Settlement Options

Most insurance policies give the beneficiaries the option of selecting the manner in which the proceeds are paid. While the growing tendency is for beneficiaries to take the proceeds in a lump sum and invest it themselves, any decision on the part of the executor and the beneficiaries should be based on a thorough knowledge of all the available options.

These options include leaving the money to earn interest with the insurance company. Interest usually begins to accrue either from the date of death or from the date the claim is received by the company. (Check immediately, since interest may not begin to accrue until you submit a death claim.) There is also an installment option under which the beneficiary can receive a certain monthly amount for as long as the proceeds (together with interest) last. Alternatively, the beneficiary can select a term (5, 10, 15, or 20 years) and have the proceeds paid monthly, together with interest, during that period. Proceeds of insurance are not otherwise subject to income taxes, but when the proceeds are invested, the interest on the proceeds is taxable.

Other Insurance

Be aware of all death-related benefits to which the decedent's beneficiaries would be entitled. In addition to the standard life insurance contract or other insurance and fringe benefits, the decedent might have had more limited insurance contracts in force that provide a recovery depending on the cause of death. For example, a decedent might have purchased travel insurance before being killed in an airplane accident. A decedent who traveled regularly or who was particularly concerned about accidental death may have owned *accident only* coverage, which means that payment may be limited to cases of accidental death or, more limited still, to accidental death while traveling by public conveyances or other modes of travel. In the event of death by accidental cause, make every effort to ascertain whether the decedent had insurance that specifically covers the circumstances of death. Check particularly with credit-card companies such as American Express, which may offer group term coverages on an automatic basis, and travel clubs such as the Automobile Association of America, and with the decedent's bank to see if he had insurance that paid off any debt or mortgage at death.

13 | Cash, Bank Accounts, and Listed Securities

Cash

If the decedent had cash on her person or at home or in a safe-deposit box at the time of death, make an accurate record of the surrounding circumstances. For example, "$400 found in decedent's top dresser drawer" or "$150 in envelope in decedent's safe-deposit box with decedent's son's name on the envelope." This will help establish the source or ownership of the funds, if relevant, and it is especially important when there might be a question whether the cash represents the decedent's income or the property of others. Once it has been discovered, deposit the cash in the estate's checking account for a permanent record, and invest any cash not destined to be used in the immediate future in an insured account at interest.

Handling Checking Accounts, Savings Accounts, and Certificates of Deposit

After a thorough search of the decedent's documents and papers, and after preparing an inventory (see Chapter 9), you should be aware of the extent of the decedent's bank accounts. In situations where the money is unproductive (for example, $10,000 in a non-interest-bearing checking account), immediately transfer these funds to the estate checking account and then write a check payable to an interest-bearing account, unless the estate checking account itself pays a reasonable amount of interest.

It is extremely important that you have proper documentation of all bank account moneys for the inventory, the final accounting, and the state and federal tax returns. You, or the attorney for the estate, should promptly write to each bank, giving the account number and title and requesting an up-to-date statement of the moneys in each account—especially the date-of-death value. While most banking institutions post interest at stated intervals, it is necessary to have the interest stated to the date of death. Also request the date on which the account was first established, and ask whether the decedent had any other accounts or safe-deposit boxes in that bank.

If there is any indication of the potential existence of other bank accounts, send a letter to all banks in which the decedent had any prior accounts, as well as to other banking institutions in the area in which the decedent worked or resided. Be sure to write to banks in cities where the decedent had a vacation home, as well as cities where he did business (see Appendix for sample letter).

Certificates of Deposit

It is especially important when dealing with certificates of deposit to be aware of the maturity dates and the terms of the certificates. Often when a certificate matures, you need to take steps to change the investment, or else it is automatically rolled over into a new certificate or placed in a low-interest savings account. On the other hand, there is no necessity for you immediately to cash in certificates in the decedent's name that are paying an attractive rate of interest. Unless the cash is otherwise needed by the estate, you may permit the money to remain at the current interest rate until the certificate matures.

Banking regulations usually permit the death of the insured to accelerate the maturity date of a certificate of deposit. For example, suppose someone who dies in March 1995 has a certificate that matures in January 1996. You can probably cash it in and receive full interest to the date the certificate is terminated, without the usual penalty imposed for cashing it in before the maturity date.

Jointly Owned Bank Accounts

If the decedent held a checking account, savings account, or certificate of deposit jointly with another person at the time of death, ascertain the precise interest of the estate in the account. Determine who has the legal right to possession and ownership, who is responsible for paying taxes on that particular property, and who now has the right to spend the money in the account. If, for example, the decedent had a $10,000 certificate of deposit in his name and his wife's name, as joint tenants with the right of survivorship, in most states the money automatically belongs to the surviving spouse. However, you have to include that property in the federal estate-tax return, and in the state death-tax return if required. If in fact the account was taxable, you might want some guarantee that funds would be available to pay the proportional share of the tax attributable to that jointly held property.

If the decedent had a bank account in her name in trust for another person, in most states the account is taxable to the decedent, but the property passes to the beneficiary. This is called a *Totten trust* (named after the individual involved in the first case that dealt with this technique), sometimes known as the "poor man's will." By this device the decedent can pass property to another without having to prepare a will. This, however, leaves you in a precarious position because of the tax, and it might be wise to request that the bank arrange to have the state death tax paid, or money withheld, at the time of distribution of the proceeds to the beneficiary (see Chapter 17).

Whenever any question arises regarding the respective rights of the estate and the surviving co-owner (or co-owners), you should act only after obtaining legal counsel about the respective ownership rights of the parties. Many states have specific laws governing *multiple party accounts* in financial institutions, and the attorney for the estate should review these laws.

Handling the Decedent's Securities

While the decedent's personal records may indicate what—if any—securities were owned at the time of death, ascertain the full extent of his investment portfolio. Obtain this information by contacting all known brokerage houses with which the decedent conducted business in the three to five years preceding death. This is especially important if any securities that were purchased were not personally received by the decedent but were held by the brokerage house in its own account. (Look through canceled checks and tax returns of the previous five years for records of such transactions.)

In some cases the decedent's broker might have had standing orders or authority to purchase and sell securities on the decedent's behalf. Therefore, prompt notice of death should be given. Stock purchases made after the decedent's death might be interpreted as actions taken on behalf of you as the executor (and for which the beneficiaries may try to hold you personally liable in the event that the investment in question is a poor one).

Immediately take possession of all of the decedent's securities; write to the brokerage houses in question for a complete record of the decedent's transactions; request that all stock certificates and other evidences of investment be turned over to you immediately; and request that all standing orders be canceled immediately. It will be extremely helpful to obtain copies of all transactions made by or for the decedent for the previous few years. If these records are not among the decedent's papers, request them from the broker.

You also must know the purchase date and purchase price of the securities and their value as of the date of death (see Chapter 21). You can obtain this information from the brokerage house in question; from the stock pages of the *Wall Street Journal*, the *New York Times*, or your local newspaper; or from your bank or trust company. (Save the copy of the *Wall Street Journal* published on or following the date of death.)

Usually you have the right to sell securities unless the decedent's will states otherwise. If you are not certain about the advisability of selling securities, obtain the written consent of the beneficiaries before converting the stock into cash. This is particularly desirable in cases when the beneficiaries might prefer to receive the securities themselves as part of the distribution; this assumes that other sources can readily be drawn on to cover the various expenses of the estate.

How to Transfer Securities

While brokers' procedures as well as state regulations differ somewhat with respect to the sale of securities, some general guidelines are applicable in most cases. If the stock is registered solely in the decedent's name and you sell the stock, considerable delays can result, with consequent loss in value, dividends, or the availability of funds to the estate. Some brokerage firms put through a sell order immediately when the executor sells the decedent's stock, but delay making payment of the funds until the time-consuming process of changing title from the decedent to the executor has been completed. This process can last from three to five weeks and can create hardship if the funds are needed immediately. Therefore, whenever it seems to be necessary to sell the stock or convert it into cash within a reasonably short time, have the stock transferred from the decedent's name to your name (in your capacity as executor of the estate). Alternatively, the stock can be placed in a bank custody account, which would put it in a "street name."

The stock certificate should be registered in the name of "Mary Roe, Executrix of the Will of Richard Roe, Deceased" (or whatever wording is used in your locality). Once the stock has been transferred to you, it can be sold and payment made within the customary five business days.

Stock transfers can be made through the broker with whom the decedent (or you) regularly conducted business, or you can write directly to the transfer agent indicated on the security itself (usually a bank or trust company). The documents usually required by transfer agents are a *short certificate* (often the requirement is that the short certificate be updated to within 60 days of the date of transfer) and the stock certificate signed by you. If there are many certificates, or for other convenience reasons, you can execute a *stock power*, evidencing a transfer of ownership of stock but kept physically separate from the stock for security purposes. Stock-power forms can be obtained from stationery stores. The transfer agent often requests that signatures be guaranteed at a commercial bank familiar with your signature.

In addition, transfer agents can require an affidavit of domicile attesting that the decedent was domiciled in the state where the will was probated. Depending on the circumstances or on the particular regulations of the transfer agent, other documents may be requested.

Obtaining the necessary information and having securities processed through brokerage houses and transfer agents can be time-consuming. Start the process as quickly as possible once the decision has been made to sell the securities. If the securities are in the joint names of the decedent and a survivor, similar information must be furnished to the transfer agent in order to have the securities placed in the name of the survivor, but a short certificate usually is not required.

Securities that are in *bearer form*, such as municipal bonds and similar instruments, should be placed immediately in a secure area, preferably a safe-deposit box titled in your name, so that there can be no doubt that the property in question is an asset of the estate.

Investment Responsibilities

If you are acting under a will that gives you extensive investment powers, your authority to handle the decedent's securities and other investments is broader (and safer) than is the case if you had to rely solely on state investment law.

If the decedent specifically limited your duties, or if the decedent gave instructions that all securities were to be sold immediately following her death, then comply with this request as expeditiously as is reasonably possible under the circumstances. In the absence of specific authority, you are governed by the "reasonable and prudent man" rule. Some states have held that when the executor has particular expertise, he or she (or "it" where a corporate executor is involved) can be held to a higher standard of care than a nonprofessional executor. The following steps can protect you in these circumstances:

1. As soon as possible after death, review the decedent's investment portfolio with professionals. These include the trust or investment departments of local banks and securities brokers.
2. Consider the needs of the estate and the beneficiaries. If cash is needed for taxes or other liquidity problems or to meet beneficiaries' immediate needs, then you

may not have the luxury of gambling on a possible future increase in the value of the securities. Under these circumstances it might very well be necessary immediately to sell the investments and not risk a loss in value that could result in tax deficiencies, lack of needed capital, or personal hardship to the beneficiaries (as well as personal liability on your part).

3. When the size of the estate warrants it, talk to tax counsel and/or certified public accountants. If the decedent had employed the services of an accountant or tax attorney familiar with his personal affairs and overall tax picture, then obtain from one or both of these professionals their evaluation of the decedent's financial status. However, since the ultimate decision is yours, a second or third opinion is a good idea if you feel you are not getting proper advice. A well-intentioned executor who receives poor advice from the wrong source can still be held personally liable for unsatisfactory results.

4. Keep on top of all investments. The easiest way to get in trouble when administering investments is to ignore them. Market conditions change, and decisions that make sense at any given time may be wrong only a short time later. Then, too, investments are not always passive, and many involve timely decisions. For example, stock options might become available that must be exercised quickly.

5. Take every reasonable step to locate all of the decedent's assets. If, for example, the decedent had regularly purchased securities from different brokerage houses, a check of withdrawals and checkbook stubs for the preceding five years might indicate the purchase of a security or an investment not otherwise evidenced. Keep a close watch on incoming mail, especially for dividends and other investment information. There

may also be situations in which the decedent owned securities jointly with other persons (see Chapter 17).

Mutual Funds and Tax-Free Securities

Your obligations in regard to mutual funds, tax-free bonds, and other investments are similar to those for securities in general. While many municipal-type bonds or bond funds are exempt from federal income tax (and in some cases from state income tax), they are in most cases subject to death taxes, and they are still, of course, assets of the estate to be administered by you. While listed securities might fall in value more precipitously than municipal bonds, you still have to decide whether to sell or to retain more conservative types of investments, such as corporate bonds and Series E bonds. In these cases, however, since almost complete safety is assured and the downside risk, if any, is greatly minimized, your potential liability in retaining such assets is diminished proportionately.

14 Real Estate

Most states treat real estate differently from other property. Unlike title to other property, title to real estate usually passes automatically at death. Title can pass to a surviving joint owner, to the beneficiaries of the real estate under the will, or, in cases of intestacy, to the decedent's heirs.

Rented Property

If the decedent did not own real estate but was renting at the time of death, review the lease to determine the contractual obligations of the estate. Many landlords are sympathetic in these circumstances, and many are indifferent. Find out how long the estate will be obligated to continue the rental payments and make whatever arrangements are legally and practically possible to reduce the estate's liability. If there is any question about the legal liability of the estate, consult legal counsel, since you can be held personally accountable for making rental payments in excess of what would otherwise be legally required.

Determining the Decedent's Interest

If the decedent owned real estate at the time of death, the first question is to determine her interest in that real estate. If the property in question is titled solely in the decedent's name, look no further. In many instances, however, real estate is titled in the names of two or more persons. It then becomes essential to determine the interest of the estate or heirs or named beneficiaries of the real estate. In many instances the family home will be titled in the name of the decedent and his spouse. At the death of one spouse, the property in most cases is owned solely by the survivor, and for all practical purposes you have few responsibilities in regard to the home. However, ascertain the state's legal requirements before you relinquish responsibility for the home.

If the decedent was one of several owners of commercial real estate, a question of major consequence is whether the decedent's interest passed to the surviving joint owners or to the heirs. If the decedent's property passed by survivorship, as in cases when the property was owned *jointly with right of survivorship*, then the survivor not only takes over ownership of the property but also, in most cases, the responsibility for care and management of the property. If, however, the property was owned by the decedent and others as *tenants in common* and not as joint tenants with the right of survivorship, then the decedent's interest in the property passes to her *devisees* (the person or persons to whom the decedent bequeathed the property under the will) or, in the absence of a will, to the decedent's heirs at law. In these cases, while title usually vests immediately in the beneficiaries or heirs, you may, depending on local laws, be responsible for the property until the estate's administration has been completed.

In order to determine the ownership interest in real estate, secure the originals, or obtain copies, of all deeds and other evidences of title. If a deed indicates that the property was owned solely by the decedent, there should be no problem in regard to title. If the property was in the names of the decedent and his spouse, then ascertain the legal consequences. The result in most instances is that the surviving spouse becomes the sole owner of the entire property. If property was owned jointly by two or more persons and the other joint owner or owners are not the spouse of the decedent, obtain a legal interpretation of the documents in question as soon as possible after your appointment has been formalized.

Appraisals

While the question of whether the executor or the title owner has the right to administer the property varies depending on the state and jurisdiction involved, it is usually the executor's responsibility to file the necessary death-tax returns for the estate. In order to determine the value of the real estate in question, as well as for other tax purposes (such as computing the date-of-death value of real estate that is to be sold), accurate appraisals are necessary.

The kind of appraisal required depends on the relative value of the property as well as the value of the entire estate. In the case of a decedent and surviving spouse with a relatively small estate, if their jointly owned home is valued at $75,000, for example, and the remainder of their probate estate at $20,000, an appraisal by a real estate appraiser familiar with the area in which the decedent resided should suffice. If, on the other hand, there is valuable commercial property, then, in order to substantiate the valuation for tax purposes or for other purposes involving the sale or distribution of the property, obtain an in-depth appraisal from an appraiser who is a member of a professional society or association of appraisers. The appraiser should take into consideration other relevant factors, such as rental income, or particular features that might affect valuation (see Chapter 26). Check the requirements of local taxing authorities. For sale purposes or for filing death-tax returns, local law or practice might require, for example, two separate appraisals from appraisers who are qualified to act before the respective taxing authorities.

Administering and Maintaining Real Estate

Since title to the property in almost every instance passes at the decedent's death to the beneficiaries or heirs, ascertain exactly what your duties are in regard to administering and supervising the property. These duties depend on two factors: (1) the nature of the property itself, and (2) the applicable state law. If, for example, the property in question is a home owned jointly by the decedent and his wife, and if the wife continues to reside in the home, there will be little, if anything, for you to do to maintain and administer the property. Once it is ascertained that the appropriate insurance coverage is in effect and provisions are made for payment of any outstanding mortgage, the decedent's spouse should be able to assume responsibility for the normal day-to-day maintenance of the home. Serious problems can arise, however, in cases when the real estate interest of the decedent is otherwise.

Among the responsibilities of anyone charged with administering real estate are the following:

1. Maintaining the premises in general. If the property is rented, not only must the rent be collected, but you must check the premises to make sure they are being kept up properly. Problems can arise in the case of vacant property. Routine activities such as cutting the grass must be provided for if the property is not to appear vacant and so constitute an open invitation to vandalism and theft. If there is any question whatsoever about who has the ultimate responsibility for caring for the real estate, you and the beneficiaries should make a joint determination about who is responsible for maintaining the real estate.
2. Checking insurance policies to make certain that coverage is adequate and premiums have been paid.
3. Covering monthly or other periodic payments for such expenses as utilities (water, gas, electricity, sewer) and property taxes.

Mortgages, Liens, Leases, and Contracts

The real estate to be administered by the personal representative must be limited to the amount of the decedent's interest in the property at the time of death. Therefore, in valuing and describing the decedent's real property, take into consideration outstanding obligations or liens. If the decedent had made an agreement to sell or lease the property, then you are responsible for carrying out the terms of that contract. In all cases make a diligent search to ascertain the exact status of the real estate, because in many jurisdictions liens can be placed against the real estate for failure to comply with mortgage provisions and payments. In the case of an outstanding mortgage, payments should be kept current until a final determination is made in regard to the property—whether to sell it and pay off the mortgage or whether to continue the mortgage—which might be preferable if the outstanding mortgage had a much lower interest rate than the prevailing market rate.

Sale of Real Estate

State laws vary about the executor's right to sell real estate; consult the law before you unilaterally decide to sell. Some states give you the right to sell real estate in every instance, while others give you the right to sell real estate in order to raise necessary cash to pay taxes and other expenses. Many states require you to obtain permission from the court before selling real estate and distributing the proceeds of the sale. The right to sell real estate can be specifically given under the terms of the will or can be agreed to by you and the beneficiaries.

To be sure that you are acting properly in selling the decedent's real estate, follow these procedures:

1. Have the property accurately and adequately appraised to determine its fair market value.

2. Obtain written permission from the beneficiaries to sell the property at the indicated price; or obtain court approval for the sale at the specified price, with the indicated distribution (in certain jurisdictions, courts may require you to post bond or additional bond to cover the proceeds from the sale of the real estate until the proceeds are distributed to the beneficiaries).

3. Have the entire procedure surrounding the sale reviewed by legal counsel *before* you sign any documents.

Real Estate Located in Another State

Most states maintain the right to tax real estate located within their borders at the death of the owner of the property. Therefore, a personal representative usually must be appointed to administer the property and see that taxes are paid. You do not, however, have authority to handle the decedent's real estate in another state unless you have complied with that state's requirements. Your responsibility in this regard, in most instances, should be limited to making certain that either you or another executor or administrator (usually called an *ancillary* administrator or representative) is appointed in that state. You are also responsible for including reference to that out-of-state property in preparing federal estate-tax returns and state tax returns (even though the property will be taxed in the state where it is located and not in the state of the decedent's domicile).

15 Investing Estate Assets

Generally speaking, you are under no specific obligation to invest funds belonging to the estate. This does not mean, however, that you cannot be held accountable by the beneficiaries if you leave estate assets idle. Your obligation to "protect" estate assets implies that you have a duty to invest funds prudently and earn interest. Furthermore, your obligations may be specified in the will or in your state laws. In addition, if there is an unusual delay in settling the estate and making the final distribution, you will be expected to keep estate assets productive during the intervening period.

Your best and safest route in investment is to start with the provisions of the will and stay within those guidelines. If the will does not expressly authorize you to invest estate assets, have your attorney apply to the probate court for permission. Another course of action is to make investments that conform to state law. Many states provide a list of investments (or types of investments) that are deemed "reasonable." These are fairly conservative.

Most important, before you invest, be certain that after you make the investment, the estate will have enough ready cash for quickly paying debts, taxes, and administration expenses, and that the appropriate distribution can then be made to the beneficiaries.

You are really caught between the proverbial rock and a

hard place. You have to keep estate assets reasonably invested, yet at the same time keep investments liquid enough to pay the estate's debts, taxes, and expenses, and distribute each beneficiary's share when you complete probate.

Where to Start

Since you can't invest assets you don't have, locate assets or secure pertinent information so you can identify and inventory each asset (see Chapter 13).

To be extra safe, contact Commerce Clearing House, Inc. (4025 West Peterson Avenue, Chicago, IL 60646), and purchase its reprint of *Examination Technique Handbook for Estate Tax Examiners*. The handbook is used as a guideline by the IRS in auditing federal estate-tax returns. It is a good source of information for locating, inventorying, and properly valuing estate assets.

Need for Liquidity

Once you know how large the estate is and what types of assets the estate encompasses, you can begin to estimate what debts the estate must pay and what specific cash bequests you will have to make. You also have to "guesstimate" how much money you'll need to pay taxes and administration expenses. You have an obligation to determine whether the estate has sufficient liquidity to meet financial demands. If the estate does not, it is your duty to formulate an orderly investment plan to increase estate liquidity.

If there isn't enough cash to pay these expenses when the time comes (but there was enough value when you took over as executor), you could be surcharged for "speculating on the continued maintenance of estate values."

To avoid these problems, take the following steps:

1. Value assets as quickly as possible.
2. Draw up a list of estimated debts, taxes, expenses, and other cash needs.
3. Compute the difference between "liquidity" (the cash you'll have) and cash needs.
4. See how much of the estate consists of cash or "near cash" (bonds or savings instruments with a maturity date prior to the date you'll need cash).
5. Decide which permanent asset(s) should be sold to meet the estate's needs if your analysis shows you don't have enough cash.
6. See if any assets should be disposed of immediately to avoid destruction or loss (including stocks or bonds that may fall in value or vacant non-income-producing real estate).
7. Consider selling small or odd-lot holdings as well as underproductive assets. Confer with the beneficiaries and obtain their *written* approval *before* you make *any* sales. Obtain written approval from them or see if they would like you to hold certain assets (also obtain written consent for "holding" assets you otherwise feel you should sell).
8. Surrender certificates of deposit to the issuer before maturity. You can do this without penalty when the owner dies. (If the bank gives you any trouble, mention Federal Reserve Regulation Q.)

How to Invest Money

Almost all commercial banks offer money-market accounts that are federally insured. Make certain that your investments in any one institution do not exceed the amount for which federal insurance is available. Obviously, daily money-market accounts offer the most flexibility and liquidity; in the event that money is needed quickly, they should be given the first consideration. If a large sum of money will not be needed for longer periods of time, then consider six-month Treasury bills.

In certain situations it is more beneficial to have tax-exempt investments in order to reduce the income-tax consequences. In that event, contact a stockbroker or banker to make certain that any tax-exempt investments provide the greatest degree of safety.

Whenever it seems inadvisable to invest all of the funds in an insured money-market account or in United States government securities, obtain investment advice from a stockbroker, banker, or insurance agent (preferably a CLU or ChFC).

Do not become involved in long-term investment decisions. These should be left to the judgment of the beneficiaries or to the trustee of the trust to which you will turn over estate assets.

16 Handling a Family Business

The most difficult asset to administer in any estate is a family business. There are at least four major problems: (1) lack of liquidity—not enough cash to pay administration expenses, death taxes, and specific bequests; (2) lack of investment diversification—often all or most of a decedent's wealth is in one (often, because of the decedent's death, financially shaky) business; (3) non-marketability—it's hard, and sometimes impossible, to sell a minority interest in a family-owned business (since ownership of less than 51 percent of the voting shares can't control the actions of the board of directors, force the payment of dividends, or ensure the hiring or firing of corporate employees or the payment of dividends); and (4) the family's emotional involvement and company-employee relationships—difficulties are often encountered because decisions are not always rationally made.

Before You Accept

Before you accept the formidable responsibility of an estate consisting mainly of a business interest, be sure you obtain a satisfactory answer to the following questions:

- Does the company have (or can it get) experienced and qualified management?
- Is there enough business-generated income, after paying reasonable salaries and bonuses, to pay appropriate dividends to the beneficiaries?
- Can the business survive in the hands of others? (It's unlikely that a personal-service business, such as a professional practice, will survive the death of its owner.)
- Is retention of the business primarily to create employment opportunities for family members who are qualified or willing to run it?
- Are you as executor capable (either personally or through agents) of managing the business? (Geographically, how far away is it?)
- Is there adequate liquidity—outside the business (through life insurance proceeds or other cash-equivalent investments)—to cover death taxes and administration expenses and to provide for the surviving spouse and children not actively engaged in the business?
- Can you effectively control the direction of the business? (Or do you have to share control with cofiduciaries who may have conflicts of interest or may not have good business judgment?)

The General Rule

As a general rule, the executor does not have the legal right to continue the decedent's business. Your job is to conserve estate assets and liquidate them as soon as reasonably possible. This means that without state law, court, or specific authority in the decedent's will, you continue the business at your own risk. Any income and gains go to the beneficiaries, while you are responsible for any losses. And don't let the nature of the business mislead you into thinking that you can handle it without proper authority. A situation as uncomplicated as that of a single practitioner's medical practice recently resulted in a lawsuit when the doctor's widow, without court approval, tried to continue the practice by hiring a new doctor, found it wouldn't succeed because the new doctor couldn't relate to the patients, and then sold the practice at a price significantly below what it was worth when her husband died.

Exceptions to the General Rule

You can safely continue a business under certain conditions. First, the will may specifically allow you to do so without personal risk. Second, state law may allow business continuation (check with your attorney and obtain written confirmation). Third, you may have your attorney petition the probate court for permission to continue the business. Fourth, you could safely continue the business with the written consent of all interested parties as long as they were fully informed of the facts and as long as they were all competent adults. If you are going to run the business using provisions in a will as your authority, note that those provisions must be both definite and explicit. It must be clear that the decedent gave you such permission.

If you are going to continue the business under the authority of state statutes, you probably will be permitted to continue only long enough to "wind up" the business. This does not mean you have to close the doors the day after a person dies, but you cannot continue running the business indefinitely. Here again, obtain written advice from an attorney.

The safest authority for continuing a business is a written court order. Your attorney can obtain a court order allowing you to continue the business for several months or up to a year or longer, depending on the circumstances.

Legal Responsibility

As an executor managing a business of a deceased person, you can be sued by any number of people for any number of reasons. You could be sued by a recently divorced spouse, a beneficiary, a stockholder of the deceased individual's corporation, a creditor, or anyone else interested in the estate for mismanaging any phase of the business or for the improper use, operation, or distribution of the enterprise.

In managing a business, you are held to the standard of care that an ordinary, prudent businessperson should exercise. If loss or injury occurs, therefore, you must be adequately insured or pay the expenses personally. Of course, if your actions were prudent, you will not be surcharged, but you may still incur significant court costs and legal expenses in the process of defending yourself.

Who decides whether your acts are those of an ordinary, prudent businessperson? If the parties cannot agree, then the courts will have to decide. This can often result in long delays and a great deal of inconvenience and expense to the estate and to the executor.

Where Does the Money Come From?

Before you accept the position of executor of an estate with a family business, determine the amount of the operating funds of the business. You may not have the right to use money from the decedent's general estate for operating the business. Typically, the only funds you can safely use to carry on the business are those invested in the business at the time the decedent dies.

Even obtaining loans to run the business may be difficult under state law. In order to mortgage estate property as security for any loan, you must have express or implied authority from the will or from state laws. If you continue an unincorporated business, you subject every asset in the estate (in addition to assets invested in the business) to the liability of any new business creditors.

Who Does the Work?

You are obligated personally to perform all acts and duties requiring the *exercise of discretion*. You can hire others to do only *ministerial duties*. In fact, you must act as a prudent person in both what you do and whom you hire. You can be held accountable for hiring somebody who is not suited for the job.

How Much Authority Do You Have?

If you decide to operate an unincorporated sole proprietorship, you have complete authority to make business decisions (and complete responsibility for decisions you make). You can be personally liable for any losses that resulted from these business decisions.

If the decedent owned stock in a corporation, you have a much narrower scope of rights and responsibilities. The property for which you are responsible is the corporate stock, and you must protect the estate's interest through the exercise of that right. The more stock the decedent owned, the more power you have, as executor, in the management of the business. You are obligated to act as a "reasonably prudent stockholder" would under the circumstances.

Typically, if the decedent was a partner, you cannot become a partner unless the other partners consent. Your rights are as follows: (1) to receive income earned by the partnership (to the extent of the decedent's partnership interest), and (2) to obtain reasonable information about what is going on in the business. In most circumstances a partnership, unless otherwise provided for, terminates on the death of one of the partners.

Keeping It Up

You cannot make repairs to business property unless the will expressly or implicitly authorizes you to do so. The question is, What is a repair as opposed to an improvement? Business equipment quickly becomes old and ineffective. Should you buy new machinery or office equipment? First, check for specific authority in the will. Then try to obtain court permission. If the will does not give you clear and unequivocal guidance, and if you cannot obtain court permission and the business cannot be run effectively with its present equipment, sell or liquidate the business.

Can I Make It Grow?

It should be obvious that you need specific guidance just to continue a decedent's business. You must have even greater authority if you want to expand the business or its products or services. Your job is to conserve estate assets rather than to continue or expand the enterprise. Therefore, be extremely conservative about expanding an existing business without proper authority. It's a one-way street. The beneficiaries have everything to gain, while you have everything to lose.

What Should I Do?

Have an attorney examine the will and give you a written interpretation of it vis-à-vis the business. Be sure that the advice you receive is clear; have your attorney state that she has studied the will and state law and that either you can (or cannot) safely continue the business. If the will is silent or ambiguous and state law provides no help, either petition the court for permission to continue the business or obtain the written consent of all beneficiaries.

In any event, adequately insure and protect the business

and keep it running until the decision is made whether to sell it or continue it.

Family Business Checklist

Before you determine whether the business should be sold or continued, document—in writing—answers to the following questions:

- What type of business is it, and are there people capable of running it?
- What is the condition of the physical assets involved?
- Who are the individuals running and operating the business, and are they capable of continuing it over an extended period?
- What are the net worth and overall financial condition of the business?
- Is the business expected to become more—or less—profitable in the future?
- What is the morale of the employees after the owner's or partner's death?
- Is there reliable second-line management who can step in and take the place of senior management, or can other outside people be brought in at a reasonable expense?
- Is there a buy/sell agreement? If so, what are its terms? (The existence of a buy/sell agreement might eliminate all other problems. If the agreement is effective and adequately funded, you will receive cash and no longer be tied to the financial fortunes of the business.)
- What are the current, long-term, or potential liabilities of the business?
- How quickly do beneficiaries need cash, and do they have other large capital needs?

- Can the business be sold, and if so, to whom and at what price?
- Can money be borrowed to maintain, improve, or expand the business?
- If the business is unincorporated, should it be incorporated? (If so, consider what assets should be retained by the estate and its heirs and which should be contributed to the corporation.) Should the corporation make an election to be taxed as a partnership (the so-called "S" corporation election)?
- Can the business provide cash to pay the estate's other expenses?

17 | Jointly Owned Property

The executor administers all of the decedent's probate property. This consists of property in the decedent's name alone as well as property that was jointly owned by the decedent and other persons at the time of death and in which the decedent's interest passed to the estate and not to the other surviving joint owners of the property.

Tenancy in Common

Two or more people (such as a mother and daughter or uncle and nephew) often purchase property and hold title to it as *tenants in common*. Each person owns a proportionate share (e.g., four tenants in common each own one-fourth) and can sell it, give it away, or leave it to whomever he wishes. Each party has an "individual interest." This means that if one party dies, the decedent's interest passes under his will and therefore becomes subject to probate. It does not pass to the surviving joint tenant in common (unless it does so under the decedent-tenant's will or by the laws of intestacy). If an asset was held by someone as a tenant in common, you must treat it as an asset of the estate and dispose of it as dictated under the terms of the will (or intestacy law, if appropriate).

Tenancy by Entireties

A *tenancy by entirety* is a form of property ownership that is available only to husband and wife. Neither party during his or her lifetime (except with the consent of the other) can dispose of his or her interest. At the death of either tenant, the property is owned solely and completely by the survivor—regardless of what the will or intestacy law may provide. Technically, such property is not a probate asset, so you have no legal obligation to assist the family with it. In practice, however, you will be called on to advise the surviving spouse and assist in collecting and distributing such assets.

Joint Tenancy with the Right of Survivorship

Joint tenancy or *joint property* exists when two or more persons (who need not be husband and wife or even related in any way) hold property in such a way that upon the death of either, the property passes automatically to the survivor.

Checklist for Title Transfer

1. You can transfer the title to stocks, bonds, or other securities held by the decedent as a tenant by the entirety or as a joint tenant with right of survivorship through the transfer agent designated on the stock certificate or through a stockbroker. Typically, you will need:

   - The original stock certificate
   - An *assignment of title* (often called a "stock power" or in the case of a bond a "bond power") signed by the surviving joint tenant(s) and guaranteed by a commercial bank or stockbroker
   - A death certificate
   - An affidavit of domicile

2. Ask your stockbroker to assist you with the transfer of title and tell you what specific steps you must take.
3. Title to bank accounts held jointly (either as tenants by entireties or held jointly with right of survivorship) is transferred by submitting a death certificate to the bank.
4. Examine all jointly owned assets to ascertain whether they are subject to probate. Remember also that even nonprobate assets are often subject to federal and/or state death taxes.

Keep in mind that the valuation you place on those assets will have an impact on the potential gain to be realized on a future sale, since death-tax valuation generally establishes an asset's income-tax basis (see Chapter 26).

18 Trusts and Guardianships

The executor often has to cope with a variety of trusts or guardianships that have been established either by the decedent during her lifetime or under the provisions of the will, to take effect after death. Therefore, it is necessary that you understand the purpose and function of trusts and guardianships, and be aware of the duties and responsibilities in regard to property that is now, or will become, trust property.

Guardianships

The Need for a Guardian

In just about every state and jurisdiction, the law does not permit an executor to distribute property of considerable value to a minor or to an incompetent unless an individual or an institution has been appointed to administer the property during the period of minority or incompetency.

Some cases are easy to classify. A gift of $25,000 to a three-year-old child obviously requires that someone handle the money until the child comes of age. But how about a bequest of an automobile to a 17-year-old? Or what if you transfer a large sum of money to an elderly person whose overt manifestations of senility might have been apparent had some investigation been made? Suppose the son has a car accident or the recipient loses or squanders the money? Are you liable?

If you have any question at all about making payment to a beneficiary or heir of an estate for any of the above reasons:

- Ascertain the age of majority in your state.
- Be aware of the local rules for making payment of limited amounts or distributing specific articles without the necessity of formalized appointments.
- Be hypersensitive to any indication of a possible problem, such as a large bequest to a mentally slow, retarded, or elderly person, or gifts to minor children, or the fact that a beneficiary has been recently institutionalized.
- Take the following steps: (1) secure legal counsel, (2) have the court appoint guardians if necessary, and/or (3) obtain the court's approval for the distribution in question.

Guardian of the Person

In most jurisdictions only the surviving parent can appoint a *testamentary guardian of the person* of his minor children in his will. If no testamentary guardian is appointed and a minor beneficiary is involved, it will probably be necessary for the court to appoint a guardian. The guardian stands "in loco parentis"—in the place of a parent—to the child. In most cases this means that the child will live with the guardian and the guardian will supervise the child's day-to-day care, sign her report card, purchase clothing, and perform the usual tasks of a parent. These do not include investing the child's money, but the funds needed for the child's care and maintenance are funneled through the guardian of the person.

If there are minor children and if the children's mother (or father) is still living, then money for the care of the children that belongs to the children and not to the mother (or father) can be paid to the mother (or father) for their daily care and maintenance. If, however, you are the executor of an estate without surviving parents and funds are needed for the care of children prior to the final distribution of the estate, then you can and should make payments to the testamentary guardian if one has been named in the decedent's will. As with all payments from the estate's assets, keep careful records and receipts for all payments. When money must be paid for the care of minor children and no parent or guardian is available, take the necessary steps to have a guardian appointed.

Guardian of the Property

When property is left directly to minor children and no testamentary guardian or trustee has been named in the will, it is necessary, with few exceptions, to have a guardian appointed to administer the property for the minors until they attain their majority. If the proceeds of an insurance policy are payable to a minor child, the life insurance company usually requires the appointment of a guardian. For example, if a bequest in a will leaves $15,000 to a 12-year-old son, then at the time of making distributions from the estate, be certain that a guardian has been appointed to receive these proceeds.

Usually, this is a fairly routine procedure. A relative, friend, or bank or trust company is selected to handle the money and make any necessary payments during minority. A petition to that effect is filed with the local court having jurisdiction over minors and estates, and the court usually approves the appointment expeditiously after ascertaining that the guardian will, in fact, handle the funds for the benefit of the minor involved. The guardian is usually required to file an account with the court at the time that final distribution is made to the minor at majority.

dian Ad Litem

A *guardian ad litem* is usually a lawyer or other qualified individual appointed by the court to represent the interests of minors or incompetents in a specific matter before the court. If, for example, a question arises over the interpretation of a clause in a will that might in effect reduce the share to be received by a particular class of minors (such as the grandchildren of the deceased individual), then the court might have a guardian *ad litem* appointed, either on its own initiative or at someone's request on behalf of the minors. The guardian *ad litem* conducts an investigation, makes a report to the court, or represents the minors in any legal proceedings.

Trusts

Inter Vivos *or Living Trust of the Decedent*

In the case of a trust set up by the decedent during her lifetime and providing for disposition of the trust assets following death, these assets will continue to be handled by the trustee of the trust (see Chapter 30) and will not constitute part of the estate's probate assets (but may be part of the gross estate for computation of the federal or state death tax). In such cases your only responsibility in regard to the assets of the trust is to determine the legality and validity of the trust, by making certain that the property is not, in fact, part of the estate. If, on the other hand, the decedent had set up a trust with the proceeds payable to her estate or payable under her will at death, then these proceeds are part of the probate estate, to be handled and administered by you.

Living or Inter Vivos *"Pourover" Trust*

One of the most popular estate-planning tools is the *pourover trust*. Under this type of plan, assets are "poured over" from the probate estate into a preexisting trust. An individual sets up a trust during his lifetime that may or may not be funded with income-producing assets. In some cases, assets can be placed in the trust during the lifetime and the trustee can invest these assets and pay out the income, with additional assets being paid into the trust at death. Often, one of the principal sources of post-death funding for these trusts is life insurance. The proceeds are paid directly to the trust and bypass the estate.

Another often used feature of this type of plan is that it allows the decedent's will to leave property to the trust. For example, the will might first dispose of personal property (leaving that to the spouse and children), with the residue of the estate (all other property in his name alone) paid to the trustee of the living trust. (The trust must be in effect before the will, so that the will may leave property to the trust—but usually both are prepared at the same time, the trust being executed just prior to the will.)

If you are the executor of an estate in which a trust is a beneficiary, pay particular attention to your accounting procedures. Usually, the only difference between making payments to a named beneficiary or to a trust is that in some cases a more detailed accounting is required for payments to a trust. Maintain a clear distinction between what is "principal" and what is "income" so that a final, accurate accounting and distribution to the trustee can be made. (Incidentally, the terms *principal* and *income* may have been specifically defined in the trust document. If not, state law will provide a definition for these terms. The distinction is important both for tax purposes and also to determine "who gets what."

Executor/Trustee Duties

Your duties and responsibilities as executor are considerably different from those of the trustee. The executor's duties are to collect the assets of the estate, satisfy the outstanding obligations, and make payment to the beneficiaries. Once you have made payment, you will be discharged as executor.

The trustee, on the other hand, is in fact one of the beneficiaries of the estate. The trustee's duties do not begin until you as executor have transferred the assets or trust property to the trustee. From that point on, the trustee's duties and responsibilities are governed by the trust instrument itself. For example, the trust might say that the trustee is responsible for paying certain income to the decedent's spouse for her lifetime, or holding the property in trust until the children reach certain ages and then making distribution to them.

In spite of the differences, a common thread ties together the executor's and the trustee's duties and responsibilities: They may both handle the same property. Since the executor handles the property until it is turned over to the trustee, the trustee has a considerable and vital interest in what the executor does with the potential trust property. Consult with the trustee, when feasible, on such important matters as death taxes and income taxes on the property in question or the sale or exchange of potential trust property during the administration of the estate.

Testamentary Trust

A trust established under the provisions of a will is called a *testamentary trust*. Testamentary trusts do not take effect until death. When the will establishes a trust, your duties as executor are similar to those in which the property in the will is poured over into an *inter vivos* (living) *trust*. You are responsible for administering the property in question, collecting all assets, paying all debts, and then making distribution to the trustee rather than to an individually named beneficiary. The trustee is therefore another named beneficiary under the will, and upon ultimately receiving the property from you, he will then hold and administer the property pursuant to the trust provisions set out in the will.

Keep a careful accounting of the trust property, and in those jurisdictions that require it, make a clear distinction between principal and income. Also consult with the trustee for major decisions about taxes or about the sale or distribution of, or change in, the trust property. In most cases, especially when banks or other corporate trustees are involved, a formal accounting and approval by the court are required before the trustee accepts the trust property from the executor.

Trustee Ad Litem

Although the court does not frequently do so, it can appoint a *trustee ad litem* (also called a *guardian ad litem*), usually an attorney, to represent the interest of unascertained persons in a particular matter before the court. In most situations that involve distribution of the estate to close family members, no problems of this nature arise. Sometimes, however, a question may arise about the rights of unascertained beneficiaries (for example, an unborn grandchild). To protect yourself and ensure fair and conclusive administration and accounting of the estate, you can request the court to appoint a trustee *ad litem* (if the court on its own volition does not appoint one) to represent the interest, if any, of these unascertained persons or beneficiaries.

19 | Debts and Expenses

Funeral and Last Expenses

One of the first bills—and frequently one of the largest you must pay—is the funeral bill. Funeral expenses, cemetery expenses, and related costs—e.g., the costs of religious services, cremation, or grave markers—are normal estate expenses and should be paid out of the estate's assets, unless you feel that the charges are unreasonable or are not as previously agreed on.

If the decedent was ill for some time prior to death, then there may be unpaid medical bills. Ascertain the extent of all of the decedent's medical insurance coverage. Conduct a careful search of the decedent's documents to make sure that all private insurance, work-related coverage, and government benefits have been exhausted before utilizing the estate's assets to cover these costs. Promptly acknowledge receipt of a bill to avoid any legal action. Remember, however, that it is much easier to pay a bill late than to obtain estate funds back from a medical provider when the provider has already received remuneration from an insurance carrier or government agency.

Administrative Expenses

Executor's fees and attorney's fees frequently are the largest element of the administrative expenses and, as such, almost always are subject to court approval. Any contractual agreement between the executor and the attorney with regard to fees can still be questioned by the beneficiaries when the estate is called for audit (an accounting of what came into the estate, what went out, and to whom these amounts were paid). This also applies to any fees charged by the executor. Of course, it is reasonable to pay for services on a periodic basis, but if you pay an attorney a fee that the court later holds to be excessive, you could be surcharged by the court for the amount of the overpayment. Beneficiaries can question fees. The procedure may—or may not—be a judicial proceeding, depending on the state. Some courts do not allow the payment of legal fees without court approval—especially if the fiduciary is an attorney.

Allocate and set aside the appropriate amount for your own and the estate attorney's services, but withhold payment until the court has approved your final accounting. However, if it seems that the administration of the estate will be protracted, perhaps over a period of years, this obviously is not a fair procedure. In this case periodic payments in an amount that would be unquestionably reasonable can be made—with the understanding that, regardless of any other agreements made, the court will have the final say on the reasonableness of the amount of the fee.

Aside from the executor's and attorney's fees, other reasonable costs can be paid when they are incurred (for example, travel expenses, postage and shipping costs, storage and insurance expenses, and the normal and reasonable costs of administering the estate).

Other Debts and Obligations of the Estate

A date-of-death balance sheet that lists (in addition to assets) all of the decedent's obligations is the best way to ascertain the total amount of outstanding bills. These obligations, plus other continuing obligations of the decedent (and now of her estate), are your responsibility. Usually, a will contains a clause directing the payment of all unpaid debts. Even in the absence of such direction, most obligations have to be satisfied before any moneys are paid to beneficiaries. Problems can arise when assets are insufficient to pay all debts and satisfy bequests in the will, and also when any property is mortgaged or otherwise encumbered.

For example, if the decedent left real estate with an outstanding mortgage to his son, who is responsible for paying the mortgage—the son or the estate? Suppose that, at death, the decedent had left debts in the amount of $10,000, a bank account to his daughter with a balance of $8,000, and an automobile worth $15,000 to his son. From which of these assets must you obtain the money to pay the creditors?

First, examine the will to see if it contains helpful directions ("I give and bequeath my real estate located at 651 Shore Drive to my son, DAVID DOE, *free and clear of all encumbrances*"). Second, consult the law of the state of domicile to determine how that state treats this particular problem in legal terms. Obviously, it is imperative to seek legal assistance.

Before satisfying any creditor's claim, be certain that the claim is genuine. By advertising the existence of the estate (as discussed in Chapter 9), you have given notice to all creditors of the decedent's death and have indicated where claims against the estate should be presented. Any unsubmitted claims will be discharged at the same time that the court discharges you of your responsibility. If you have a question about the amount or nature of the claim, inform the court. The court then rules on the validity and amount of the claim prior to the *final adjudication of the executor's account* (the accounting you must submit and have approved before being released from your obligations). State laws and local court regulations vary in the exact procedure required when submitting a formal claim to an estate; therefore, in any case involving a disputed claim, obtain legal advice before making or permanently withholding payments.

20 | State Death Taxes

Almost every estate incurs some state death tax. In some cases the state death tax equals or exceeds the federal death tax. The amount of these taxes should be "guesstimated" by the estate's attorney or accountant so that you can begin to assemble enough cash to meet the demands. If you must sell estate assets to raise cash, your goal must be to obtain the highest price and best terms possible. The sooner you begin the process of analyzing liquidity needs, the less likely it is that this forced sale will turn into a fire sale.

Types of Property Subject to Tax

There are three types of property—real property, tangible personal property, and intangible personal property.

Real property (such as land, commercial buildings, and houses) can be taxed only by the state where the property is located (the so-called *situs* of the property), regardless of where the decedent was domiciled at the time of death.

Tangible personal property (such as furniture, cars, art, or jewelry) can be taxed only by the state where the property is located. (This rule is identical to the rule governing real property.)

Intangible personal property (such as stocks, bonds, bank

) is taxed by the state in which the decedent was domiciled at the time of death, regardless of where the securities or other evidences of ownership are located. But intangible personal property may also be taxed (with the possibility of double or even multiple taxation of intangible personal property) by any other state that "afforded some direct protection to the decedent's rights in such property."

The Concept of Domicile

While every person has one and only one domicile for death-tax purposes, states often disagree on which state that is. The problem is that each state claiming domicile can tax all the intangible personal property of the decedent regardless of where the property is located (see Chapter 6). In one case, an estate composed largely of intangible personal property was almost completely consumed by the death taxes imposed by four states. Fortunately, many states have enacted legislation that minimizes or eliminates unfair double or multiple taxation. Many states expressly exempt the intangibles of nonresidents or provide for reciprocal exemption. In other words, one state won't tax the intangible personal property of a nonresident if the state of residence will provide the same protection for the other state's domiciliaries.

Inheritance Tax Defined

Almost every state levies a tax at death. Many states impose an inheritance tax, which is imposed on the right to inherit property. This should be compared with an *estate tax*, which is a tax imposed on the right to transfer property. The distinction is important because an inheritance tax is levied on the share of each beneficiary individually and not on the estate as a whole. The importance of this distinction is that the closer the relationship to the decedent, the greater the exemption (if there is one) and the lower the rate of tax. For instance, some states don't tax transfers to surviving spouses, while others provide a lower rate of tax for transfers to children, parents, or surviving spouses.

The Estate Tax

Some states impose an estate tax in addition to or in place of the inheritance tax. Typically, the estate tax is levied in addition to the inheritance tax, and it is designed to absorb the credit allowed against the federal estate tax. In simple terms, federal estate-tax law allows a credit for the state death taxes the estate pays (a dollar-for-dollar reduction of the tax) to be applied against the federal estate tax payable. This federal credit is for state death taxes actually paid. The instructions to the federal estate-tax return (Form 706) have tables that show the maximum limits on this federal estate-tax credit. The additional estate tax is designed to guarantee that—to the extent there is a credit and that credit has not already been "used up" by the inheritance tax—it will be used up by an additional state estate tax. In essence, the state is saying that a given amount of tax is going to be collected, either by the federal government or by our state, so it might as well be—up to those limits—our state.

The form and amount of such "additional estate taxes" vary considerably among the various states. Check with a local attorney or examine your state's death-tax laws. In many cases when the decedent is survived by a spouse, the federal law will not allow a credit for state death taxes, and therefore no additional state estate tax should be imposed.

What Transfers Are Taxable?

All states tax property transferred by will or by intestacy laws, so the property actually owned by the decedent at the time of death is subject to state death taxes. There are exceptions, however. For instance, if an individual renounces her legacy (that is, disclaims all rights to that transferred property), no tax is imposed on that individual's share of the estate. In a will dispute, most states tax the original beneficiaries regardless of the way that property is actually distributed. Some states, however, impose their inheritance taxes in accordance with the actual distribution of property after a compromise, rather than by the terms of the will.

What if a decedent has forgiven a debt that someone owed him? The forgiveness of a debt in a will results in the debt's being treated as a taxable transfer, on the assumption that the debtor is solvent and the debt is still legally binding. Bequests to executors in place of regular commissions are taxable. The state has the right to tax a bequest to an executor just as though it were a normal bequest. Likewise, if an individual signs a prenuptial agreement that requires that property be transferred at her death, when property is transferred pursuant to that agreement by will, it is taxable under state death-tax laws.

Gifts in Contemplation of Death

Most states tax transfers that are made within prescribed periods before death. Typically, if an individual makes a transfer within one, two, or three years before death, the state law may treat that transfer as if it were still in the estate at the time of death.

Many states use what is known as a *contemplation of death* statute. This means that nothing is taxable unless the state can prove that the decedent gave the gift with the intention of avoiding the state death tax. If the survivors can prove that the decedent had a "living" motive (such as the desire to minimize income taxes), this would mean that the gift was not made in contemplation of death and therefore is not subject to a state death tax.

The trend is for state death-tax laws to follow the federal

law. Under the current federal statue, but with notable exceptions, gifts made within three years of death are *not*—generally—brought back into the estate.

Transfers "Taking Effect at Death"

Most states tax transfers "taking effect at death." These include transfers under which the decedent retained a life income ("You can have the stock now, but I'm keeping the dividends as long as I live") or life estate ("The house is yours, but I'm going to live in it until I die") or the right to designate who will receive either the property or the income or both. Transfers taking effect at death also include property placed in revocable trusts. Since these trusts can always be changed, a transfer does not take place for tax purposes until the death of the person who established the trust. A third type of transfer is one in which the rights of the donee (the recipient of the gift) are not certain (or, as lawyers would say, "vested") until and unless he survives the person who made the gift. A fourth type of transfer is one under which the decedent had retained power (either in himself or in conjunction with someone else) to alter, amend, or terminate the donee's enjoyment of the gift. For instance, if an individual establishes a trust but reserves the right to alter, amend, revoke, or terminate the trust, state death taxes will be imposed when that individual dies, just as if the trust had never been established (see Chapter 30).

Powers of Appointment

Powers of appointment sometimes attract state death taxation. A *power of appointment* is a right given to one person to designate who will receive property placed in trust by someone else. For instance, a father could leave $100,000 to a trust and give his daughter the right to specify who will get that money. Under a *general power* of appointment, individuals who are given the right to designate the recipients of the property can take the property themselves or name as recipients their estate, their creditors, or the creditors of their estate. If the daughter could name herself as recipient, the power would be "general." A *special power* is one in which individuals with the right to appoint property can appoint it *only* to a specified or limited group of people (which does not include those individuals themselves, their estate, their creditors, or the creditors of their estate). So if the daughter could only name one of her children as recipient of the $100,000 left in trust by her father, the power would be "special" (some attorneys call this a "limited" power).

Some states tax the property subject to a power of appointment in the estate of the donee (the person with the power to appoint the property) only if the power is general. Other states impose a tax only if the general power is exercised. In most states, transfers under limited or special powers are not taxed. In at least one state (Pennsylvania), if an individual dies while possessing a general power of appointment, none of the assets are taxable.

Jointly Owned Property

Jointly owned property (property the decedent owned jointly with right of survivorship) becomes the property of the survivor immediately on the death of the other owner.

Some states tax such jointly held property under the *percentage of contribution* rule. This means the entire value of the property is subject to state death taxes except to the extent that any survivors can prove their contribution. If survivors can prove that they contributed 90 percent and the decedent contributed 10 percent of the purchase price, then only 10 percent of the date-of-death value of the property is subject to tax.

Other states use the *fractional* method, where the date-of-death value of the property is divided by the number of owners. For example, if there are four owners, only one-fourth of the value of the property is includable in the decedent's estate. Some states do not tax property owned jointly with the right of survivorship if that property is owned jointly by husband and wife.

Community Property

Community-property states typically impose an inheritance tax on one-half of the community property at the death of either spouse. There are eight community-property states—Arizona, California, Idaho, Louisiana, Nevada, New Mexico, Texas, and Washington. Wisconsin and several other states have laws very similar to community-property laws.

Life Insurance

Most states treat life insurance—if it is payable to the estate of the insured (or the executor or administrator of the insured)—like any other property. Life insurance is also taxable if it is paid directly to a creditor of the insured. Some states (for example, Pennsylvania) exempt life insurance proceeds—regardless of amount—no matter who the recipient is.

Many states exempt fully or partially the proceeds of life insurance payable to a named beneficiary or to a trustee for the benefit of specified beneficiaries.

Qualified Retirement Plans

Payments under qualified pension and profit-sharing plans—IRAs, HR-10 plans (self-employed retirement—often called Keogh—plans), and other retirement plans or systems—are sometimes exempted fully or partially from state death taxes. Unfortunately, many states follow federal law, which no longer allows an exemption. If the proceeds are payable to the plan participant's estate, any exemption usually is lost. Under federal law, much if not all of what is received at death from a retirement plan is also subject to income taxes. Some states also impose an income tax on pension proceeds, since the employer's contribution to such plans was not taxed to the employee during lifetime.

Preparing and Filing State Death-Tax Returns

Each state usually has its own forms for inheritance-tax or other death-tax returns. Obtain these forms at the earliest possible date so that you will be aware in advance of your responsibilities and can accumulate the necessary information during the administration of the estate.

As soon as reasonably possible, become familiar with the time requirements for filing the state death-tax returns. Some states give a discount for early payment, and this early payment can be due several months after death. The tax return often is due in less than a year, with penalties for late payment. If you do not take advantage of discounts when they make good financial sense, and if you do not pay the tax on time, with no justification for failure to pay, you can be personally liable for penalties and interest.

Sometimes it is impossible to pay the tax on time—such as in the case of undiscovered assets or assets whose values cannot be determined easily. It may also be impossible if, for example, the only asset is real estate of considerable value that must be sold in order to produce the funds to pay the taxes. Most states have requirements for requesting extensions within which to pay the tax, and these requirements must be complied with in all cases. Quite often it might be wise to make a payment on account, so that interest (or penalties) will not accrue on the full amount of the unpaid tax. If requests for extensions are filed in a timely way, the estate is relieved of penalties for failure to pay the tax, although interest still accrues in most cases.

Most states allow certain deductions, credits, and exemptions that differ from those indicated in Chapter 21 for the federal estate tax. For example, some states have a *family exemption*, which is available if the beneficiaries were members of the decedent's household at death. Some states have a *homestead allowance* for the family home. Other states have credits and exemptions for close family members. Some relieve married persons from any tax on jointly held property, while in other states the amount of the exemptions and credits might relieve the entire estate from all tax obligations.

Allocation of the Tax Among the Beneficiaries

In most states the executor is responsible for paying state death taxes, but this responsibility applies only to property passing through the probate estate. In many cases, non-probate property is also subject to inheritance tax. Property held in the names of two brothers, for example, might pass to the surviving brother. The surviving brother, and not the executor, has the responsibility of paying the state inheritance tax on the share of the property owned by the deceased. In spite of this, however, the executor may still be responsible for advising the state of the fact that the decedent died owning property jointly with his brother. Therefore, be careful to include all required information concerning the decedent's assets on the state death-tax return.

If the decedent left a will, then examine the provisions of the will to determine where the tax burden lies. For example, if the decedent bequeathed certain gifts to his children and left the residue of his estate to his wife, and if the will indicates that all taxes shall be paid from the residue of the estate, the children will receive their gifts free of any tax obligations.

Examine state death-tax laws to determine whether a particular tax should be apportioned *pro rata* among the estate's beneficiaries, charged to certain named beneficiaries, or paid from the residuary portion of the estate. In the case of property left to an individual under a will, that individual is often responsible for the inheritance tax on that property. Unfortunately, every case is not that clear, and you therefore have two distinct responsibilities: (1) to be certain of the amount of the tax and make payment, and (2) to allocate the tax burden to the proper beneficiary.

21 | The Federal Estate-Tax Return

An executor must complete and file Form 706—United States Estate and Generation-Skipping Transfer Tax Return—if the size of the estate exceeds a specified amount ($600,000 in 1997, increasing in steps to $1,000,000 in 2006). To obtain Form 706, write to any local IRS office or to the Government Printing Office in Washington, D.C. Although a great deal of the mathematics involved is simple and the compilation and gathering of data seem to be merely legwork, this task should *not* be attempted without the assistance of tax counsel. The tax payable, the options forfeitable, and the penalties that may be imposed are too high for the layperson to attempt to prepare this form without counsel. Missing an election or even filing a late estate-tax return can cost hundreds of thousands of dollars.

Nevertheless, you can be of great assistance and can save a great deal of time and money if you are aware of what must be done and how that task (and it can be a very difficult one) is to be done.

Many of the words and phrases in this chapter are used in a special way by tax attorneys and accountants. In most cases a definition follows, and you will find a more complete definition in the Glossary.

When to File Form 706

Form 706, the federal estate tax return, must be filed within nine months after a person's death. (It is possible to receive an extension of time for both filing and paying the tax. These extensions are discussed below.) There are penalties both for late filing and for late payment unless there is reasonable cause for the delay. If the tax is paid late, the IRS charges interest on the unpaid tax using a daily compounding rate.

Who Must File Form 706?

Form 706 must be filed by the executor. To guarantee that someone will be responsible, the tax law defines *executor* very broadly. Essentially, for estate-tax purposes an executor is the person(s) named in the will, or—if there is no valid will—the person named by the court to act as the decedent's administrator. If no executor or administrator has been appointed by the court, anyone (and everyone) who has actual or "constructive" possession of any of the decedent's property is considered an executor and therefore is legally responsible (which means personally liable) for filing a federal estate-tax return.

Form 706 must be filed for the estate of any person who was a U.S. citizen or resident if that person's (1) *gross estate* (defined below) *plus* (2) her *adjusted taxable gifts* (the taxable portion of gifts made after 1976) exceed $600,000 (as of 1997, increasing by steps to $1 million in 2006). Form 706 NA must be filed for estates of decedents who were neither residents of the United States nor U.S. citizens but who owned property in the United States at death.

A person's *gross estate* means all property in which the decedent had an interest. This definition is very broad and includes:

- Real and personal property titled in a person's name
- Certain transfers (see page 181) made during the decedent's life (not counting those made for adequate and full consideration)
- Certain annuities
- Joint tenancies in property with survivorship interests
- Life insurance proceeds
- Property over which the decedent possessed a general power of appointment
- Property paid under state intestacy law
- Certain community property

Where Must Form 706 Be Filed?

Mail the form (use certified mail, return receipt requested) to the appropriate IRS Service Center (i.e., the one serving the area in which the decedent was domiciled at time of death). Nonresidents file either in Philadelphia, PA 19255, or with the Director of Internal Operations, Washington, DC.

State	Mailing Address of IRS Service Center
New Jersey, New York City, and counties of Nassau, Rockland, Suffolk, and Westchester	Holtsville, NY 00501
New York (all other counties), Connecticut, Maine, Massachusetts, New Hampshire, Rhode Island, and Vermont	Andover, MA 05501
Florida, Georgia, and South Carolina	Atlanta, GA 31101

State	Mailing Address of IRS Service Center
Kansas, New Mexico, Oklahoma, and Texas	Austin, TX 73301
Alaska, Arizona, California,* Colorado, Idaho, Montana, Nebraska, Nevada, North Dakota, Oregon, South Dakota, Utah, Washington, and Wyoming	Ogden, UT 84201
California (all other counties) and Hawaii	Fresno, CA 93888
Illinois, Iowa, Minnesota, Missouri, and Wisconsin	Kansas City, MO 64999
Indiana, Kentucky, Michigan, Ohio, and West Virginia	Cincinnati, OH 45999
Delaware, District of Columbia, Maryland, Pennsylvania, and Virginia	Philadelphia, PA 19255
Alabama, Arkansas, Louisiana, Mississippi, North Carolina, Tennessee	Memphis, TN 32501

*Counties of Alpine, Amador, Butte, Calaveras, Colusa, Contra Costa, Del Norte, El Dorado, Glenn, Humboldt, Lake, Lassen, Marin, Mendocino, Modoc, Napa, Nevada, Placer, Plumas, Sacramento, San Joaquin, Shasta, Sierra, Siskiyou, Solano, Sonoma, Sutter, Tehama, Trinity, Yolo, and Yuba

Who Must Sign Form 706

The executor or administrator (if more than one, then all) must sign the 706. Your signature verifies the statements on the return and in every case *you sign under penalty of perjury.*

The Criminal Investigations Division of the IRS has means of uncovering assets left unlisted (such as crosschecks with past years' income-tax returns, insurance policies, and canceled checks).

In many cases an attorney or accountant prepares the return. If it is prepared by someone other than the person who is filing it, the return must also be signed by the preparer. Each individual executor must list his Social Security number on the form or on a separate, attached sheet.

Does the Will Have to Be Filed with Form 706?

A certified copy of the will must be filed with the federal estate-tax return if the decedent was a citizen or resident and died *testate* (with a valid will). Certain other documents must also be filed, including a certified copy of the death certificate. (In most estates you will need at least 10 copies of this. The cost should be paid by the estate and is deductible as part of administration expenses.) You must also file copies of any trust instruments in which the decedent held a *power of appointment* (the right to say who receives the property in the trust) and, if the state death tax has been paid, a copy of the state certification of payment.

Checklist of Documents That Should Be Filed with Form 706

___ Copy of the decedent's will
___ Copy of the order admitting the will to probate
___ Copies of any relevant trust documents
___ Real estate appraisals
___ Supporting documents to indicate how the value of a business interest was determined, including copies of

any buy/sell agreements, copies of balance sheets, profit-and-loss statements for five years preceding death

___ Letters from stockbrokers confirming the absence of value of worthless securities.

___ Verification letters from banks indicating date-of-death balances for all accounts and certificates of deposit

___ Statement verifying reason for taking discount on notes payable

___ Form 712 for every insurance policy on the life of the decedent and for every policy that the decedent owned on the life of some other person

___ Proof of the survivor's contribution to jointly owned property, such as deeds, bills of sale, or copies of gift-tax returns

___ Appraisals of valuable items or collections

___ Statement discussing valuation problem involving pending litigation

___ Copies of trust instruments containing powers of appointment

___ Affidavits from attorney and executor in regard to fees

___ Information to verify *special use valuation* (affidavits about the use of the property)

___ Evidence of payment of state death taxes

Completing the Form

On each schedule list the items that belong in that category. Land owned by the decedent in her own name, for example, is listed on Schedule A, "Real Estate." Number the items you list on each schedule. Then total all listed amounts at the bottom of each schedule. When you have completed all the schedules, enter the totals on page 3, under "Part 5—Recapitulation."

Round off the value of the items you list on the return: Drop any amount smaller than 50 cents; raise amounts of 50 to 99 cents to the next highest dollar.

Page 1

State the name and *domicile* of the decedent, as well as the year that domicile was established. Also state the decedent's date of death and Social Security number and the name(s), address(es), and Social Security number(s) of the estate's executor(s). Similar information must be given for the estate's attorney.

The second half of the page is devoted to the federal estate-tax computation, which cannot be completed until all the schedules have been filled out and the "Recapitulation" on page 3 is completed. We'll come back to the tax computation after discussing these tasks.

Page 2

Page 2 requests further general information, such as the decedent's business or occupation and marital status. It requires a breakdown of the estate to show how much of it was (or is to be) received by the spouse and other heirs. This is to ascertain the estate-tax marital deduction discussed below.

An extremely important decision must be made on this page. Part 3, line 1, requests you to decide whether the *alternate valuation* date is to be used. The alternate valuation date is the earlier of two dates—either six months after the date of death or the date on which an asset is sold, exchanged, distributed, or otherwise disposed of. This makes it imperative in most larger estates to wait until six months have elapsed in order to determine what the alternate values are. The decision has very significant estate- and income-tax implications.

The right to elect alternate valuation is forfeited unless the 706 is filed on time. As is the case with most of the tax decisions in the administration of an estate, this one should *not* be made without the advice of both an attorney and an accountant. The alternate valuation date is discussed in more detail below.

If the decedent owned a farm or other closely held (not publicly owned) business real estate, you may elect *special-use valuation* (Part 3, line 2). This allows you to value certain real estate at its farm- or business-use value rather than at the highest price it might bring on the general market. Whether or not you think you can meet the tests for this favorable provision, file a *protective election*. Basically, this means that you are retaining the right to use special use valuation even if it appears that you don't qualify when you initially file the return. This election, however, does not extend the time to pay the taxes shown on the return.

Page 3

A very important decision is the *QTIP election* (Part 4, line 6). Certain interests in property may not have passed outright, or in a manner tantamount to outright, to the surviving spouse. For example, a decedent may have left property to his wife for life (she gets the income), but at her death the property goes to his children. The wife's interest terminates at her death. Without this QTIP (qualified terminable interest property) election, such *terminable* interest property would not qualify for the federal estate-tax marital deduction. But if certain requirements are met, the entire value of such property can be deductible in the present estate. The cost of the QTIP election, however, is that when the second (surviving) spouse dies, her estate will include (for estate-tax purposes) the value of the QTIP property. This election is another major decision that should be made with the advice of counsel.

Page 3 continues the compilation of general information. This is followed by a schedule entitled "Part 5—Recapitulation," which is used to total the values in the schedules of assets and deductions that follow.

Page 4, Schedule A—Real Estate

Complete Schedule A if the total gross estate is more than $600,000 (as of 1997, increasing to $1 million in 2006) and contains any real estate owned by the decedent in his own name. Real estate owned in *joint tenancy* or *tenancy by the entirety* or as part of the unincorporated business is reported on either Schedule E (Part 1) as jointly owned property, on Schedule E (Part 2) as part of the "All Other Joint Interests" category, or on Schedule F as part of the valuations of an interest in a partnership or unincorporated business.

List and number each parcel of real estate owned solely by the decedent (or that the decedent had contracted to purchase in her own name). Describe it in enough detail so that the IRS can inspect and value it if necessary.

When property is subject to a mortgage, record the full value of the property if (1) the creditor can proceed against assets of the decedent other than the property subject to the mortgage (a *recourse debt*), or (2) the decedent was personally liable for the debt. For instance, in the typical home mortgage, the documents the borrower signs entitle the lender to proceed not only against the house itself but also against the personal assets of the borrower who fails to make payments. So if you buy a $100,000 house in your own name, borrow $60,000 and die, the full, fair-market value of the home ($100,000) is listed on Schedule A. (In this example the unpaid amount of the debt, $60,000, may be taken as a deduction of the estate on Schedule K.)

If the estate is not personally liable for the mortgage and the property itself is the only security for the loan (a *nonrecourse debt*), report only the net value of the property—the value of the property minus the indebtedness. For example, say you bought a $1 million office building and borrowed $900,000 to help finance it. If the bank could proceed only against the building and had no right to attach your personal assets for nonpayment of the mortgage, you enter only the *net value*, $100,000, on Schedule A. In this case there is no Schedule K deduction.

As with other property listed on Form 706, real estate must be listed at its *fair-market value*, the highest price at which property would change hands between a hypothetical willing buyer and willing seller who both have knowledge of the relevant facts (an exception is made for special-use valuation property).

Hire a qualified independent appraiser who should consider the following factors:

1. The prices obtained on the prior sales of the property in question or for similar properties located nearby.
2. The size, age, condition, use, and income-generating capacity of the property in question or of similar properties.
3. The value of the property according to a capitalization of the net annual income it produces—in other words, what an investor would pay for the property if a given rate of return was assumed appropriate for the type and condition of the property, and the net income was known. For example, if a given building produced a net annual income of $50,000 a year and an interest rate of 15 percent was appropriate, the property should be worth about $333,333. This is found by dividing the $50,000 a year net income by the 15 percent rate of return it is assumed an investor would demand on the capital in the situation.

Before you do your best to lower the value you enter on the return, here's something to consider. As in the case of the estate-tax valuation of stocks, bonds, and other assets likely to be sold before the death of the beneficiary of the estate, the lowest valuation is not always the most advantageous. This is because the fair-market value that is settled on for estate-tax purposes becomes the recipient's income-tax basis for determining gain or loss when the property is later sold. Likewise, it is the recipient's income-tax basis for determining the limit on cost recovery (depreciation) deductions. High estate-tax valuation (which may or may not mean a higher estate tax), will result in a higher income-tax cost basis, which means less gain and therefore less income tax on a subsequent sale of the property, or higher depreciation deductions if the property is depreciable.

For example, if you buy real estate (or any other asset) for $1,000 and sell it for $5,000, your gain is the difference between the amount you realize on the sale (here $5,000) and your cost (tax professionals call this your *basis*). At a person's death the basis of most assets changes. The basis of assets is "stepped up" (or down) to its federal estate-tax value; so, in the example, if death occurred when the property was worth $8,000, when the property is sold for $8,000 after the owner's death, there is no gain because the amount realized on the sale, $8,000, does not exceed its $8,000 basis. So be sure to consider the income-tax as well as the estate-tax implications of your valuations. (More on this important planning technique—and others—appears in chapters 25 and 26.)

Describe any property listed on Schedule A according to the examples given in the instructions for Form 706. Attach to the 706 all supporting documents and appraisals. Without such documentation and description, the estate tax examiner is much more likely to audit the return.

Page 6, Schedule A-1, Section 2032A Valuation

"Highest and Best Use" Rule

As a general rule you must value property at its *highest and best use value*. This means the highest price at which a willing buyer and a willing seller would come to terms. But if certain conditions are met, you can value the estate's real property devoted to farming or closely held business use on the basis of the property's value according to its current use.

Special (Current) Use Valuation

Farmland is a good example of the type of property for which the *special or current-use election* is advantageous. As a general rule farmland is valued at the price it might bring if it was to be used for residential or industrial development rather than the price it is worth as farmland. But if certain conditions are met, you are entitled to value the farm on the basis of a formula that more realistically represents its special-use value as farmland. One such formula works like this:

Dick owns 400 acres of farmland. About the same acreage of nearby land generates an average of $20,000 in annual gross cash rentals. Average annual state and local real estate taxes are $3,000. Assume the average annual effective interest rate for loans from the Federal Land Bank is 10 percent. Under this special-use valuation formula, Dick's land is worth $170,000, or $17,000 ($20,000 less $3,000) divided by 10 percent.

Here's a more detailed example of how to do this special-use valuation computation:

SPECIAL-USE VALUATION
Estimated Land Bank Rate—0.114

Years Prior to Death	Gross Rent of Comparable Land	Real Estate Taxes	Capitalize Value
1991	$120,000	$ 5,000	$1,005,245
1990	$ 90,000	$ 4,500	$ 747,378
1989	$ 80,000	$ 4,000	$ 664,336
1988	$ 70,000	$ 3,500	$ 581,294
1987	$ 60,000	$ 3,000	$ 498,252
Totals	$420,000	$20,000	
Averages	$ 84,000	$ 4,000	

Special (Current) Use Value—$699,301

Source: NumberCruncher Software (610-527-5216)

Do not use this general valuation formula if there is no comparable land from which average annual rentals can be determined. In that case value the farmland by another method.

To take advantage of this special valuation, list each *qualified heir* (essentially the decedent's immediate family plus descendants and certain other relatives) who will receive an interest in the property to be specially valued.

Various other documents must also be filed with this schedule, including:

- Statement signed by every person who has an interest in the property with information about the adjusted value and how it was ascertained
- Copies of written appraisals of the fair market value of the real property
- A legal description of the specially valued property
- Consent statement by all the parties with an interest in the property that if the property is sold or no longer used as farmland (or has no other special use), they agree to a *recapture* (payback) to the IRS of all or some of the taxes that would have been paid if this advantageous election had not been allowed.

Page 8

Protective Election Agreement

Whether or not you think the estate meets the requirements for special- or current-use valuation, file a *protective election*. You protect the right to value property according to its current use by completing Schedule A-1 and checking the box on line 2 of Part 3 of Form 706. You'll need to list: (1) the decedent's name and taxpayer identification number, (2) the relevant qualified use (such as farming), and (3) the location of the real property that you are claiming is used for farming or business.

Page 10, Schedule B—Stocks and Bonds

All stocks and bonds that were titled by the decedent in her own name must be entered on this schedule.

Checklist of Required Stock and Bond Information

Stocks

___ Number of shares
___ Common or preferred
___ Exact name of corporation
___ Price per share
___ Stock exchange where sold

Bonds

___ Quantity and denomination
___ Name of obligor
___ Date of maturity
___ Interest rate
___ Interest due date
___ Stock exchange where sold

Obtaining Stock Prices

Prices of stocks can be obtained in a local library. Check in the *Wall Street Journal* for the relevant date. Many stockbrokers subscribe to computerized services that can list this information quickly. The broker's printout probably will be acceptable as an attachment to this schedule.

Valuing Stocks in General

The fair-market value of publicly traded stock is the mean between the highest and the lowest quoted selling price on the valuation date.

Valuing Bonds in General

Corporate bonds are valued similarly to stocks. The mean of the highest and lowest selling prices on or near the applicable valuation date is used.

If there were no sales on or reasonably close to the valuation date, the value of the bonds is determined by:

- Ascertaining the soundness of the security
- Comparing the interest yield on the bond to yields of similar bonds
- Examining the maturity date
- Comparing prices for listed bonds of corporations engaged in similar types of business
- Checking the extent to which the bond is secured
- Weighing all other relevant factors such as the opinions of experts, the business's position in the industry, and the economy in general

Valuing Closely Held Stock

If the estate holds stock that is not traded on an exchange or over-the-counter, eight factors should be considered (and here an accountant working with an attorney can be invaluable): (1) the nature and economic history of the business; (2) the economic outlook in general and the outlook for the specific industry; (3) the book value of the corporation and financial condition of the business; (4) the company's earning capacity; (5) the corporation's dividend-paying capacity; (6) the existence or nonexistence of goodwill; (7) stock sales and size of the block of stock to be valued; and (8) the fair-market value of stock of comparable corporations engaged in the same or a similar line of business.

No single fixed formula of valuation has been devised that is applicable to all closely held corporations. Consider all the factors that would add to or subtract from value.

A reduction in value may be allowed because the shares being valued represent a minority interest. Executors typically take from 10 to 30 percent off the value because the stock isn't a controlling interest. Certainly, stock has less value if its holder is unable to force the payment of dividends, compel the liquidation of the corporation, or control corporate policy.

Effect of Buy/Sell Agreement on Value

Stock has less value if it cannot be traded freely or if there is no active market for it. Most closely held stock is subject to some type of restriction on its marketability. A buy/sell agreement, for example, may set a ceiling on the price that will be paid for stock. The IRS and the courts typically go along with the price that was set in the buy/sell agreement if the following conditions are present:

- The agreement was made between the parties as the result of arm's-length bargaining.
- The price set in the agreement was fair and adequate at the time the agreement was signed.
- The decedent was bound to offer the stock back to the corporation or its shareholders during his or her lifetime before he could offer it to anyone else.
- The decedent could not sell the stock for a higher price during her lifetime than the estate was entitled to at death. (This is required to prevent an artificially low death-time price designed to result in a lower estate tax.)

- The executor is bound to sell the stock at death at the price fixed in the agreement.
- The price per share payable for the stock either is specifically fixed by the agreement or is determinable according to a formula in the agreement.

Buy/sell agreements between family members are very closely scrutinized by the IRS to determine whether they are bona fide business agreements or merely devices to pass the decedent's shares to the objects of his bounty for a price that does not reflect the stock's fair-market value.

Recent legislation has tightened the rules described above to prevent abusive intrafamily schemes designed to shift business wealth through artificially low prices or unrealistic terms in the buy/sell agreement. Now the general rule is that a buy/sell or any other type of agreement carries no weight in setting tax value for transfer-tax purposes when the agreement is between family members. Fortunately, the new law carves out an exception. If three tests are met, the IRS and the courts will recognize the value-depressing effect of an option, agreement, right, or restriction in a buy/sell agreement.

These three requirements are as follows:

1. "Bona fide business arrangement" rule: The agreement must be part of a bona fide business arrangement.
2. "Device" rule: The agreement must not be a device to transfer the property to members of the decedent's family for less than full and adequate consideration in money or money's worth.
3. "Comparability" rule: The terms of the agreement must be comparable to similar arrangements entered into by persons in an arm's-length transaction.

The "business purpose" and "device" tests are independent. The executor should document facts that indicate that the arrangement was not a device to pass the property to members of the decedent's family at a bargain price.

Under the comparability test, in order to fix estate-tax value, there must be a showing that the arrangement was one that could have been obtained in an arm's-length transaction. Would the decedent have entered into such an arrangement with an unrelated third person? This requirement of comparability applies not only to price but also to all the terms of the contract between the parties. Factors the IRS will take into account include: (1) the expected term of the agreement, (2) the present value of the property, (3) its expected value at the time of exercise, and (4) the consideration, if any, offered for the option. Thus, as in the case of a transfer of stock and a partnership interest, there may be some inherent minimum value in the appreciation element of common stock.

A fixed price based on the value at the time the arrangement was entered into will be challenged and seldom prove successful. On the other hand, a price determined by a realistic formula (or qualified independent appraisal) is most likely to be accepted by the IRS. However, certain formulas, such as those based solely on book or adjusted book value, may not be viewed as the kind of arrangement that unrelated third persons enter into. The validity of the formula must be established with respect to generally practiced valuation methods. Capitalization of earnings or discounted cash flow will probably be recognized. In addition, the general appreciation rates of businesses within the same industrial segment must be taken into account. Statistics found in trade journals and magazines often are quite helpful in establishing the appropriate discount rates and justifying other assumptions.

Whenever an estate includes closely held stock, submit copies of the corporation's balance sheet (particularly the one nearest to the valuation date). The IRS also requires copies of the corporation's previous five years' profit-and-loss statements.

Valuing Government Bonds

There are three types of bonds that may need to be valued:

- State, local, private, and foreign bonds must be shown at the mean of the bid and asked market quotations on the applicable valuation date. Interest on such bonds that has accrued from the last payment date to the date of death must be shown as a separate item.
- Series E and EE U.S. savings bonds must be shown at the total of their cost plus the increase in value due to any semiannual accruals up to the date of the decedent's death.
- U.S. Series H, J, and K bonds must be listed at par value.

Valuing Worthless Securities

Even though a security may have no value, it must be shown on Form 706. Attach letters from stockbrokers, the companies, or your state's Department of Corporations to confirm the absence of value. Such documentation may prevent an audit.

How to Handle Dividends

Dividends on stock owned by the decedent at death constitute part of the estate and must therefore be entered on the 706 if the dividend was payable but not received until after death. If the decedent died after a dividend was declared but between the *ex-dividend date* and the *stockholder-of-record date* (your stockbroker can explain these terms and help you obtain the appropriate price), the market price of the stock will have fallen by the amount of the dividend. But since the dividend was payable to the estate, list the sum of (1) the depressed market price and (2) the dividend received by the estate.

Page 11, Schedule C—Mortgages, Notes, and Cash

If any mortgages or notes were payable to the decedent at time of death, list them here. Group the items in the following categories and list the categories in the following order:

1. Mortgages. State: (a) face value and unpaid balance, (b) date of mortgage, (c) date of maturity, (d) name of maker, (e) property mortgaged, and (f) interest dates and rate of interest.
2. Promissory notes. Same procedure as for mortgages.
3. Contract by the decedent to sell land. State: (a) name of purchaser, (b) date of contract, (c) description of property, (d) sale price, (e) initial payment, (f) amounts of installment payments, (g) unpaid balance of principal, and (h) interest rate.
4. Cash and certificates of deposit in the decedent's possession (list separately from bank deposits).
5. Cash in banks, savings and loan institutions, and other types of financial organizations. State: (a) name and address of each organization, (b) amount in each account, (c) account number, and (d) nature of account (savings, checking, etc.).

Keep statements from all financial institutions. (As soon as you are officially the estate's executor, you should write to all the banks requesting that an officer provide you with a letter verifying the information.) Show the date-of-death balance for bank accounts. Savings accounts should reflect interest if that interest was both accrued and payable at the decedent's death. Reduce accordingly commercial accounts with checks outstanding (unless the checks are shown as debts on Schedule K—in which case, show the balance on this schedule).

List the balance of any note due to the decedent at death, plus any interest that has accrued, unless (1) there is substantial doubt that the note will be collected and that the security is sufficient, or (2) the rate of interest payable is well below the prevailing prime rate (for example, when the rate is less than two points above prime). In the latter case, take a discount (substantiated by a statement filed with the return that explains why the discount should be allowed and why the amount taken is reasonable).

Page 12, Schedule D—Insurance on the Decedent's Life

This schedule requires information concerning life insurance policies (including group insurance and insurance obtained through fraternal or religious organizations) on the decedent's life. List every policy, even if you feel it should not be included in the gross estate.

Reasons Life Insurance Must Be Included

Life insurance is includable in the gross estate if (1) it is payable to or for the benefit of the estate (regardless of who owned the policy), or (2) it is payable to a named beneficiary other than the estate but the decedent held an *incident of ownership* in the policy (see below) at time of death.

Insurance is considered payable to the estate if it is payable to the estate's executor (as executor); or it may be payable to a beneficiary who is obligated by contract or otherwise to use the proceeds to pay the estate tax or any other taxes, debts, or charges that are enforceable against the estate.

A decedent is considered to have an incident of ownership in a policy of insurance on her own life if she had any of the following rights:

- The right to change or name the policy beneficiary
- The power to surrender the policy or cancel it
- The right to assign the policy or revoke an assignment
- The power to pledge the policy for a loan
- The right to obtain a loan from the insurer
- A *reversionary interest* (which occurs if the proceeds are payable to the estate of or according to the directions of the insured) with an actuarial value in excess of 5 percent of the policy's value (as of the instant before the insured died)

Request from each insurance company a Life Insurance Statement on Form 712 (the home office of each insurance company will send this form to you at no charge) showing how much was paid and the method of payment. If the policy proceeds are paid in a lump sum, go to line 24 on Form 712 and enter that amount on your Form 706. If the proceeds are not paid in a lump sum, go to line 25 on Form 712 and enter that figure on Form 706.

Reasons Not *to Include Some Policies*

If for any reason you are not going to include the proceeds of a policy on the decedent's life, explain the reason for the noninclusion. In certain instances a policy on the life of a person should not be included in the estate. For example, if a son takes out a policy on his father's life and pays all the premiums from his own money, nothing should be included in the father's estate (unless the proceeds were payable to the estate or unless the son was under an obligation to use the proceeds to pay taxes or expenses of the father's estate). If the decedent owned a policy on his own life but made an irrevocable transfer of the policy *more* than three years before death, the proceeds are not includable in the estate.

Photocopy each policy and any other papers before you send an original policy to the insurance company to obtain the death proceeds.

Page 14, Schedule E—Jointly Owned Property

Enter on Schedule E all property, whether *real* or *personal* (any property or property rights other than real estate), in which the decedent held an interest as a joint tenant with right of survivorship or as a tenant by the entirety. List property held as a tenant in common on Schedule A rather than on this schedule.

Jointly held property is divided into two categories: (1) qualified joint interests and (2) all other joint interests.

Qualified Joint Interests—the 50/50 Rule

Qualified joint interests are interests whereby the decedent held title to the property as tenant by the entirety or as a joint tenant with right of survivorship if the only joint tenants were the decedent and her spouse. Qualified joint interests are listed in Part I of Schedule E. They are so called because only one-half of the estate-tax value of such interests is includable in the decedent's gross estate, regardless of which spouse dies first or when the property was purchased or how much each spouse contributed to the purchase price. So if a married couple purchases a home for $80,000 and the wife dies when the home is worth $200,000, then 50 percent, or $100,000, of the value of the home, is included in her estate. This 50/50 rule applies only if the property is held solely by the husband and wife.

Other Joint Interests—the "Percentage of Contribution" Rule

All joint interests other than qualified joint interests are entered in Part II of Schedule E. A different inclusion rule applies to such interests. Include the entire value of the property except to the extent that the surviving tenant can prove that he contributed to the purchase of the property or that a part of the property originally belonged to the surviving cotenant. The consideration paid by the cotenant is counted only to the extent that it was not a gift from the decedent.

If the survivor(s) can prove contribution, then only a percentage of the estate-tax value is includable in the decedent's estate. You may exclude from the full value of the property an amount proportionate to the consideration furnished by the survivor. Let's assume a father paid $20,000 and his adult son paid $80,000 (money he saved from salary) for a parcel of land. Let's further assume that the land was worth $500,000 at the father's death. Only two-tenths (20,000/100,000) of the $500,000 would be included in the father's estate, since the son could prove he contributed four-fifths ($80,000/100,000) of the original purchase price and could also prove none of the money was a gift from his father.

In order to use this *percentage of contribution rule* (some attorneys call this the *consideration furnished rule*) to exclude part or all of the property from the decedent's estate, you must be able to prove the extent, origin, and nature of both the decedent's and the survivor's interests. The IRS typically goes along with records of the original purchase (such as deeds or bills of sale) or copies of gift-tax returns filed by donees other than the decedent. (Remember that property received gratuitously from the decedent and contributed by the donee toward the purchase of the joint tenancy does not count as part of the survivor's contribution.) Although in some instances the IRS accepts oral and circumstantial evidence of the survivor's contribution, it often is necessary to litigate a case in order to receive credit for such testimony.

Page 16, Schedule F—Other Miscellaneous Property

Schedule F is the place to enter all the items includable in the gross estate that are not includable in any other schedule. This includes such items as household goods and personal effects, boats, debts owed to the decedent (other than notes and mortgages), interests in a sole proprietorship, royalties, income tax refunds, shares in trusts established by others (attach a copy of the trust document), livestock, farm equipment, and automobiles. It also includes life insurance owned by the decedent on the life of another.

Sole Proprietorships and Partnerships

When the decedent had owned an interest in a sole proprietorship or partnership, attach a balance sheet for the valuation date as well as for the five years preceding that date. Also file profit-and-loss statements for the same five years. The business must be valued essentially as you would value a closely held corporation. This means that any *goodwill* ("going concern") value attached to the business must be considered in your valuation process.

Jewelry, Art, Furs, etc.

Articles of intrinsic or artistic value—such as jewelry, furs, silverware, books, statuary, rugs, art, and coin and stamp collections—must be noted and fully described. If any one such article or collection is valued at more than $3,000, attach an appraisal. (The IRS has ways to uncover assets that "disappear." Typically, the IRS examiner requests canceled checks and insurance policies covering valuable collections or art objects. Since you, the executor, sign all tax returns under penalty of perjury, it pays for you to be honest.) The appraisal must be made by an independent expert, who signs the appraisal of value under oath, and it must be accompanied by a statement of her qualifications. The telephone directory probably lists the names of several such appraisers (your attorney or trust officer should be able to suggest an appropriate expert). Discuss the appraiser's fee *before* you authorize her to proceed.

Insurance on the Lives of Others

One asset that must be listed on Schedule F but is often overlooked or misplaced is insurance on the lives of others. If the decedent owned a policy on the life of some other person, the value of that policy (i.e., its replacement cost) must be included in the decedent's gross estate. This value will be figured at no cost to you by the insurer and provided to you on Form 712 (request it from the insurer). Write directly to the home office of the company or have your agent contact the company. Attach Form 712 to Schedule F.

One very important note of warning. If, as executor, you are holding a policy on the life of a person who dies after you have begun your probate, do not select the alternate valuation date without consulting counsel. If you elect the alternate valuation date (six months after the decedent's death), his estate will then include the proceeds on the life of the other insured. For instance, say Don and Gene are coshareholders and each purchases a $500,000 policy on the life of the other to fund a business buy/sell agreement. Don dies and you are named his executor. If Gene dies within the next six months and you select the alternate valuation date, the entire $500,000 of proceeds will be considered an asset of Don's estate. (This problem is discussed in detail in Chapter 25.)

Claims in Litigation

A decedent may have been litigating claims against others at the time of her death. If there is pending litigation that could result in an estate asset, enter the estimated value of such a claim on Schedule F. If the value of the claim is impossible to ascertain, file Form 706 and show no value but attach a statement explaining the valuation problem. Obviously, in most cases this will trigger an IRS audit (unless the surviving spouse is the sole or primary beneficiary, in which case the estate-tax marital deduction will eliminate the tax).

Amounts from the Estates of Others

In some instances a decedent will have been entitled to the proceeds of someone else's estate at the time of his death. Use actual amounts received if the distributions have been made to you as executor by the time the 706 must be filed. If any distributions are yet to be made, use an estimated amount. You'll have to file an amended return when the actual amount is known.

Page 18, Schedule G—Transfers During Decedent's Life

There are five types of lifetime transfers that must be reported on this schedule: (1) certain gift taxes, (2) certain transfers within three years of death, (3) transfers in which the decedent retained a *life estate*, (4) transfers that take effect at death, and (5) revocable transfers.

Inclusion of Gift Taxes on Gifts Within Three Years of Death

On Schedule G, enter the amount of any gift tax paid by the decedent (or her estate) on gifts that the decedent made within three years before death. Tax practitioners call this a *gross up* of the estate by the amount of the gift tax. This "gross up" rule requires you to review all gift-tax returns (IRS Form 709) filed within three years prior to death. Determine what part of the total gift taxes reported on these returns is attributable to gifts made within three years of death. Attach copies of those returns to Form 706.

Life Insurance Transferred Within Three Years of Death

Certain other gratuitous transfers made within three years of death must also be included. If an insurance policy on the life of the decedent was transferred by him within three years of death, include the policy proceeds in his gross estate.

Lifetime Gifts When a Power Is Retained

Likewise, if the decedent made lifetime gifts but retained certain powers over the property given away, and if those powers were given up within three years before death, the property subject to the powers is includable. For example, if a mother gave her son $300,000 worth of stock but retained the right to the income from the stock, the value of the stock on the date of her death is includable in her estate. Under the "gifts within three years of death" rule, the property is still includable—even if she gave up the right to the income—if she released the right to the stock's dividends within three years of death.

Transfers in which the decedent had retained for life the right to the income or enjoyment of the property or the right to designate the person or persons who would possess or enjoy the transferred property must be entered on Schedule G.

For instance, if the decedent put $160,000 of stock in

trust for his daughter but retained the right to the dividends from the stock, the entire amount of the stock would be in his estate at its federal estate-tax value. Likewise, if the decedent had given a summer home to his son, the house would be in the decedent's estate if he had retained the right to live in it (or to say who could).

The tax law also requires you to list on this schedule any lifetime gratuitous transfers of stock if the decedent had retained or acquired voting rights in a *controlled corporation*. A controlled corporation is one in which the decedent owned—actually or constructively (or had the right to vote, alone or with any other person)—at least 20 percent of the total combined voting power of all classes of stock.

Transfers that take effect at death make up another type of gratuitous lifetime transfer that must be shown on Schedule G. In essence, these are transfers in which the beneficiary cannot take possession of or enjoy the property unless she survives the decedent, and the property returns to the decedent's estate if the beneficiary does not survive. This is called a "but if . . . back to" type of transfer, because the decedent, when he gave away the property, provided, "But if you don't survive me, the property is to come back to me or to my estate." (The rules here are highly technical; before you list such property, consult a tax attorney.)

A further type of gratuitous lifetime transfer that is included on Schedule G is a revocable transfer. If the decedent had given property away but had reserved the right to alter, amend, revoke, or terminate the gift in any significant manner, its value is includable. Here are three common examples: (1) The decedent set up a trust and put property into the trust but provided in the trust that he could change its terms or decide who would receive the property in the trust or choose when trust beneficiaries would receive the property. (2) The decedent established a *revocable trust*, which he could terminate or whose terms he could alter at any time during his lifetime. (3) A woman put $8,000 into a Uniform

Gifts to Minors Act account (UGMA) for her 12-year-old daughter. If the mother is custodian for the minor child at the time of the mother's death, the value of the money in the account is included in the mother's estate because of her right as custodian to determine the time of payouts.

Schedule G requires you to list the name of the transferee, state the date of the transfer, and give a complete description of the property. When the transfer was by trust, attach a copy of the trust document to the 706.

Page 18, Schedule H—Powers of Appointment

A *power of appointment* is a right to designate who will receive someone else's property. For example, a grandfather may set up a trust to provide "income to my wife for her life, and at her death, any capital in the trust is to be distributed in equal shares to my grandchildren." The grandfather could give his wife or his son (or both) a power of appointment, a right to change the distributive pattern.

If the power is *limited* (some attorneys call this a *special power of appointment*), the holder of the power would have the right to divide trust assets among only the class of people or organizations designated by the person who set up the trust. For instance, the grandfather may have given his son a power to give income or capital to one or more of the son's children. The son could not use the property in the trust for his own benefit.

If the power was *general*, the son could exercise the power for his own benefit and obtain any or all of the trust's assets at any time. His control over trust property would be nearly the same as outright ownership.

General Power Is Includable

When a decedent had, at the time of death, a general power—an unlimited right to funds in a trust established by someone else, exercisable in favor of himself, his estate, his creditors, or the creditors of his estate—the property subject to that power must be included in his estate and listed on Schedule H. In essence, a general power gives a person the right to take the property in someone else's trust whenever she wants or to use it for her benefit or to satisfy debts. Therefore, under the estate-tax law, the right over property is taxed accordingly (even if the holder of the power, the son in the example above, never actually owned the property or never took it out of the other person's trust or never exercised his power in any other way).

No federal estate-tax inclusion is required when the decedent merely held a limited power of appointment over the assets in someone else's trust. So you don't have to list the property on Schedule H if, according to a trust provision, the son can direct that the trust assets be paid to or among only a designated class of individuals or organizations—no matter how broad that class is—as long as it does not include the holder of the power (the son) or his estate or creditors.

Attach to the 706 a certified or verified copy of the trust instrument giving the decedent the general power of appointment. Indeed, you are required to file the copy even if you feel that the power was limited and no property should be included under this schedule.

Page 19, Schedule I—Annuities

Includable on this schedule are certain arrangements that fall into two general categories: (1) *joint and survivor annuities* purchased from insurance companies, and (2) *nonqualified deferred compensation plan* payments and payments under qualified retirement plans.

Joint and survivor annuities provide that payments will be made during the joint lifetimes of two people and, upon the death of one annuitant, continued for the life of the other person. The contract provides that the same or a reduced payment will be made to the survivor. If all payments are to cease at the death of an individual, the annuity is not "joint and survivor" and is not includable, since no property will be transferred at death.

In your description of the annuity, include the name and address of the party (typically, an insurance company) paying the annuity. If the annuity is payable for a term of years, rather than over the survivor's lifetime, specify the length of the term and the date on which the annuity began. Also give the survivor's birthdate and sex.

Valuation of the Survivor's Rights

Typically, joint and survivor annuities are purchased from an insurance company. The value of a commercial joint and survivor annuity in the estate is the amount that it would cost to buy an annuity contract for the survivor that would pay the same amount under the same conditions as the contract purchased by the decedent.

Individuals or corporations can promise to pay others an annuity. These "private annuities" are valued by using actuarial tables, which can be found in government regulations and can be computed using software such as Number-Cruncher (610-527-5216). Nothing is includable in the annuitant's estate if the annuity ends when the annuitant dies (except for any payments received and not given away by the date of death).

If the annuity continues beyond the initial annuitant's life to a second annuitant, only the percentage of the purchase price of the annuity that the decedent paid is includable. So if the decedent contributed 60 percent of the purchase price, only 60 percent of the value of the actuarial value of the annuity is includable in the estate. If the decedent had contributed the entire purchase price, the entire value of the cost of a comparable contract (to provide income to the survivor) would be in the estate.

Valuing Nonqualified Deferred Compensation (Salary Continuation) Plans

A *nonqualified deferred compensation plan* (often called a *salary continuation plan*) is an employer-sponsored plan that provides income after retirement to an employee and payments after the employee's death to his designated beneficiary. Such arrangements are a form of joint and survivor annuity, since they provide that upon the death of one annuitant, payments will be continued for the life of another. The present value of the survivor's right to receive payments must be included in the decedent's estate. The value is ascertained through government actuarial tables, which are reprinted in the regulations to the Internal Revenue Code. But the IRS has an actuarial department that will assist you or your counsel in making the computations. Software—such as IRS Factors Calculator (610-527-5216) or NumberCruncher (610-527-5216)—is available from private sources to do these complex actuarial procedures.

Page 20, Schedule J—Funeral Expenses and Expenses Incurred in Administering Property Subject to Claims

Schedule J is the proper place to list deductible expenses incurred in connection with the funeral and the probate of the estate. Funeral expenses include the cost of the burial plot, the cost of monuments or gravestones and markers, the cost of perpetual care for the lot, and the expenses of religious observances.

Among the other expenses you can claim on this schedule are court costs, filing fees, transfer fees, accountant's fees, and other expenses incurred in safeguarding and distributing the estate.

Keep receipts of all expenditures, no matter how small or seemingly trivial. For instance, the costs of photocopying and postage alone add up quickly. These expenses are deductible on both federal and state death-tax returns.

Deduction Requirements

To be deductible, death-related expenses must be necessary, reasonable, allowable under state law, and have been paid (or be payable) by the estate. The IRS will attempt to disallow deductions for expenses that are not necessary to pay the debts or taxes of the estate or to preserve the estate or distribute it. For example, if property is sold that is not needed to raise funds for the estate, the cost of the sale will not be deductible, since the expense benefits the heirs personally rather than the estate.

The "reasonableness" requirement precludes the deduction of funeral expenses significantly above the decedent's station in life. (Don't panic with respect to this rule—the IRS and the courts are fairly liberal with respect to funerals.)

The requirement that the expense must be allowable under local law is to ensure that the outlay is within the local probate law's scope of legitimate expenses incurred in the estate's best interest.

Estate-tax law prohibits a deduction for expenses that will not be paid by the estate and reduces otherwise allowable deductions by the amount of any Social Security or veteran's burial allowance.

Deduction for Executor's Commissions and Attorney Fees

A deduction for your commissions as executor as well as any attorney fees is allowable to the extent permitted under local law (the local probate court serves as a watchdog in this respect). If these fees have not been paid by the time the 706 is due, take the deduction anyway. Attach to Form 706 an affidavit signed by both you and the attorney stating the amount that must be paid.

Choosing the Tax Return on Which to Take a Deduction

It is extremely important to consult tax counsel before claiming certain deductions. For example, it may pay for you to waive the executor's commission, since this is taxable to you as ordinary income.

If your income-tax bracket is higher than the estate-tax rates and you are also the sole beneficiary under the will, the additional estate tax incurred by forgoing the deduction for your commission on the estate-tax return is outweighed by the tax savings realized if you do not have to report the income.

An estate has the option to claim administration expenses either on the estate's income-tax return (while the estate is open, it is a tax-paying entity separate and apart from its beneficiaries) or on the estate-tax return. The deduction may be more valuable if taken on the fiduciary income-tax return, since the tax bracket may be higher.

The IRS accepts a reasonable estimate of expenses if you cannot determine the exact amount at the date you file the return.

Page 22, Schedule K—Debts of the Decedent, and Mortgages and Liens

Among the items that are listed on this schedule are medical expenses not reimbursed by insurance, unsecured notes, miscellaneous bills, any unpaid income taxes due when you computed the decedent's final income-tax return, and any real estate taxes that were a lien at death.

Requirements for Deductibility

A debt is deductible only if (1) the decedent owed the money personally at the time of death, and (2) the claim was legally enforceable at the date of death. If the debt is disputed or is the subject of litigation, take a deduction only for the amount (if any) you concede to be a valid claim. If you are planning to contest a claim, state that fact on Schedule K.

In addition, for a claim to be deductible there must be adequate and full consideration for the debt. This prevents a dying parent from giving children an IOU for, say, $300,000 and then allowing the estate's executor to claim that amount as a deductible debt.

An exception to this rule applies to certain pledges to charity. An enforceable claim based on a decedent's promise or agreement to make a contribution or gift to (or for the use of) a charitable, public, religious, or other similar organization is deductible to the extent that state law would allow the deduction.

In listing unsecured debts, include the following: (1) the name of the payee, (2) the face amount, (3) the unpaid balance, (4) the date and term, (5) the interest rate, and (6) the date to which interest was paid before death. Also include the exact nature of the claim and the name of the creditor.

Medical Expenses—Choosing the Tax Return on Which to Take the Deduction

A decedent's medical expenses and expenses of her last illness can be claimed on Schedule K for estate-tax purposes or on the decedent's final income-tax return (or partially but not fully on both returns). Here again, consult tax counsel about possible tax savings. Typically, it is advantageous to take the deduction on the return in the highest bracket, but you will also need to consider the effect on various beneficiaries.

Deducting Property Taxes

When deducting property taxes, you are limited to the taxes accrued before the decedent's death. Likewise, you can deduct any taxes owed on income received while the decedent was alive. Taxes owed on income received after the decedent's death are not deductible.

Inclusion Rule When Property Is Subject to a Mortgage

If the decedent was personally liable for a debt in connection with the purchase of property (i.e., if the creditor can go beyond any particular property and claim any of the decedent's assets), include the full value of the property on the appropriate schedule. Then deduct the mortgage or the lien here. But if the property itself was the sole collateral for the loan and the estate is not liable, only the net value of the property (value of the property minus the amount of the debt) is listed in the gross estate.

For example, if a woman purchased a home for $90,000 subject to a $40,000 mortgage and (as is almost always the case) the bank could go beyond the house itself and reach her personal assets if she defaulted on the debt, enter the $90,000 amount on Schedule A, "Real Estate," and then take a deduction here on Schedule K for the outstanding balance on the date of her death. But if a $1 million building was mortgaged for, say, $700,000, and the bank lending the money had agreed to accept the building as the sole collateral for the loan, enter the building on Schedule A at its net value of

$300,000 (assuming death occurred while the outstanding balance was still $300,000). No further reduction is allowed.

Page 23, Schedule L—Net Losses During Administration and Expenses Incurred in Administering Property Not Subject to Claims

Losses Incurred During Administration

If a fire, storm, earthquake, or other sudden or unexpected casualty occurs during the settlement of the estate, you may take a deduction to the extent the loss is not offset by insurance.

Describe the loss and its cause, and, if you receive any insurance, state the amount you collected.

If you elected the alternate valuation date, you probably already reduced the value of any damaged or lost item when you listed that item in the gross estate. You cannot take a deduction on this schedule for the amount by which you have already reduced the value of the item.

Choosing the Tax Return on Which to Take the Deduction

A casualty-loss deduction can be taken either on this estate-tax return or on the estate's income-tax return, but not on both. Consult tax counsel about which return is in the highest bracket and is otherwise the most advantageous place to take the deduction.

Expenses Incurred in Administering Nonprobate Property

This part of the schedule deals with expenses incurred in administering *nonprobate property*. These expenses (deductible only if paid within three years and nine months from the decedent's death) include costs incurred in the administration of a trust established by the decedent before death.

To be deductible, these expenses must have been incurred as a result of settling the decedent's interest in the property or vesting good title to the property in the beneficiaries.

List the names and addresses of persons to whom each expense was payable and the nature of each expense. Identify the property for which the expense was incurred. You can estimate an expense if you don't know its exact amount. Keep all vouchers and receipts.

Page 24, Schedule M—Bequests, etc., to Surviving Spouse

Schedule M is the appropriate place to list the items that will pass or have passed to the surviving spouse in a manner that will qualify him for the federal estate-tax marital deduction. In most cases involving married couples, this is the single most important deduction on the estate-tax return.

Rules Governing Marital Deduction

The tax law governing the marital deduction is highly complex and is strictly construed by both the IRS and the courts. In essence, the deduction is allowed for property passing outright or in a manner tantamount to outright where the surviving spouse is a U.S. citizen and receives property or an interest in property:

- As the heir under the decedent's will
- As the surviving joint tenant
- As the beneficiary of a life insurance policy, or
- As a surviving spouse taking the share of a decedent's estate allowed under state law in the event of intestacy

- As the recipient of any transfer made by the decedent at any time if the property was includable in the decedent's gross estate

Marital Deduction for Transfers in Trust

You take a marital deduction if the property passes in trust to the surviving spouse if a number of conditions are met. Because of the complexity of the tax law in this area, the advice of counsel is essential.

QTIP Rules

QTIP (qualified terminable interest property) is a term that every executor should know. It means that certain property that otherwise would not qualify for the marital deduction can qualify if certain conditions are met.

This very important election must be made by the executor; once made, it is irrevocable. The election can be made only if the surviving spouse is entitled to all the income from the property and if that income is payable annually or more frequently. For example, a man may have left property income to his wife for her life, and then, upon her death, the property is to go to their children. Such a bequest ordinarily does not qualify for the marital deduction, but it does if a QTIP election is made. There is just one catch: If you make the election on the deceased spouse's estate-tax return, when the widow dies, the value of any QTIP property remaining at her death will be included in her estate (even though she doesn't have the right to dispose of it at her death). When the QTIP technique is used, the marital deduction merely defers the tax (i.e., it becomes payable at the death of the surviving spouse).

On Schedule M, list each property interest for which you are claiming a marital deduction. Number the items in sequence and describe each item in detail. Describe the *instrument* (will or trust) or provision of law under which each item passed to the surviving spouse. Attach a certified copy of the order admitting the will to probate.

QDT Rules

QDT (qualified domestic trust) is an extremely important term for surviving spouses who are resident aliens. Property passing from a U.S. citizen to a spouse who is not a U.S. citizen will not qualify for the federal estate-tax marital deduction and will therefore be subject to federal estate tax immediately upon the first death—unless it meets special rules (explained in detail in Chapter 25). Among these rules is a requirement that an election be made on Schedule M. This irrevocable election may be made only if the property passes to the surviving spouse in a QDT—or if the property is transferred or irrevocably assigned to a QDT before the estate-tax return is filed. As executor you must make the QDT election within one year after the Form 706 is due (including extensions).

Essentially, a QDT is any trust in which at least one trustee is a U.S. citizen or a domestic corporation. It provides that no distribution can be made from the trust unless the U.S. trustee has the ability to withhold federal tax due. The trust must otherwise qualify as eligible for the marital deduction under the normal rules and meet other stringent requirements.

Page 26, Schedule O—Charitable, Public, and Similar Gifts and Bequests

Use Schedule O if the decedent left property to a charitable, religious, educational, or scientific organization. The deduction is unlimited (there is no percentage limitation) and applies to gifts made in a person's will as well as transfers to charity through life insurance policies, certain transfers in trust, and even lifetime transfers that for some reason were included in the estate.

Attach to this schedule a copy of the trust document or other instrument under which the charitable transfer was made. If the transfer was by will, attach a copy of the will and a certified copy of the order admitting the will to probate.

Page 27, Schedule P—Credit for Foreign Death Taxes

A *credit* (dollar-for-dollar reduction of the tax) may be taken for death taxes paid to one or more foreign countries. This credit is allowed if the gross estate includes property that was taxed in a foreign country.

If the credit is applicable, prepare IRS Form 706CE in triplicate. Retain one copy and send two copies to the appropriate tax official in the foreign country. Direct that person to certify one copy and forward it to the IRS office where you file the 706.

Page 27, Schedule Q—Credit for Tax on Prior Transfers

If two people die within a short time of each other and the first to die had left property to the survivor (who later died), a credit may be available to alleviate the harshness of two taxes on the same property within a relatively short period. This *credit for tax on prior transfers* is available if the later-to-die decedent had received property from someone else's estate within 10 years of her death and an estate tax was paid at the prior death.

Amount of the Credit

The credit is a percentage of the lower of two amounts: (1) the tax generated by the inclusion of the property in the estate of the present decedent, or (2) the tax generated by the inclusion of the property in the estate of the prior decedent.

The percentage is 100 if the two individuals die within two years of each other. Then it drops 20 percent every two years. So in the third and fourth years after the first individual's death, the credit has dropped to 80 percent of what would have been allowed if death had occurred in the first two years. In the fifth and sixth years, the credit drops to 60 percent. By the seventh and eighth years, the credit is down to 40 percent. In the ninth and tenth years, the credit is only 20 percent of the lower of the two taxes. If the second individual dies after the tenth year, no credit is allowed.

Page 28, Schedule R—Generation-Skipping Transfer Tax (GSTT)

There is a flat-rate 55 percent tax on every *generation-skipping transfer*. Essentially the GSTT affects transfers to grandchildren or others in that or following generations. The tax applies to transfers in trust or arrangements having substantially the same effect as a trust, such as transfers involving life estates (the right to use and possess the property for life) and remainders (the right to what "remains" when the life estate or estate for years ends), estates for years (the right to use and possess the property for a specified number of years), and insurance and annuity contracts. So if the decedent left cash or any other property to a grandchild, either directly or in some indirect manner (such as in trust with the provision that "income is to be paid to my child for life and at my child's death, principal is to go to my grandchild"), and if the amount of the transfer is large enough, this very harsh tax is imposed (in addition to any other tax that applies to the transfer).

GST Exclusion

Every individual is allowed to make aggregate transfers of up to $1 million (this may be indexed annually for inflation after 1998), either during his lifetime or at death (or some during lifetime and the balance at death), that are exempt from the GST tax.

Completing Schedule R (and Schedule R-1 for trusts) can be very difficult, with long-range effects on future generations. It is absolutely essential to consult tax counsel for assistance.

Calculating the Federal Estate Tax

You have now completed schedules A through I, which include all the property that must be entered in the gross estate, and schedules J through R, the allowable deductions and credits.

Now enter the total values of both assets and deductions under "Part 5—Recapitulation" on page 3 of Form 706 and total both the gross estate and allowable deductions.

Notice the column entitled "Alternate value." In each of the gross estate schedules, to the left of the "Value at date of death" column, there are two columns entitled "Alternate valuation date" and "Alternate value." As executor you have the right to decide whether to value assets as of the date of death or as of an alternate valuation date, which is six months after death. The purpose of the later date is to alleviate hardship. Assume that an estate values assets at the date of death and pays taxes based on these values. Assume also that the assets plunge in value in a rapidly declining market so that by the time the return is filed, the tax is larger than the estate. The right to value assets at an alternate date minimizes the potential for this unfair and harsh result.

If you elect the alternate valuation date, *all* assets must be valued as of that date. *Alternate valuation date* typically means six months after death, but it can be earlier if assets were sold, distributed, exchanged, or otherwise disposed of before that date. Use the value as of the date, distribution, exchange, or other disposal.

Another exception may be made to the general rule for alternate valuation dates if an asset is affected by the mere lapse of time—such as a patent that loses value as each day's monopoly is lost. If the asset's value dimishes merely because of the passage of time, the alternate valuation date is defined as the date of death. But adjustments are allowed for any reduction in value that is not due strictly to the lapse of time—such as an improved competing product on the market or a drastic change in technology that reduces the importance of the asset in question. For example, the value of a corporation that makes a first-generation computer drops drastically when the second- and third-generation products of its competitors are announced.

Importance of the Alternate Valuation Date Decision

Why is the right to select an alternate valuation date so important? As mentioned, the finally agreed-upon value of an asset has implications beyond the federal estate tax. The value used on the 706 determines the income-tax basis of the property in the hands of its beneficiary. In other words, the basis of an asset is changed (*stepped up* or *stepped down*) when a person dies. The new *basis* (the starting point for determining the gain or loss from a sale or the limit on cost recovery through depreciation) is the asset's federal estate-tax value. A higher value may mean higher estates taxes, but it may also mean a lower gain to report if it is sold by the beneficiary, or it may mean larger write-offs.

Alternate valuation may be elected only if the total value of all property in the estate is reduced *and* if the federal estate-tax liability is reduced.

Once the decision has been made, proceed to the actual computation on the first page of Form 706.

The Computation

Page 1 of the 706 is the place for the actual computation of the tax. The "Total gross estate" (line 1) is the sum of all amounts subject to tax ("Recapitulation"—page 3, line 10). "Total allowable deductions" (page 3, line 20) are then subtracted from the gross estate. This results in the "Taxable estate," upon which you compute the "Credit for state death taxes" (line 13). The taxable estate is not—as its name seems to imply—the amount to which the estate tax rates are applied.

Applying the Rates

It is to the "Tentative tax base" (page 1, line 5) that the rates are applied. The tentative tax base is found by adding to the "Taxable estate" (line 3) any "Adjusted taxable gifts" (line 4). These are the taxable portions of any lifetime gifts that are not already reflected in the gross estate: Add the "taxable portion" (gross gift less any allowable annual exclusion, marital, or charitable deduction) of any taxable gifts made after 1976 to the taxable state.

Now go to Table A in the instructions to IRS Form 706 and figure the "Tentative tax" (page 1, line 6).

Subtract any post-1976 gift taxes actually paid (line 7). The result (line 8) is the "Gross estate tax."

Reducing the Tax by the Unified Credit

You are allowed to reduce the gross estate tax by one or more of various credits. The first is the "Unified credit" (line 11), allowed to every person during his lifetime or at death (this is why it is called "unified"). It offsets the tax on a dollar-for-dollar basis. This $192,800 credit is roughly equivalent to sheltering the first $600,000 from tax. (If you figured the estate tax on $600,000 of taxable assets, the tax would be $192,800.) The $600,000 applicable exclusion (sheltered) amount is for 1997. In other words, if the property actually subject to tax in 1997 was $600,000 or less, there would be no federal estate tax (assuming the decedent had not made large taxable gifts and used up any of the credit during her lifetime). For persons dying in 1998 the applicable exclusion amount is $625,000, for 1999, $650,000, $675,000 in 2000 and 2001, $700,000 in 2002 and 2003, $850,000 in 2004, $950,000 in 2005, and $1 million in 2006.

Reducing the Tax by the Credit for State Death Taxes

After subtracting the unified credit from the gross estate tax, you may also be entitled to a "Credit for state death taxes" (line 13). Go back to the "Taxable estate" amount (line 3). Subtract $60,000. (This is a fixed statutory amount that must be subtracted at this point.) Use the net result to compute your credit according to the applicable rates in Table C in the instructions.

The amount you have just computed is your *maximum* allowed credit for state death taxes. Actually, the credit allowed is the lower of two amounts: (1) the amount you have just computed, or (2) the amount the estate actually paid to the state as a death or inheritance tax. (You may claim the credit you anticipate and figure the federal estate tax on the return before the state death taxes are actually paid.) The credit is allowed for state inheritance, estate, legacy, or succession taxes.

File the following documents with your federal estate-tax return:

1. A certificate from the state showing the tax paid, the amount of any interest and penalties, the total amount

paid in cash, and the date of payment. (This is important because the federal credit will not be allowed unless the state tax is paid within four years after the return is—or should be—filed.)

2. Any additional proof of payment.

Reducing the Tax by Other Types of Credits

You may be entitled to a credit for federal gift taxes if those transfers were included in this estate (Schedule O).

Credits are also allowed for foreign death taxes (Schedule P) and for taxes paid on prior transfers from another decedent (Schedule G).

22 | Gift-Tax Returns

If the decedent made a taxable gift during his lifetime but did not file the required gift-tax return, it is your duty to file the return and, if appropriate, to pay the gift tax. The gift tax is levied on the right of one individual to transfer money or other property to another. It is based on the value of the property transferred.

The gift tax is computed on a progressive schedule (i.e., the rates get higher as the amount of total gifts increases) based on cumulative lifetime gifts. In other words, the tax rates are applied to the total of "taxable gifts" (all gifts less exclusions and deductions) made over the decedent's lifetime rather than *only* to the taxable gifts she made in the calendar year of death.

Computing the Tax on Gifts

Gift-tax rates are applied to a new figure (the taxable gifts). Before you compute the tax on a gift, you are allowed to make certain deductions: (1) "gift splitting," (2) an annual exclusion, (3) a marital deduction, and (4) a charitable deduction.

Gift Splitting

The tax law permits a married donor—with the consent of the nondonor spouse—to treat a gift to a third party (a child or some other person) as though each spouse had given one-half. You may elect such *gift splitting* on the gift-tax return of the donor spouse.

Gift splitting is an artificial mechanism. For computational purposes, even if one spouse makes the entire gift, you may treat that single transfer on the gift-tax return as though each spouse had made only one-half of the gift. One advantage of gift splitting is that the tax rate for each spouse is calculated separately on the basis of prior gifts made by each one individually. This may lower the rate considerably.

The second advantage of gift splitting is that it "creates" another *annual exclusion* (see below).

The privilege of gift splitting is available only with regard to gifts made while the couple was married. Gifts made before the marriage may not be split, even if the couple was married later in the same calendar year. Likewise, gifts made after the couple was legally divorced or gifts made by a survivor after one spouse dies may not be split. But gifts made before one spouse dies may be split even if that spouse dies before signing the appropriate consent or election. As executor you can (and, in most cases, should) elect to split the gift.

Annual Exclusion

Each person is allowed to make up to $10,000 (indexed annually for inflation after 1998) worth of tax-free gifts to each of any number of persons or parties each year. If a male decedent was unmarried and in the course of one year made outright gifts of $2,000, $8,000, and $16,000, respectively, to his brother, father, and son, the $2,000 gift and the $8,000 gift would be fully excludable, and the first $10,000 of the $16,000 gift to his son would also be excludable. If the same individual was married and his spouse consented to splitting the gift, each spouse would be deemed to have made one-half of the gift. As a result, both spouses would receive annual exclusions, and none of the $26,000 worth of gifts would be subject to tax. Take advantage of this "extra" annual exclusion through gift splitting.

As the executor of an individual who was married at the time a gift was made, you may sign the gift-tax return with the surviving spouse regardless of who made the gift. (In fact, the Internal Revenue Service has said that if no administrator or executor has been appointed, the surviving spouse may consent to the gift split even if he has not been legally appointed.)

Gift-Tax Marital Deduction

An individual who transfers property to a spouse during her lifetime is allowed an unlimited deduction (subject to certain conditions) known as the gift-tax marital deduction. The purpose of this marital deduction is to enable spouses to be treated as an economic unit. The deduction eliminates any tax on interspousal transfers made during a lifetime. (A similar deduction, allowed at death, is explained in Chapter 20.)

Gift-Tax Charitable Deduction

A donor making a transfer of property to a qualified charity is allowed a charitable deduction equal to the value of the gift (to the extent not already covered by the annual exclusion). The net effect of the charitable deduction—together with the annual exclusion—is to eliminate any gift-tax liability.

There is no limit on the amount, free of gift tax, that an individual is allowed to give to a "qualified" charity. (Qualified charities include the federal government; state or political subdivisions; certain religious, educational, scientific, or charitable organizations; some fraternal societies; and some veterans associations.)

Calculating the Gift Tax

The actual gift tax payable should be calculated by the estate's attorney or accountant. The process begins with a determination of the amount of taxable gifts made in the year of the decedent's death. To compute taxable gifts, first value all gifts made. If appropriate, split the amount and consider the decedent as having made one-half of the gift. Then apply any annual exclusion and marital or charitable deductions to the extent appropriate.

Reporting of Gifts and Payment of Tax

Typically, no gift-tax return must be filed unless a gift made to one individual in one year exceeds $10,000 (indexed for inflation after 1998). File a return on a calendar-year basis when a gift to one person in one year exceeds $10,000, even if no gift tax is due. For example, if a married woman gives $15,000 to her son, the transfer is free of gift tax (because each spouse has a $10,000 annual exclusion and the $15,000 is split between them). However, you have to file a gift-tax return because the gift exceeds the annual exclusion amount (and also because the gift is "split," and filing a return is a prerequisite for splitting a gift).

The gift-tax return must be filed and the gift tax, if any, due on reported gifts must be paid no later than the date on which the donor's federal estate-tax return is due (regardless of any extensions for filing the donor's income-tax return and the fact that the gift-tax return normally is due on April 15 of the year following the calendar year of the gift). The date is nine months after the decedent's death.

23 | Estate's Income-Tax Return

An estate is a taxable entity just like a person. In other words, during the period of administration, if the gross annual income of the estate exceeds $600, you must file IRS Form 1041, the U.S. Fiduciary Income Tax Return (the income tax return for an estate). The estate, as a taxpayer, continues to exist until you have distributed all the assets of the estate to its beneficiaries.

The estate's income-tax return is due on the fifteenth day of the fourth month after the estate's tax year closes (assuming you select a fiscal year other than a calendar year).

The estate should have its own identification number, which is used on all federal income-tax and federal estate-tax returns. Complete and file IRS Form SS-4, Application for Employer Identification Number (EIN), as soon as possible after being appointed.

As executor you are obliged to file an income-tax return for the estate and to pay any tax on income received by the estate up until the date you are formally discharged.

Extension of Time to File

The IRS typically allows you extra time (six months maximum) to file the estate's income-tax return. Use the Application for

Extension of Time to File U.S. Partnership, Fiduciary, and Certain Exempt Organizations Return (IRS Form 2758).

Requesting Prompt Assessment of Tax

To obtain faster relief from the personal liability you have assumed as executor for payment of the estate's income taxes, you can request the IRS to make a prompt assessment of the tax due. This reduces the IRS's time for assessing any additional tax (normally three years) to 18 months from the date you request prompt assessment of any additional income tax.

Electing the Estate's Taxable Year

You have the right to choose a calendar or a fiscal year as the reporting period for the estate's income and deductions. Your objective is to minimize the overall impact of taxes on all the parties concerned—the estate and its beneficiaries.

Work with the estate's accountant and attorney, and estimate what future income will be received and what expenses will be incurred by the estate. If the estate has a great deal of income in its early stages and few offsetting deductions, you may want to elect a short first fiscal year.

Here is one useful planning technique for selecting a taxable year: If you pay administration expenses just before the estate ends, and if those deductions exceed the income of the estate, the excess deductions may be carried over to the individual income-tax returns of the beneficiaries. In other words, your payment of administration expenses can be utilized to offset the personal income of the beneficiaries.

Another technique involves timing. If an estate distributes all of its income, that income must be reported by the beneficiaries. It has the same character (ordinary, capital-gain, or tax-free income) in the hands of the beneficiaries that it had in the hands of the estate. The beneficiary is taxed on the distributions, but not until his taxable year in which the estate's taxable year ends. For instance, assume the estate's taxable year ends on January 31, 1997. The beneficiary who must report any income from the estate doesn't have to report it until his tax return for 1997 is due. That means no tax is payable until April 1998. Therefore, if you carefully select the estate's taxable year, you can defer the beneficiaries' payment of the tax for a considerable period (and earn money on the amount you would otherwise have paid in tax).

Another timing technique involves your ability to accumulate income received by the estate. To the extent that you hold income within the estate, it is taxable to the estate. Once you distribute that income, it is taxable to the beneficiary. Because you can choose how much to pay out and how much to accumulate, you have the flexibility to allocate tax liability between the estate and its beneficiaries. Consult with the estate's attorney and accountant, and decide which taxpayer is in the highest tax bracket. Then try to equalize the incomes of the respective taxpayers so that all income is in the lowest possible overall tax brackets.

When the time comes to distribute the estate, any *loss carryovers* (losses that are tax-deductible) not fully used by the estate can be used by the beneficiaries.

24 | Decedent's Final Income-Tax Return

It is your duty as executor to prepare a final federal (and state) income-tax return for the decedent if she would have been required to file a return had she lived. That return covers the part of the taxable year of the decedent during which she was alive.

The federal return is due on or before April 15 of the year following the year of death. Check with the decedent's accountant to find out when the state income-tax return is due.

You may have a duty to file even if it appears that the decedent's income was insufficient to require the filing of a return. This can occur because of a possible refund of tax withheld or estimated tax paid.

To obtain the necessary information to file someone else's return, examine prior tax returns, deposit slips, and canceled checks. The easiest course is to contact the accountant who prepared the decedent's income-tax returns in the past and hire that individual to prepare the final income-tax returns. The fees you pay the accountant on behalf of the estate are deductible for federal estate-tax purposes as an administration cost (or can be deducted on the income-tax return if this deduction results in a greater benefit).

Extension of Time to File

The IRS will grant you an automatic two-month extension to file the decedent's last federal income-tax return after you complete Form 4868 (Application for Automatic Extension of Time to File U.S. Individual Income Tax Return). However, even though you can extend the time to file, you *cannot* extend the time to pay. When you send in your completed Form 4868, you must also enclose payment for any tax due. (Obviously, you will not know the exact amount; make the best estimate possible at the time.)

If you are delayed by circumstances beyond your control, you may be able to obtain an additional extension to pay the tax due. File Form 2688 (Application for Additional Extension of Time to File U.S. Individual Income Tax Return) and state why timely filing and payment are impossible.

Requesting Prompt Assessment of Tax

You are personally liable for payment of all the decedent's taxes if you make distributions to beneficiaries before having fully satisfied your tax obligations. You may therefore want to request that the IRS assess the tax due more promptly than it usually does and thus settle the issue. Contact an accountant and/or tax attorney before making such a request (which is likely to trigger an audit). The request must be sent separately from the tax return itself and must be made within three years of filing the return.

To be discharged from your personal liability for payment of the decedent's income taxes, write for a prompt assessment. The IRS will notify you of the amount of the tax within nine months of the date it receives your application. Once you pay that amount, you are discharged from personal liability even if a deficiency is found later.

Obtaining a Refund

In many cases a refund is due to the estate. Complete IRS Form 1310 (Statement of Claim Due Deceased Taxpayer) and attach it to the income-tax return. Also enclose a *short certificate*, the shortened version of your authorization to act on behalf of the estate, as granted you by the Register of Wills.

Right to File Joint Returns

As executor you have the right to file a joint return with the decedent's surviving spouse (even if you *are* the decedent's surviving spouse), or you can file a separate return for the decedent. You probably will file a joint return if those overall tax rates are more favorable than filing for the decedent as a single individual. You may also want to file jointly if the decedent had significant tax losses or deductions that might otherwise be wasted. (Note that the executor loses the right to file a joint return if the surviving spouse remarries before the end of the calendar year in which the decedent died.)

Election for Certain Government Bonds

If the estate holds Series E or EE bonds, you have the right to report the increase in the bonds' value year by year, or you can defer reporting the income until you redeem the bonds. If you report the interest currently (which makes sense if the decedent had little or no income), the accrued interest must also be reported in the current year.

Medical-Expense Deductions

You have the right to deduct the decedent's final medical expenses either on the decedent's final income-tax return or on the federal estate-tax return (or take some of the expenses as deductions on each return). Have the decedent's accountant make a comparison of the relative tax advantages. If you take the deductions on the decedent's return, file a statement that you have not already claimed (or will not claim) the same expenses as a deduction on the federal estate-tax return.

Personal Exemption and Dependency Exemptions Allowed

When you file the decedent's last income-tax return, you must report all income the decedent earned, but you are entitled to deduct the decedent's personal exemption and dependency exemptions in the same manner as if the decedent had lived.

25 Tax Elections

An executor can choose to use—or not to use—a multiplicity of income-tax and estate-tax deductions. These elections or options can greatly diminish the overall tax burden facing the estate and its beneficiaries, and can result in a dispositive arrangement that meets the needs of the beneficiaries more effectively. (None of the elections should be made—or allowed to lapse—unless they are considered carefully by counsel.)

Examine each of the elections discussed in this chapter and determine:

- Does this estate qualify for this election?
- Should the election be taken in light of *all* the surrounding circumstances? (What are the tax *and* nontax effects?)
- How much time do we have to make the election?

Create a checklist and keep a written record indicating the date on which each of these issues has been addressed.

Joint Return with Surviving Spouse

The decedent's accountant and attorney should decide whether or not the decedent's income, earned and reportable up to the date of death, should be shown on a return that also includes the surviving spouse's income. You may file a joint return income-tax return with the surviving spouse's income for the entire year.

To be eligible for this election, the surviving spouse must not remarry until after the regular tax year ends. The surviving spouse must join you in signing IRS Form 1040 and thereby consent to the election. (You sign as the surviving spouse *and* executor if you are both.)

The advantage of filing a joint return is that the income-tax rates are lower, making the overall income tax lower. A secondary advantage is that the surviving spouse might have incurred losses that can offset the income of the deceased spouse, or the deceased spouse may have had tax losses or other deductible items that can offset the income of the surviving spouse.

This election must be made by the due date of the decedent's final income-tax return.

Series E Bond Accrued Interest

Interest accrued on Series E government bonds (as well as H and HH exchange bonds) can be reported in one of four ways:

1. Report accrued interest on the final income-tax return of the decedent.
2. Report the income on the estate's income-tax return.
3. Report the accrued bond income on a later return.
4. Cash in the bonds.

There are no special requirements for any of these options as long as the bonds pass to you at the owner's death. However, if the bonds pass to someone other than the executor (for example, if the bonds were held jointly with rights of survivorship), you could not report the accrued interest on the estate's income-tax returns.

The major advantage of this is flexibility. Rather than piling this additional income on top of substantial amounts of other income, you can place it on the income-tax return, where it is subject to lower rates.

If you report this accrued interest on the decedent's final income-tax return rather than on the estate's income-tax return, a deduction that might otherwise have been available to the recipient of the income—the deduction for "income in respect of a decedent"—is lost. (Income that was earned but not received by a calendar-basis taxpayer before death is subject to both federal estate tax and federal income tax. The recipient of such income is entitled to an income-tax deduction based on the federal and state death taxes generated by the inclusion of this income. The greater the death taxes generated, the larger the income-tax deduction.)

One advantage, therefore, of reporting accrued bond income on the decedent's final return is that it creates an income-tax liability that in turn may be taken as a federal estate-tax deduction. There is a second advantage. Suppose the decedent died early in the tax year, before she had realized much income. If you report all the "built-in" gain from the Series E bond in that tax year, you obtain the low marginal tax rate applicable to that very short year. Keep in mind, however, that once you elect to report the income from the bond, you have to continue to report it annually. If the tax you have to pay is large, you have a high-cost-of-money factor to consider (you have to pay the tax now, but you have no cash until you cash in the bond).

Accrued bond interest is reported on the appropriate tax return by the applicable due date.

Unpaid Medical Expenses

You can deduct unpaid medical expenses either on the federal estate-tax return or on the decedent's income-tax return for the year in which the expense was incurred. Note that the income-tax deduction will be disallowed unless the medical expense is in fact paid within one year of death.

Take the deduction on the return that produces the greatest tax benefit—typically, the return in the highest tax bracket. If the decedent left property to a surviving spouse in a manner that qualifies for the federal estate-tax marital deduction, there may be no estate tax. Obviously, the deduction is wasted if it is not taken on the decedent's final income-tax return.

If medical expenses are very large, consider dividing the deduction. In other words, deduct some of the expenses on the decedent's last income-tax return and the balance on the estate-tax return. The medical deduction must be taken on the appropriate return by the due date of that return.

Whenever possible, the family should pay medical bills prior to death. This has the twofold effect of generating an income-tax deduction and reducing the gross estate by the amount of the payment.

Administration Expenses

You can deduct administration expenses on the estate's income-tax return or on the estate-tax return, or split the deduction between the two.

Deductible administration expenses include executor's commissions, attorney's fees, court costs, accountant's costs, appraiser's fees, and other death-related expenses.

Be careful. When you take a deduction on the estate's income-tax return, you may be increasing the estate tax. This means that the estate's *remaindermen* (those who receive property after the income beneficiary's death) receive less. The income-tax deduction benefits the income beneficiaries. Check the will for authorization to take the deduction on either return, or discuss the matter with an attorney.

Distributions from the Estate

Taxation of the income produced by property generally follows the property itself. When the estate makes a distribution of property to an heir, the heir, rather than the estate, is taxable on the income produced by the property.

To accomplish this income shift, it is necessary actually to distribute the property during the estate's fiscal year (the income-tax consequences will also be shifted to a beneficiary if the will requires the income to be distributed even if in fact it is not). By distributing property, the tax burden can be shifted to a number of taxpayers (thereby lowering the effective rate of tax) and can be shifted to family members who are in the lowest brackets. You can apply the same tax-saving principle by making an early distribution to a trust (which is also a separate taxpayer and in a separate tax bracket).

You can make distributions from the estate until the end of the estate's fiscal year. If the decedent's assets produce a great deal of income, significant tax savings can be realized by keeping the estate open. In other words, by continuing the estate as a separate taxpayer, you can divide income by holding some and paying out the rest. The estate is taxed on what it receives and does not pay out. The estate's beneficiaries are taxed on what they receive.

The estate is permitted to remain in existence for "a reasonable period of administration"—defined as the period actually required for you to collect the estate's assets, pay its debts, and distribute any legacies and bequests. The longer you can extend the administration, the more income-tax savings are possible.

Waiver of Fee by Personal Representative

You are entitled (unless the will specifically prohibits it) to a fee for the services you render on behalf of the estate. But you may *waive* (formally give up) your right to the fee or to a portion thereof (see Chapter 21).

If you decide to waive your fee, inform the principal beneficiaries in writing. Give notice quickly—if possible, within six months of your appointment as executor. Of course, if you are the principal or only beneficiary of the estate, it is highly doubtful that taking a fee and paying income tax on it would ever be in your financial interest. If you don't take the executor's fee, it passes to you as beneficiary, free of income tax. On the other hand, suppose you are one of several beneficiaries. By waiving your fee, you can shift the amount you could have taken to a younger generation of relatives. Best of all, no gift tax will be payable.

Election Against the Will

In almost every state, a surviving spouse has the legal right to a share of a decedent's estate regardless of what the will says. This *right of election* is specified under state statute. The *statutory share* is typically one-third of the probate estate of the decedent (the amount varies from state to state).

One reason to consider an election against the will is that it may give the surviving spouse a larger portion of the estate than she would receive under the will. A larger portion of the estate translates into a larger marital deduction, which means lower federal estate taxes.

This right to "elect or take against the will" is generally easy to exercise. There is no need to contest the will or to show any fraud, duress, undue influence, or improper execution. Check with counsel about your state's provisions. It is necessary to file a written election with the local probate court. Election must be made within the time specified under local law—typically, six months after the public announcement of the appointment of the estate's executor or within one year of death. Failure to file the election within the prescribed period results in permanent loss of the surviving spouse's right to "take against the will."

In some states children have a similar right, determined by statute, to a share of a decedent's estate, regardless of what the will provides.

Alternate Valuation

An executor can choose one of two dates for valuation of assets on the federal estate-tax return. The first is the date of death. The second date is six months after the date of death—the *alternate valuation date*. If property is sold, exchanged, distributed, or otherwise disposed of between the date of death and six months after death, the latter becomes the alternate valuation date.

If you are required to file a federal estate-tax return (Form 706), you are eligible to elect the alternate valuation date.

An obvious advantage of the alternate valuation date is that if the value of estate assets has dropped between the date of death and the alternate valuation date, this election may reduce federal estate taxes. (To the extent that property qualifies for the marital deduction, this is not true, since no federal estate tax would be payable regardless of the value of the property.) For example, suppose a widow died owning assets worth $800,000. Assume these assets had dropped in value to $730,000 six months later. By valuing assets six months after death rather than on the date of death, you save estate tax on $70,000 ($800,000 less $730,000).

In some cases you should choose the date on which overall estate values were highest. This technique is especially useful in an estate with a great deal of highly appreciated assets that are likely to be sold by the heirs. A higher value is also important when the estate contains highly depreciated assets, such as buildings. You may want to pick the date on which assets have a higher value because the federal estate-tax value of an asset also becomes its *basis*—the starting point for determining gain or loss in the event of a sale, or the limit for cost recovery through depreciation deductions. The higher the seller's basis, the lower the gain on a later sale. Likewise, the higher the basis, the greater the income-tax deductions that can be enjoyed by the recipients of depreciable property.

Choosing the alternate valuation date to obtain a higher value is especially indicated if the state and federal combined income-tax brackets of the estate and/or its beneficiaries are higher than the estate-tax bracket of the estate. Obviously, if all or a large portion of the estate qualifies for the estate-tax marital deduction, lower or no rates are applied against estate assets, regardless of their value. So it would seem to be excellent planning to select the date that would result in the highest estate-tax valuation. Unfortunately, this technique is not available. An estate may use alternate valuation only if the election has the effect of reducing (1) the total value of the gross estate and (2) the amount of the estate-tax liability.

Make the alternate valuation election on page 2 of IRS Form 706 by the date the form is due to be filed. (An exception to this rule allows the election to be made on a return filed late, but only if that return is the first filed for the estate, is otherwise properly made, and is filed within one year of its due date.)

Special-Use Valuation for Farm or Closely Held Business Real Estate

Real estate used as a farm or closely held business can be valued according to its actual use (for example, as pastureland) rather than its "highest and best use" (for example, at the price it would bring if offered to a real estate developer), but only if certain tests are met (see Chapter 21).

The amount of the decrease between the property's highest and best-use value (the valuation required for most assets) and the special-use value is limited to $750,000 (indexed for inflation after 1986). Have an appraiser figure both the normal fair-market value and the special value (although there are formulas that you can use; see Chapter 21).

There are various disadvantages to the special-use valuation. For example, personal liability is required of all heirs to the property; and if the property is disposed of within 10 years of the decedent's death, all or a portion of the estate-tax savings will be *recaptured*—that is, the money the estate "saved" in taxes must be paid back to the IRS.

There also may be administrative problems (as is inevitably the case where minors are involved) as well as intrafamily conflicts of interest. The IRS will probably want a special lien placed on the property until the statutory period for recapture of the tax break has expired.

The current-use valuation election must be made on a federal estate-tax return timely filed (including extensions).

Family-Owned Business Interest Exclusion

If certain requirements are met, an estate can elect to exclude from the estate tax calculation all or a portion of a family-owned business. Together with the increased unified credit, this exclusion can't exceed $1.3 million.

Among the many requirements to qualify for this exclusion are these:

- The value of the business must comprise more than 50% of the decedent's estate.
- The principal place of business must be in the U.S.
- The interest cannot be publicly traded within 3 years of the decedent's death.
- The decedent must have been a U.S. citizen or resident.

Note that the IRS will "recapture" all or some of the estate tax benefits realized if, within 10 years of the decedent's death, the business is sold to an outsider or certain other "triggering events" occur.

Qualified Terminable Interest Property (QTIP)

Generally, property qualifies for the estate-tax marital deduction only if it is left to the surviving spouse either outright or in a manner tantamount to outright. These *terminable interests* can qualify for the marital deduction if you make a QTIP election (see Chapter 21).

Although the QTIP election makes it more likely that no one other than the individual(s) selected by the decedent will obtain the property when the surviving spouse dies, it does not fully ensure that result. For example, in some states a surviving spouse still has a right to "elect against the will" and take the same share of the estate that would have been available had the decedent died intestate. Still, the odds are higher that the decedent's objectives will be accomplished.

Make the QTIP election on the federal estate-tax return, filed by the appropriate due date.

Installment Payment of Estate Tax

If certain tests are met, you can elect to pay the federal estate tax generated by the inclusion of a closely held business in installments. During the first four years only interest on the unpaid tax is due. Over the next 10 years the estate must pay principal and interest (equal annual principal payments with interest on the declining balance).

To qualify, the enterprise in question must in fact be an active trade or business, not a mere investment.

It is appealing to be able to put off principal payments on the federal estate tax for four years and pay a modest rate of interest during that time. Many smaller estates will pay only 2 percent interest on the unpaid balance of tax. If the business exceeds a specified value, the interest on a portion of the unpaid tax will be at 45 percent of the rate that the IRS generally charges on unpaid taxes. This rate is changed twice a year and is compounded daily. It was 9 percent in 1997.

This 6166 election does not provide funds to pay the tax; it merely delays the day of reckoning. Furthermore, you become personally liable for the tax if you distribute estate assets to the beneficiaries before paying the tax. You will be discharged from personal liability only if you furnish a bond (you can charge the cost of the bond to the estate) or have all the parties who have an interest in the property consent to a lien and to the imposition of additional liens if the value of the original property is—or falls—below the total of the unpaid taxes and the aggregate interest owed. It would be extremely dangerous to make final distributions to estate beneficiaries before the expiration of the entire 14-year period.

This installment election (tax practitioners call this a *6166 election* because Internal Revenue Code Section 6166 spells out the eligibility requirements) defers only the federal estate tax attributable to the closely held business. It does not defer administration expenses or the need for cash to pay state death taxes, debts, the remaining portion of the federal estate tax, income taxes, etc.

To take advantage of this election, submit notice to the IRS when you file the federal estate-tax Form 706 and check off line 3 of Part 3 on page 2 of the form. Discuss with your attorney and CPA how to coordinate code section 303 stock redemptions (see page 227) with the need for cash under code section 6166.

Deferral of Estate Tax on Remainder or Reversionary Interest

A *remainder interest* is a future interest in property that comes into existence after a prior interest terminates. For example, a decedent may have set up a trust under her will and provided in the trust that her husband is to receive the income from the property in the trust for his lifetime, and that the principal at his death is to go to their children. The children receive what is left (the remainder) when the husband's interest terminates. For this reason, the children are called *remaindermen*. A *reversionary interest* is a right to recover property at some time in the future. For instance, a person may set up a trust under which a parent will enjoy the income so long as the parent lives. When the parent dies, the principal of this trust will revert to the person who set up the trust (the *grantor*).

Federal tax law recognizes the imposition that would be placed on estates that contained remainders or reversions of great value; there would be tax imposed on the actuarial value of the right to recover the asset, but the estate would not have the asset to sell, pledge, or otherwise pay the tax. For this reason the law (Internal Revenue Code Section 6163) provides that the estate tax attributable to the value of either a remainder or a reversionary interest can be deferred up to six months beyond the date on which the preceding legal interest ends. In the examples above, the executor would have six months from the date the husband (the income beneficiary) died in the case of the remainder interest and the same length of time from the date the parent died in the case of the reversion example.

This Section 6163 election to defer payment of the federal estate tax is available to any estate in which a remainder or reversionary interest is includable in the gross estate. Make the election if the estate needs cash or if the value of the interest is large relative to the values of other estate assets.

Make the election by checking yes on line 4 of page 2 of Form 706 or by filing a notice to the IRS on or before the due date for filing the federal estate-tax return. Include a copy of the document that created the remainder or reversionary interest.

You must also furnish a bond to the IRS for twice the amount of the tax and estimated interest.

Reasonable-Cause Extension to Pay Federal Estate Tax

Under Code Section 6161 the IRS may (entirely at its discretion) allow an estate to extend the due date for payment of the federal estate tax, one year at a time, for up to 10 years.

To obtain the Section 6161 extensions, you must prove to the IRS one of the following:

1. You are unable to marshal assets to pay the estate tax at the time it is due.
2. A substantial part of the estate consists of rights to receive payments in the future.
3. The estate has insufficient cash to pay the tax and is not able to borrow the money except on unreasonable terms.
4. Sufficient funds are not available, after the exercise of due diligence, to pay the tax in a timely manner.
5. There is some other "reasonable cause" for the extensions to be granted.

All of the problems discussed in connection with the 14-year installment payout also apply to this election. The big advantage is that it relieves the immediate need for liquidity, but eventually you must raise the cash to pay the tax or be liable personally. To apply for this deferral, file IRS Form 4768 with the federal estate-tax return by the due date of the return.

Section 303 Stock Redemption

The tax law recognizes the hardships caused by a forced sale of a closely held business, and it provides a way for a corporation to make a distribution in redemption of its stock that will not be taxed as a dividend. Specifically, Section 303 allows a corporation to provide cash and/or other property in return for its stock without its being treated as a dividend, and to provide cash for the estate to pay death taxes and other expenses.

This protection is limited: A distribution is afforded "sale or exchange" treatment. (Only the difference between the estate's basis and the amount it receives for the stock is taxable, and that gain, if any, usually receives capital-gains treatment.) Typically, there is no reportable gain, since the estate's basis for the stock is stepped up to the stock's fair market value as of the decedent's death. The new basis, therefore, is equal to the price the estate receives for the stock, and there is typically no reportable gain. The distribution is protected from dividend treatment only to the extent that the seller of stock must pay or is liable for the decedent's death taxes or other expenses.

A major advantage of Section 303 is that it affords protection to family-owned corporations from *attribution* (constructive ownership) problems, whereby redemptions of only a part of a family member's stock are almost always taxable as dividends. (If a distribution is classified as a dividend, the entire amount received is taxable at ordinary income rates, as compared to the rates for long-term capital gains.)

Section 303 is typically implemented by an agreement between the corporation and the selling shareholder. A price for the stock is established. Then the corporation pays cash and/or property and in return receives stock of equal value.

The redemption must be accomplished within three years and 90 days from the due date of the federal estate-tax return; or, if there is a contest regarding the estate's tax liability, within 60 days of the time a tax-court decision on the subject is final. A longer time is allowed if the estate is also utilizing a Section 6166 installment payout of estate taxes.

Disclaimers

A *disclaimer* (some practitioners call it a *renunciation*) is an unqualified refusal to accept benefits. For federal estate-tax purposes, the person disclaiming is regarded as never having received the property disclaimed. As a result of this treatment, no transfer is considered to have been made by the disclaimant for estate-tax or gift-tax purposes.

The ability to shift an interest in property without paying gift tax can lead to exciting planning possibilities. For example, if an individual with children and a large estate receives a bequest that would only compound his estate-tax problems, disclaiming causes the bequest to pass to the next in line. So if the decedent left $1 million to his multimillionaire nephew if he was living, and otherwise to the nephew's children, the nephew, by disclaiming, in essence makes a tax-free gift of $1 million to his children. The disclaimer can be used to shift not only capital but also income.

If property is left to a child if living, and otherwise to the decedent's surviving spouse, a disclaimer by that child means that the property will be considered as having passed directly from the decedent to his surviving spouse and may therefore qualify for the estate-tax marital deduction. Likewise, if property is left to a child if living, and otherwise to a qualified charity, a disclaimer by the child will result in a charitable deduction in the decedent's estate.

A disclaimer has the desired tax effects only if it is "qualified." A *qualified disclaimer* is an unqualified refusal to accept an interest in property. It must be in writing and must be received by the legal representative of the decedent within nine months of death (or the day the transfer became complete, if earlier), or within nine months of the date on which the beneficiary reaches age 21. The disclaimer must be made before the property or any of its benefits have been accepted. The interest must pass (or have passed) to the recipient without any direction on the part of the disclaimant.

Although the disclaimer may be effective in spite of local law, be sure to check and meet all local law requirements for disclaimers as well as those outlined above.

Fiscal Year of the Estate

The fact that the estate is a tax entity separate from its beneficiaries can result in a great many planning opportunities (see Chapter 23).

To obtain the benefit of a short fiscal year, file the estate's income-tax form, Form 1041, by the fifteenth day of the fourth month after the end of that fiscal year.

Estate Administration Expenses

The expenses of administering an estate include attorney's fees, probate costs, accounting fees, and many other fees. You may deduct these costs on either the estate's income-tax return (Form 1041) or the federal estate-tax return (Form 706). You may also apportion the deductions to both returns, partly as income-tax deductions and partly as estate-tax deductions (see discussion earlier in this chapter).

Make the election by claiming the appropriate amount of deductions on the return you have selected. If you claim a deduction on the income-tax return, file a waiver stating that you agree not to take the deduction on the estate-tax return filed later.

Estate Selling Expenses

There is great flexibility with respect to the expenses an estate incurs when you must sell estate assets to pay taxes or expenses or to meet any other obligations or responsibilities of the estate. You can deduct estate sale expenses—such as brokerage fees, seller's commissions, or other transfer costs—on the federal estate-tax return as part of the cost of administering the estate. Alternatively, when you report a gain on the sale of an item, you can reduce the sale price in computing the gain. Here again, you are comparing the rates of the two returns and typically take the deduction (or reduction) on the return with the highest rate.

The only requirement for this deduction is that the amount of the expense be reasonable and allowable under state law and necessary to the administration of the estate. If the expense is not deemed necessary and benefits the beneficiaries more than the estate itself (for example, if the expense is incurred to settle a dispute among the heirs), then it cannot be taken as a deduction on the estate-tax return. It may be used, however, to reduce the amount reportable if there is a gain on the sale of an item.

Claim the deduction on the appropriate return before the expiration of the limitations period.

QDT (Qualified Domestic Trust)

A *QDT* (qualified domestic trust) election qualifies a transfer at death to a spouse who is not a U.S. citizen for a delay in the federal estate tax. Make this election by answering yes to the question on line 3 of Schedule M (page 24) of IRS Form 706. But remember the true effect of the QDT election: The estate tax is not forgiven; it is merely delayed.

The federal estate-tax marital deduction is the largest and typically the most important of all estate-tax deductions available to married couples. But the marital deduction is allowed only if the surviving spouse is a U.S. citizen. (Congress was concerned that an alien spouse, having received the estate, but not having paid any estate tax, would literally take the money and run back to a foreign country and beyond the reach of the IRS.)

Denial of a marital deduction, of course, is irrelevant if the estate does not significantly exceed the amount of the unified credit equivalent—$600,000 in 1997, increasing in steps to $1 million in 2006. But in other cases loss of the deduction can be devastating.

For instance, Michael and Carol have been married for 20 years. He is an entrepreneur from England. She is a housewife, born in Florida, who inherited a small amount of real estate and, through superior investment skills, parlayed it into $2 million. On the advice of their attorney, she made gifts of $600,000 worth of land to a trust benefiting their children. Carol's will provides that her entire remaining estate ($1,400,000) goes to Michael at her death. Carol expects that if she predeceases Michael, there will be no death tax because the $1,400,000 she leaves to Michael will qualify for the unlimited federal estate-tax marital deduction and the $600,000 given to the children will qualify for the unified credit. Compare what Michael and Carol *expect* to happen with what *will* if death occurs in 1997. This couple's heirs will receive $588,000 less than expected!

Clients' Expectation	Actual Result
Carol's gross estate $1,400,000	Carol's gross estate $1,400,000
Marital deduction 1,400,000	Marital deduction - 0 -
Adjusted taxable gifts 600,000	Adjusted taxable gifts 600,000
Tentative tax 192,800	Tentative tax 780,000

Clients' Expectation	Actual Result
Unified credit $192,800*	Unified credit $192,800*
Federal transfer taxes - 0 -	Federal transfer taxes 588,000
Received by Michael* 1,400,000	Received by Michael 812,000

*Increases year by year until 2006

Exceptions to loss of marital deduction rule. There are exceptions to the general rule that no marital deduction is allowed if the surviving spouse is a resident alien:

- When the surviving spouse becomes a U.S. citizen before the decedent's estate-tax return is filed and has been a U.S. resident at all times after the death and before becoming a U.S. citizen.
- If the property passing to the surviving spouse goes into a qualified domestic trust (QDT)

The QDT limitations. A QDT must meet all the following requirements:

1. Generally, at least one trustee must be a U.S. citizen or a domestic corporation.
2. The trust must provide that no distribution can be made from the QDT unless the U.S. trustee can withhold any federal tax due.
3. The executor must make an irrevocable election for QDT treatment.
4. Certain other requirements must be met to ensure the collection of any tax imposed on the trust.
5. The QDT must otherwise qualify as a transfer under the normal rules applicable to marital transfers.

Three events can trigger an immediate estate tax on QDT assets:

1. *Any* distribution—*other* than (1) income to the surviving spouse or (2) a distribution to the surviving spouse because of hardship—made prior to the surviving spouse's death.
2. If the QDT fails to meet any QDT requirement, the estate tax will be imposed as if the surviving spouse had died on the date the trust failed the requirement.
3. If the QDT pays the estate tax imposed on the second triggering event, that payment is considered a taxable distribution that sets off yet another tax. In other words, the QDT's payment of the estate tax on a distribution is itself a taxable distribution (equal to the amount of the tax) subject to a further estate tax.

The tax imposed on the occurrence of a taxable QDT event proves the QDT to be a cleverly devised trap for the unwary for the following reasons:

• The QDT tax is imposed at the highest marginal rate of the citizen spouse. This is an unusual penalty on the resident alien, particularly if the survivor has insignificant individual wealth and was in a lower tax bracket.
• The QDT tax cannot be avoided by the consumption of corpus by the surviving spouse (absent permissible hardship distributions).
• The surviving spouse's unified credit is not available to the surviving spouse for QDT taxable events. Thus, the surviving spouse's unified credit is wasted unless the surviving spouse has sufficient individually owned property to qualify for the credit.

Generation-Skipping Tax

If there is a possibility of the imposition of a generation-skipping tax on any beneficiary, either now or in the future, make the appropriate elections, and if given discretion under the will or trust, reallocate the estate's assets to trust for grandchildren to eliminate or greatly reduce the negative impact of the generation-skipping tax (see Chapter 21). These highly technical elections and options should be made only with the help of tax counsel.

26 | Valuation of Assets

One of the most complex and uncertain processes is the valuation of property for federal and state death-tax purposes.

Value is a variable. Reasonable minds can and often do differ over the proper value of any item of property. You must use appraisals by qualified experts, obtain documentation of recent sales of similar property, and submit photocopies of any buy/sell agreements to the IRS.

General Rules of Estate-Tax Valuation

As executor you must value every asset at its fair-market value—the price at which the property would be acquired by a hypothetical willing buyer from a willing seller, assuming that neither of them is under any compulsion to buy or to sell. A further assumption is that both parties have reasonable knowledge of any and all relevant facts. The value you place on property may differ greatly from what the government thinks that property is worth. So take a reasonable but aggressive position. If your purpose is to reduce federal and state death taxes, place the lowest possible reasonable value on the property. On the other hand, if you are interested in obtaining a high cost basis for the beneficiaries in order to lower potential gain if the property is later sold, or to increase cost recovery (depreciation) deductions, place a high but reasonable value on the asset.

Direct appraisers to document those factors that support your position and that, if litigated, would likely be sustained by the courts.

There is a substantial estate- or gift-tax valuation understatement penalty. If the value of any property is listed on an estate- or gift-tax return at 50 percent or less of the amount determined to be correct, the penalty is 20 percent of the underpayment attributable to the estate- or gift-tax valuation understatement. (No penalty is imposed if the tax due because of a valuation understatement is $5,000 or less.) Beware of "gross valuation misstatements." The penalty is 40 percent of the underpayment attributable to such misstatements. A gross valuation misstatement is one in which the claimed value of any property on an estate-tax or gift-tax return is 25 percent or less than the amount determined by the IRS and/or courts to be correct.

Date of Valuation of Assets

Generally, federal estate taxes are based either on the fair-market value of property as of the date the decedent died or on the value of property six months later (the *alternate valuation date*). Once selected for valuation purposes—date of death or alternate valuation date—that date applies to all assets in the estate.

If you select the alternate valuation date and you distribute, sell, exchange, or otherwise dispose of property within six months of death, you must value it as of *that* date—not the "six months after death" date.

Certain types of property diminish in value over time. For example, the value of a patent diminishes each year, as does the value of an annuity. Value a property interest whose value is affected by the mere passing of time as of the date of death.

Of course, if some external factor has affected valuation (as a new invention might reduce the value of an existing patent), that factor can be used in the valuation process.

Valuation of Real Property

The value of any real property as of a given date is subject to widely differing opinions. If there is no market for the property, it should be valued at (a) the highest price available, or (b) the amount it will bring as salvage, whichever is greater. If there is a market for real property held by the estate, the factors that you (and/or a professional appraiser) should consider are the following:

- The nature and condition of the property, its physical qualities and defects, and the adequacy or inadequacy of its improvements
- The size, shape, and location of the property
- The actual and potential use of the property and how it is affected by development trends and economic conditions (Is the neighborhood getting better or worse?)
- How suitable the property is for its actual or intended use
- Changes in zoning restrictions
- The size, age, and condition of the buildings (degree of deterioration or obsolescence)
- The market value of other properties in the same area
- The value of the net income realized from the property (Rentals are often *capitalized*, which means the value of the rent is projected to derive a value for the asset. For example, a building that yields $10,000 a year in net rentals probably is worth some multiple of $10,000, such as five times. Once rental has been capitalized, it must be adjusted for depreciation.)
- Prices at which comparable property in the same area was sold at a time near the applicable valuation date

(providing it was an arm's-length transaction for the best price obtainable)
- How much it would cost to duplicate the property after taking depreciation into account (Your appraiser must separate the cost or value of land from the total value. The cost of reproducing the building, using present cost figures, has to be estimated, and then the loss in value due to depreciation is subtracted from the total of the other two figures.)
- Unusual facts

If property in the estate is sold within a reasonable time after death, the IRS usually accepts the amount received as its value. This assumes, however, that it was sold in an arm's-length transaction. If property is sold at auction, the price is generally accepted if it appears that no other method would have resulted in a higher price.

Land may have substantial value for federal and state death-tax purposes even though it doesn't produce income and even though there is no active market. If land is in or adjacent to a settled community (such as at the edge of an expanding shopping center), it might be worth far more to the shopping-center developer than to a potential buyer in the residential market. Real estate, just like all other assets, must be valued at its "highest and best use" price rather than at the lowest figure the property might bring.

Special Valuation of Certain Farm and Certain Business Real Property

Let's assume the decedent was a farmer. Let's also assume that the farmland is surrounded by new housing developments. The estate-tax value of the land as farmland might be considerably lower than the value of the land if it were subdivided and used for single-family dwellings. The tax law allows you to value farmland (and certain business real property) at its "special use" value. For example, you could value farmland as such rather than as land subdivided and developed.

Essentially, the requirements for *special-use valuation* are the following:

- On the date the decedent died, the property must be in use as a farm for farming purposes or in a trade or business other than farming.
- The property must make up a significant portion of the decedent's gross estate.
- The property must pass to a "qualified heir"—a member of the family, an ancestor, a lineal descendant, the spouse, the spouse of a descendant, or a lineal descendant of a grandparent.
- The property must have been owned by the decedent or a member of her family and been used as a farm or closely held business for at least five of the eight years prior to death; during that time the decedent or a member of her family must have been materially involved in the operation of the farm or other business.

You can choose one of various formulas to reduce the value of the farmland from its "highest and best use" value (such as the price a developer might pay) to its value as farm (or business) real property (see Chapter 21).

If there is no comparable land, or if you choose to value the farm in the same way you might value qualifying closely held business real estate, do one or more of the following:

- Capitalize the income that the property can be expected to yield for farming purposes over a reasonable period of time under prudent management using traditional cropping patterns for the area (taking into account soil capacity, terrain configuration, and other relevant factors).

- Compare sale prices of other farms or closely held business land in the same geographical area but far enough removed from metropolitan resort areas to eliminate nonagricultural use as a significant factor in the sale price.
- Consider any other factor that fairly values the farm (or closely held business) property.

Watch out for *recapture*: If, within 10 years after the decedent's death and before the death of the "qualified heir," the heir disposes of it (by selling or giving it to someone outside the family) or no longer uses it as a farm or for business purposes, the estate-tax benefit because of the lower valuation is "recaptured." The tax savings is lost and all the tax that would have been paid by choosing the "highest and best use" valuation must now be paid (see Chapter 25).

Valuation of Life Insurance

Life insurance on the decedent that is received by or for the benefit of the estate is taxed in the estate. (Note that many *state* death taxes do not require inclusion, or provide special partial exclusions for life insurance proceeds.) The amount should be the amount received by the beneficiary—including any dividends and premium refunds paid to the beneficiary.

If the beneficiary selects a *settlement option* (i.e., takes the money in a form other than a lump sum), the amount that would have been payable as a lump sum is the amount you include in the decedent's gross estate. If the policy did not allow a lump-sum payment in the first place, the amount you include is the *commuted amount* used by the insurance company to compute the settlement-option payments. In other words, it's the total sum the insurance company would apply to make the promised monthly or annual payments to the beneficiary.

What if the decedent owned insurance on the life of

someone else? The value of a policy that has not matured and is owned by a decedent on the life of someone else is included in the policyholder's gross estate when he predeceases the insured. The amount includable depends on whether the policy is "new," "paid up," "active" (still in the premium-paying stage but beyond its first year), or "term insurance."

If a *new policy* (a policy in its first year) is involved, list the gross premium paid as the policy's value.

If the policy is *paid up* (i.e., no more premiums were payable when the decedent died), or if it was a *single-premium policy*, the value is the policy's *replacement cost*. This is the single premium that that company would have charged for a comparable contract with the same death benefit on the life of a person who was the same age as the insured at the date of the decedent/policyowner's death.

If it is a *whole-life policy* on which premiums were still being paid, the value is (slightly oversimplified) the policy cash value plus the portion of the premium paid beyond the date of death of the policyowner.

If it is a *term insurance policy*, the value is the premium paid beyond the date of death of the policyowner.

You do not have to compute these valuations. Request in writing that the insurance company supply IRS Form 712 for each policy, with the appropriate figures, which it will do at no charge.

Look out for this tax trap: If the insured dies within six months of the policyowner and you elect the alternate valuation date, you must include the full amount of the proceeds rather than the "living" value of the policy. In other words, the entire proceeds are includable in your decedent's estate.

Valuation of U.S. Government Bonds

Series E bonds are valued at the redemption (market) price as of the date of death.

Even if such bonds are not used to pay federal estate taxes, courts have consistently held that, to the extent they *could* have been so used, they should be valued at the higher of the two—market value or par value. But to the extent the bonds could not have been applied to pay the federal estate tax, their value is the market value—the mean quoted selling price as of the date of death. Your stockbroker can obtain U.S. government bond valuations for you.

Valuation of Household and Personal Effects

In valuing household and personal effects, itemize each asset, room by room. Generally, when valuing household property and personal effects (watches, rings, clothing, etc.), use the *willing buyer/willing seller rule*. Hire an independent appraiser if household goods include articles of artistic or intrinsic value, such as jewelry, furs, silverware, paintings, engravings, antiques, books, statuary, Oriental rugs, and coin, stamp, gun, or other valuable collections. Call your local bank's trust department and ask them to recommend one or more appraisers.

Valuation of Listed Stocks

For federal and state death-tax purposes, the fair-market value per share of a stock traded on an established exchange governs. The fair-market value is based on selling prices when there is a market for the stock. This is the mean between the highest and lowest quoted selling price on the valuation date (see Chapter 21).

Valuation of Corporate Bonds

Value bonds similarly to the way you value listed common stock. If there were no sales on the valuation date, take the weighted mean of the selling prices on or near the applicable valuation date.

If there were no sales and no "bid" or "asked" prices within a reasonable number of days before and after the valuation date, consider the following factors to determine the value of the bonds: (1) How sound was the security? (2) How does the interest yield on the bond in question compare to yields on similar bonds? (3) What is the date of the bond's maturity? (4) How do prices for listed bonds of corporations engaged in similar business compare? (5) Is the bond secured? If so, by what? (6) Does the business have goodwill? What is the industry's outlook? What is the company's position in the industry? How sound is the company's management?

The *Wall Street Journal* can be used to find a bond price. Again, your stockbroker and accountant may be helpful in documenting a value.

Valuation of Stocks of Closely Held Corporations

If you are the executor of an estate that holds closely held stock, you have a difficult, time-consuming, and potentially costly problem if there is no buy/sell agreement (see Chapter 21).

Work closely with the estate's attorney, and particularly with the business's accountant (or an accountant of your own selection). If the stakes are high enough, the estate administration team may also want to hire a person or company that specializes in the valuation of closely held stocks.

Be aggressive but reasonable in valuing closely held stocks. Definitely take a reduction in value if the shares being valued represent a *minority* (i.e., less than controlling) interest in the business. A minority interest discount (10 to 30 percent) is often allowed because such shares have no power to force the corporation to pay dividends, liquidate the corporation, or control corporate policy. This weakness limits the potential market for the stock. It is probably only the controlling shareholders who would be interested. Therefore, the price at which such shares might be purchased (if at all) would be much lower than other factors would tend to indicate. (Conversely, if the shares in question represent a controlling interest, the IRS may attempt to increase the value of the stock because control does justify a higher value for a specific block of stock.) Remember this particularly if you are taking a charitable deduction for stock left to charity.

For the price and terms in an intrafamily buy/sell agreement to be persuasive to the IRS and the courts, the agreement must meet all three of the following rules:

1. Bona fide business arrangement rule: The agreement must be part of a bona fide business arrangement.
2. Device rule: The agreement must not be a device to transfer the property to members of the decedent's family for less than full and adequate consideration in money or money's worth.
3. Comparability rule: The terms of the agreement must be comparable to similar arrangements entered into by persons in an arm's-length transaction.

Lowest Value Not Always Best

While the federal estate tax is based on the value of the property interest in the estate, the lowest possible valuation of an asset is not always the best objective. One example is the estimation of the value of a business interest. A buy/sell agreement that provides a higher price per share results in more cash for the estate and its heirs than a formula resulting in a lower price.

Second, the additional tax payable because of the increased valuation of closely held stock may be more than offset by the advantages of qualifying for a *Section 303 stock redemption* or a *Section 6166 election* to pay federal estate taxes attributable to the business interest over as many as 14 years (see Chapter 25). To qualify for either of these favorable elections, the value of the business interest must *exceed* 35 percent of the value of the gross estate after certain adjustments.

Third, and most important, you must be aware not only of the estate-tax implications of your actions but also of the income-tax results. If the asset in question is likely to be sold shortly after the decedent's death, a higher estate-tax valuation can lead to a lower income-tax gain in the future. This is because of the *step-up-in-basis* rules, whereby most property included in an estate acquires a new basis for income-tax purposes. This new basis is the fair-market value of the property at the date of death (or the applicable alternate valuation date). The higher the estate-tax value, the higher the income-tax basis. Then, because the beneficiary's basis is high, there is a lower income tax liability when the property is later sold by the beneficiary. For example, assume a decedent owned stock traded on a national exchange. If that stock was worth $100 a share when purchased and $1,000 a share on the date of death, its new basis is $1,000 per share in the hands of the estate or its beneficiaries. If the stock was sold later for $1,001, there would be a $1 long-term capital gain, and the tax payable would be negligible. You should be aggressive—but only after you have decided what your objective is. A higher valuation (especially if there is an unlimited estate-tax marital deduction) may in fact be better than a lower valuation. This is yet another reason to work with qualified and experienced tax planning professionals.

27 Charitable Bequests

Identifying the Charity

Often a will fails to pinpoint the specific charity that is intended. References to "Boy Scouts" or "Methodist Church" clearly indicate the general intention of the maker of the will to benefit a particular class or group, but they still leave considerable room for interpretation. The courts can apply the doctrine of *cy pres*—they can construe the bequest in accordance with what they consider the general intent of the decedent. So if a will contained a bequest to "our local Boy Scout chapter to place an additional wing on its lodge in Briar Park," and if Briar Park has since been sold to a real estate developer, the courts can construe the bequest to be a general one to the Boy Scouts of America or to the local Boy Scout chapter.

In any event, whenever a will contains a bequest to a charity, be certain the charity can be identified precisely. Specificity averts litigation. Payment to the wrong beneficiary, or even the wrong organizational chapter, Scout troop, church, or synagogue, can lead to legal action against you. If there is any doubt whatsoever, file a formal statement of your interpretation of the identity of the charity so that court approval can be given before any money is paid.

Notice Requirements for Charitable Bequests

Because charitable bequests are in the public interest, most states require that the attorney general of the state in which the will is probated be notified of a gift to charity. This ensures that the charity will have representation in the event the bequest is not paid in full. Consult local and state laws to make certain that these notice requirements are complied with at every step prescribed in the probate or distribution process.

Also send written notice to each charitable beneficiary, stating the date of death and the county where the will has been probated, and also stating that the charity has been named as a beneficiary.

Exemption Certificate

Almost all states provide an exemption from the state inheritance tax for transfers of property to or for the use of religious, charitable, scientific, literary, or educational organizations. Some states require you to apply for a certificate of exemption from the state inheritance tax for charitable bequests. Check with counsel before making any distributions to charities.

Gifts for Religious or Charitable Purposes Made Shortly Before Death

A potential problem area is that of the "last-minute charitable gift." A few jurisdictions have laws (called *mortmain* statutes) that invalidate last-minute charitable gifts (typically gifts within 30 days before death). The theory is that the decedent, being near death, was not acting rationally in leaving her money to charity, or might have been unduly influenced to leave her money to a particular religious charity.

Form of the Charitable Bequest

There are different methods by which to give money to charity under the terms of a will, with varying tax consequences, depending on the form the bequest takes.

Outright Bequests

In the case of an outright gift to charity, such as "I give the sum of $10,000 to XYZ University, to be used for the general purposes of the university," there is no question of the validity of the bequest, the identity of the recipient, or the fact that this is an outright bequest. Under state and federal death-tax laws, the bequest to charity will be tax-exempt (see chapters 20 and 21), and as long as you comply with the notice requirement and the other procedural requirements, payment can be made with no further problems.

Qualified Charities

Contributions to charities—either by will or by another means of conveyance, such as life insurance—are generally deductible for both federal and state death-tax purposes, but only if the charity is "qualified."

Qualified charities include:

- A state, a U.S. possession or political subdivision, or the U.S. government itself.
- A community chest, corporation, trust, fund, or foundation organized or created in the United States, if it is operated exclusively for charitable, religious, educational, scientific, or literary purposes, for the prevention of cruelty to children or animals, or to foster national or international sports competitions (this category includes most schools, colleges, churches and synagogues, and many hospitals and medical-research organizations)
- Certain veterans organizations

- A nonprofit volunteer fire company
- Certain other charitable organizations

Charitable Remainder Interests

The decedent may have kept, for the lifetime of some other individual such as a spouse, the right to use, possess, or enjoy property and/or its income. At the same time the decedent may have given a specified charity the right to the property at the end of that given time. There are four forms such a charitable remainder interest may take:

- A personal residence or farm
- The assets of an "annuity" trust
- A unitrust
- A pooled income fund

Such gifts often pose questions for both federal and state death-tax valuation, so the assistance of counsel is essential. An immediate deduction is allowed for the present (actuarial) value of the charity's right to (someday) receive the property.

Remainder interest in a personal residence or farm. A typical example of such a bequest is the case of a decedent who has signed a deed transferring a home or farm to a charity subject to the right of the decedent and his spouse to live in the house for the rest of the decedent's life. The home need not be the principal residence, so a vacation home or condominium can qualify.

Charitable remainder annuity trust. This is, for example, an arrangement in which a sum of money, stocks, bonds, or other income-producing property has been transferred in trust to the charity, but a specific amount in dollars had to be paid from the trust to the decedent and his spouse each year. At the end of a specified period—or at the death of a special beneficiary—the property or money in the trust is transferred to the charity. For example, assume $500,000 was placed into a trust at an individual's death with $25,000 a year payable to the donor's 60-year-old brother for life; then, at his death, the assets in the trust pass to a qualified charity. At the date of death, the federal discount rate was 10.6 percent. The estate would receive an estate-tax charitable deduction of $314,425 (63 percent of the trust's value).

Charitable remainder unitrust. Essentially, the unitrust is similar in concept to the annuity trust; income has been retained by the donor's designated beneficiary, but at the end of a given period (or at the death of the income beneficiary), the principal goes to a designated charity. The difference is that in a unitrust, the donor does not receive a guaranteed specific amount of cash each year from the trust. Instead, the income recipients are paid a fixed percentage of the fair-market value of the trust's assets—as revalued each year. So if assets in the trust grow in value, more income is paid. If unitrust assets shrink, annual payments to the income beneficiaries are lower. Assuming a 60-year-old recipient and a 10.6 federal discount rate, if the $500,000 trust provided variable income equal to 5 percent of its value—as revalued each year—the estate would be entitled to an estate-tax deduction of $203,340 (41 percent of the trust's value).

Pooled income fund. Instead of establishing a personal trust at the decedent's death, the decedent may have joined many others in transferring cash or property under her will to a community organization that pools each donor's contributions. Each donor (or, in this case, the decedent's beneficiary) would be paid a proportionate share of the income of the fund. The income payment is not fixed in amount and varies with the growth of the pooled funds just like a mutual fund.

A multiplicity of problems can arise if the estate includes any of the four categories of charitable gifts. Tax counsel is highly recommended.

28 | Anatomical Gifts

If a person wants to make an anatomical gift, he should know how to do it. Conversely, anyone who is strongly against such a gift should be protected from violation of his desires.

What It Is

The Uniform Anatomical Gifts Act (UAGA) has been enacted in whole or in part in every state and the District of Columbia. Its purpose is to encourage organ donations and to avoid inconsistency among the various jurisdictions.

The UAGA provides that any person over 18 may donate her entire body or any one or more of its parts to any hospital, surgeon, physician, medical or dental school, or various organ banks or storage facilities. Organ gifts can be made for the purposes of education, research, therapy, or transplant. These gifts become effective at death and can be made by will. The act also provides that no body or organ gift may be made if there is an express objection to such a gift either by will or in some other document.

How It Works

There are two ways a gift can be made under the UAGA. One is for the donor to designate a specific individual to receive the gift. For instance, a person might specify that an eye be given to a blind sister. A hierarchy of donees can be established, and various body parts can be specified to go to certain donees.

A second way is to grant persons other than the decedent the power to make the gift. In other words, a family member can donate a person's body or organs.

Without any evidence that the decedent did *not* want to make an anatomical gift, his spouse, adult children, parents, or siblings (in that order of priority) can make a donation. The gifts can be made by these third parties unless there is actual knowledge that the decedent would not have wanted to make an anatomical gift, or someone in the same or higher "class" opposes the gift. Donations can be authorized by third parties either before or after death. Obviously, because of the possibility that an ill-intentioned relative would use anatomical gifts to obtain postmortem revenge, a person's intention regarding such gifts should be specified clearly one way or the other.

Requirements

The UAGA requires that gifts be made in writing by the donor and attested to by at least two witnesses. The donor must be of sound mind at the time of the writing (although there is no procedure for proving legal capacity in a manner similar to that used in probate). There is no requirement that the will or other documents be delivered by the donor to make the gift valid. When gifts are made by family members, a written document is not a legal requirement, and a telegram, audio- or videotape recording, or taped telephone conversation may satisfy statutory formalities.

Many states provide for the making of anatomical gifts through a notice on a driver's license. But many authorities feel that because of the wide variety of forms the gift may take and the potential for problems with regard to revoking gifts made in such a way, it is better either to make or object to an anatomical gift through a document.

Documents meeting the requirements of the Uniform Anatomical Gifts Act should be prepared separately and apart from the will. A codicil to the will can state intentions regarding anatomical gifts in a way that does not disclose the other provisions of the will. If possible, a person should designate a specific donee, such as a family member or medical institution (and there should be "backup" donees in case the primary one cannot or will not accept the gift). (See the Appendix for a sample anatomical gifts form.)

When Is the Donor Dead?

The UAGA gives no specific definition of death. Most states define death as "a total and irreversible loss of brain function" and require the opinion of at least two physicians to that effect. The UAGA forbids the physicians who certify death (and all members of the medical team involved) from participating in any organ removal or transplant procedure.

If only a part of the body is donated, the surviving spouse or next of kin or other person responsible for the burial must make final disposition of the body after that part is removed.

Objections to an Anatomical Donation

If someone does not want a gift of body parts to be made, such desires should be expressed clearly and strongly. A *nonconsent document* should have been prepared, and you should check the will. Some wills provide that any bequests made to an individual who consents to an anatomical gift will be void.

29 | Distribution

Who Is Entitled to a Decedent's Property?

After all the assets of the estate have been assembled and made secure, and the debts and taxes have been paid, you as executor are in a position to distribute the assets to the beneficiaries. Who gets the property depends on the terms of the will. If the decedent had no will, then distribution is governed by the intestacy laws of the state of domicile. Review your state's intestacy laws and check with counsel about their interpretation.

If the decedent's estate consisted solely of cash and the will leaves everything to the spouse, who in fact was living at the time of the decedent's death, there is no problem with distribution. But beneficiaries can die before receiving their share of the distribution. Also, property left to a particular individual may have been sold or given away or lost prior to the testator's death.

Property No Longer Owned by a Decedent at Death

If the decedent left specific property to a particular beneficiary in her will but sold it or otherwise disposed of it before death, then that gift to the beneficiary (a gift under a will is called a *legacy* or *devise*) is said to have been *adeemed. Ademption* means that the property is not available for distribution to the beneficiary. Assume, for example, that a female decedent said in her will, "I give and bequeath my 1956 antique Thunderbird automobile to my nephew, Jack." But several years before her death, after making her will, the decedent had sold the Thunderbird. The gift to Jack would be adeemed. Jack is not entitled to any other property from the estate in place of the car or its value.

Exceptions to the rule are possible. If the will of a father specified a gift of "my automobile to my daughter, Jane," the courts could decide—or could interpret prior cases to hold—that the decedent did not make a gift of a specific automobile, but of the automobile he owned at his death. How can you determine whether the gift is specific ("my 1956 Thunderbird") or general ("my automobile")? In all cases where doubts arise, refer to state law, and make distribution only with the court's approval, or the approval of all interested parties.

Suppose a mother's will specified a gift of "$5,000 to my son, Steven," but six months before the decedent died, she gave Steven $5,000. In that case the law in many states would say that the gift to the son under the will was "satisfied" by the gift during the decedent's lifetime. The courts could hold that this lifetime gift was an "advance"—the purpose of the law being to secure equality among the children. In this situation the controlling factor would be the decedent's intent when she made the lifetime gift. You therefore need a formal, legal interpretation about whether in fact the lifetime gift satisfied the bequest in the will. This could be obtained by having the schedule of proposed distribution approved by the court (after you have given all beneficiaries written notice and ample opportunity to testify or object), so that any objections can be raised prior to payment of the legacy to the son.

Assets Insufficient to Satisfy a Bequest

Suppose a male decedent's will left "$5,000 to my daughter, Amy." What happens if assets, after paying administration costs and debts, are insufficient to pay Amy $5,000 and to distribute other gifts and bequests? How can you properly apportion assets?

If there are no assets to satisfy the bequests, or if the assets available are insufficient to satisfy all of the gifts in full, then the gifts or bequests are said to *abate*, either entirely or proportionately, according to state law. Therefore, look to the law of your state to determine the order of *abatement*. Property bequeathed specifically to a spouse and children usually has priority. Obtain court approval (or at least the approval of *all* interested parties) before making distribution.

Beneficiary's Death Before Decedent's Death

What happens if a father's will includes a bequest of "$5,000 to my daughter, Mary," and Mary dies before her father? In many cases Mary's estate is not entitled to the $5,000, unless the will made it clear that Mary did not have to survive in order to receive the money. Mary's bequest would therefore *lapse*. However, if the will left "$5,000 to my daughter, Mary, if she survives me, otherwise to her children," then clearly Mary's children are entitled to the $5,000. The wording in many wills is not as clear as in this example, so consult state law and obtain court approval when there is any question about the possible lapsing of a particular bequest.

If the beneficiary cannot be located, and if you are not certain whether the beneficiary is alive or dead, then, after a reasonable attempt to locate the beneficiary, obtain court direction on how to handle the bequest.

Common Disasters

If a question arises about the order of death of the decedent and a beneficiary, distribution of the estate can be seriously affected. Many wills contain *common disaster clauses* that direct the executor, when the order of death is not certain, in deciding whether the beneficiary or the decedent is presumed to have survived. In other wills, certain "marital deduction" tax clauses might indicate that the spouse of the testator is deemed to survive if the order of death is not clear. Most states have specific statutes dealing with common disasters. Consult the state law and, when in doubt, obtain court approval before making distribution.

Distribution Affecting the Marital Deduction

When the estate is large enough to be affected by the federal estate tax, make certain that any distribution of marital property includes only property that qualifies for the marital deduction. Whenever in doubt, consult with counsel to make sure that the spouse receives only property that can qualify for this particular tax shelter (see Chapter 21).

Minors or Incompetents

Never make distribution directly to a minor or to anyone you feel has a mental disability (see Chapter 18). If no guardian or trustee has been appointed to receive the property of such an individual, it is your responsibility to see that someone is appointed to handle the funds of the minor or incompetent before any distribution of the estate's assets is made to that person.

Other Legal Impediments to Distribution

In some cases, bequests to beneficiaries that are otherwise in order can be held by the state of domicile to be improper because they violate state law. For example, in some states beneficiaries to a will can forfeit the right to receive property under it if they have also signed as witnesses. (As a general rule, we recommend that three adult persons who are unrelated to the testator and not beneficiaries should sign as witnesses in one another's presence. In states that permit self-proving notarized wills we suggest this device be used.) Many state laws do not permit anyone causing a person's death to receive property under the will. Also, in some states a highly technical *rule against perpetuities* prohibits long-term gifts that do not take effect within 21 years of the death of someone who is alive on the date of the gift. For instance, if a will provided that a home was to go to a friend, Marie, but could not be sold by her until 50 years after the death of a certain individual, the gift to Marie may not be valid. In such cases, before making any distribution, determine how state law affects the particular situation.

Informal Distribution

Let's assume you are satisfied that no problems exist, that you have handled the administration of the estate in a responsible manner, that all outstanding debts and taxes have been paid, and that the beneficiaries are pleased with your handling of the estate. In that case a formal accounting and discharge by the court may not be necessary (or may not even be advisable). A great deal of time and effort go into preparing and filing a formal account and giving the required notice. Filing fees, advertising expenses, and legal fees also raise the cost to the estate. Therefore, in close family situations when everyone is satisfied with the administration of the estate, a *family settlement agreement* can be entered into by all the parties involved. The beneficiaries enter into a written agreement with the executor stating that they have received an account of the income, expenses, and property available for distribution in the estate; that a copy of the accounting is attached to the agreement; and that all the beneficiaries agree to the proposed distribution.

Even when questions do arise regarding the respective rights of the beneficiaries or the handling of the estate, if all the interested parties (including all the beneficiaries) sign an agreement on the handling of the estate and the proposed distribution, that agreement usually is enforced by the courts.

In most states the executor files the family settlement agreement (depending on the law of the jurisdiction), and the agreement is on record as a final settlement of the estate.

When all parties agree to waive a formal accounting in simplified estates or in estates involving close family members, the estate can be settled without even using the family settlement agreement. Supply the beneficiaries with an informal accounting and obtain their approval of the accounting and their share of the distribution. This is usually accomplished by obtaining a *receipt* from each beneficiary for her distributive share of the estate as well as a *release* from any further liability or obligation to that beneficiary. This simplified *receipt and release procedure* can be used if no formal accounting is required and if you are satisfied that there are no outstanding questions to be resolved. It is often advisable to hold a certain sum in an escrow account for a period of time after distribution in the event any claims are made, or tax liabilities arise, at a later date (see Appendix for a sample release).

Small Estates

Most jurisdictions provide for the settling of small estates without a formal accounting. For example, a statute might provide that if the estate does not exceed $10,000—exclusive of real estate, wages, and salaries—a petition may be filed with the court, with an accounting attached, asking the court to approve the petition; order distribution in accordance with its terms; and discharge the personal representative of further responsibility. The court usually requires that notice be given to all interested parties, including beneficiaries and creditors, of the filing of the petition and its contents.

Accounting

Perhaps your single most important duty is to file a formal accounting with the court. This means preparing financial statements that give the court, the beneficiaries, and everyone in the estate a clear picture of the property available for distribution, as well as presenting a history of all the transactions involving the estate's assets dating back to the time you took control of the property. The accounting is simultaneously a balance sheet, a record of income and expenses, and a vehicle for tracing the history of the original assets left by the decedent and any changes in their form or value during the period of the estate's administration.

The accounting is prepared and filed at the conclusion of the administration of the estate. It forms the basis for the court's order to approve the accounting, direct distribution of the assets, and discharge you from duties and liabilities. It also relieves the requirement of any bond, if one has been filed. If for any reason you choose not to file a formal accounting, a beneficiary or other interested party in the estate may ask the court to require you to do so.

Time, Place, and Notice Requirements

The account usually is filed at the end of administration of the estate, unless required earlier by the court on request by an interested party. For example, if a beneficiary feels that you are unduly delaying the administration of the estate or have handled the estate's funds improperly, that beneficiary may request the court to demand that you file an account at that time, so that any improprieties can be brought to the court's attention immediately.

Review state and local laws before preparing the accounting to determine the form, notice, and advertising requirements. State laws usually require that creditors, beneficiaries, and other interested parties be given sufficient notice of the time and filing of the account and the court in which the account will be filed. This is to give them an opportunity to present any objections to the accounting at the time it is handed up for *audit* (i.e., review and approval by the court). At the time of the audit, you usually must furnish proof to the court that notice was in fact given to all parties. Without such notice it is always possible that an interested party will later challenge your handling of the estate. Local courts often require that the filing also be advertised in local newspapers.

Form of the Accounting

The form of account to be used depends on the rules of the court in the jurisdiction in which the estate is probated. Sample forms usually are available at the courthouse in the county where the decedent lived, or they are included in the local rules of the court having jurisdiction over these matters. In most cases, because of the complexity of the account, its contents should be reviewed (and preferably prepared) by counsel and/or an accountant.

Audit

Audit (accounting) procedures vary considerably with local court custom and state law, and must be consulted by you or counsel. In general, the purpose of the audit is to have the formal accounting approved by the court and to prove to the court that anyone with an objection to the account will have the opportunity to be heard; therefore, notice requirements and advertising procedures must be strictly complied with. In many jurisdictions the court itself publishes the legal advertisement of the audit.

Depending on local customs, you might prepare a proposed schedule of distribution to be presented on the audit date, or prepare one by direction of the court after the accounting has been approved. In any event, approval of the audit will be accompanied or followed by an approved schedule of distribution.

Receipt and Satisfaction of Awards

Following the court's approval of the accounting and distribution, wait until the time has elapsed for appealing the *adjudication* (the court's formal approval of the accounting and distribution). The time varies from state to state but typically does not exceed three months. Thereafter, you are in a position to deliver the property in question to the beneficiaries in accordance with the court's adjudication, obtain a receipt from each beneficiary for the property transferred, and take the necessary steps to have any bond terminated. Then—*and not until then*—you will be relieved of all liability and responsibility for your administration of the estate.

30 The Duties of a Trustee

Suppose, instead of appointing you as executor under his will, Uncle Stanley had appointed you trustee of his revocable living trust. The duties of a trustee are often similar to those of an executor. But to understand your duties as a trustee, you should first understand what a trust is and how it works. (*The New Book of Trusts* [610–527–5216] is a comprehensive, up-to-date, and objective source of information.)

What Is a Trust?

Trust. Picture in your mind a box. Let's call that box a *trust*. Into that box you can put cash, stocks, bonds, mutual funds, the deed to your home, or even life insurance. When you put property into the box, you are "funding" the trust. You can put almost any asset into a trust at any time. For example, you can name the trust as the beneficiary of your life insurance, pension plan, IRA, or HR-10. Then, at your death, the trust would be funded.

A trust is therefore a legal relationship that enables one party, the *trustee*, to hold money or other property (trust *principal*) transferred to the trust by a second party (the *grantor* or *settlor* or *trustor*) for the benefit of one or more third parties (the *beneficiaries*), according to the terms and conditions of a written document called a *trust agreement*. That document spells out the following: (1) how the assets of the trust are to be managed and invested, (2) who will receive income and assets from the trust, (3) how that money is to be paid out, and (4) when principal or income is to be paid (for example, at what ages or in what circumstances the beneficiaries will receive their shares).

The key is that you, the trustee—for investment, management, and administration purposes—hold legal title to the property in the trust. But you may use the property—and the income it produces—only for the benefit of the beneficiaries (which may include the grantor).

Trustee. Someone is needed to safeguard and invest—and then pay out—the assets in the box, including income and/or capital from those assets. This is the *trustee*. This obligation may last only a few years or it may run for generations. There can be more than one trustee, and they can be individual and/or corporate trustees such as banks. When several parties are named, they are *co-trustees* and make decisions jointly (and are jointly liable for mistakes).

Beneficiaries. The people for whom the grantor set up the trust are the beneficiaries, who receive income from the trust assets—and/or principal—at the age and under the terms and conditions specified. The first people to receive distribution from the trust are the *primary beneficiaries*. For instance, if the trust instrument says that the grantor is to be paid all the income for as long as she lives, she is the primary beneficiary. If a child is to receive what remains in the trust at a mother's or father's death, he is the *remainderman*.

Living Trust. A trust set up during the grantor's lifetime is a *living (inter vivos) trust*. That trust could hold assets that the grantor put in during his lifetime or could receive assets he owns at death. The will could "pour over" assets into the previously established trust.

Testamentary Trust. If the trust is created under a will, it is a *testamentary trust*. Assets owned in the grantor's name pass from the will into the trust. Attorneys use a testamentary trust to reduce the number of documents; with a testamentary trust, the will and the trust are both in one document. A living trust and a will require two separate documents (and if the grantor funds the living trust during her lifetime, there will be ongoing expenses). The drawback of the testamentary trust is that if for any reason the will is not probated or is successfully attacked, the testamentary trust may never come into existence. Testamentary trusts save neither income nor estate taxes, since the grantor owns the assets and the income that those assets produce until death.

Revocable Trust. Now picture a string on the box. That string enables the grantor to pull back the box and reach in. He can revoke the trust, take back what he has transferred to it, alter it, amend it, or even revoke and terminate it. This is a *revocable trust*.

Irrevocable Trust. Cut that string and it's an *irrevocable trust*. No property can be removed from the trust and nothing can be changed.

Benefits of a Trust

People set up trusts for many reasons:

1. The beneficiary is unwilling or unable to invest, manage, or handle the responsibility of an immediate outright gift. Families with minor, handicapped, or financially or emotionally immature children should consider trusts.
2. Full ownership can be postponed until the beneficiary is in a position to handle the property or income properly or until the grantor (or someone she names)

is ready or able to part with it. For example, the grantor may want to keep the income from a trust for a given number of years—or for life—and then have the principal remaining go to charity (a *charitable remainder trust*).

3. The financial security of property can be spread among a number of individuals when the asset (for instance, an apartment house or a life insurance policy) does not lend itself to fragmentation.

4. The grantor may have particular dispositive plans in mind so that control is essential—for example, to prevent the beneficiary from disposing of the family business or family home to persons outside the family.

5. Assets can be protected from the claims of creditors (only irrevocable trusts can accomplish this objective).

6. Children or grandchildren can be treated equally if the grantor owns some property that may appreciate and some property that may fall in value. By placing both properties in trust and giving all the children (or grandchildren) equal shares of the trust, both benefits and risks are equalized.

7. The uncertain (and sometimes costly) process of probate can be avoided.

8. A trust can—in many states—reduce the probability of a will contest or an "election" by a spouse to take a state-mandated portion of the estate (roughly one-third) regardless of what the will provides.

9. All the details of one's finances can be kept as private as legally possible.

10. A trust can relieve oneself of the burden of investing and managing property and can serve to protect oneself in the event of physical, emotional, or mental incapacity. (A *step-up trust* or *standby trust* steps up and takes over when the grantor doesn't want to or cannot manage property.)

There are many management, conservation, dispositive, and control objectives that can be met through one or more types of trusts that are not possible with a direct gift.

Revocable Living Trusts

Revocable living trusts (RLTs) are *not* designed to produce income or estate-tax savings. Because assets put into a revocable trust can be regained, the grantor is taxed on the income the trust produces. The principal in an RLT will also be included in the estate.

So if there are no tax savings, why are RLTs so popular?

- All assets (such as life insurance, pension plan, IRA, and personal property) can be "poured into" a revocable living trust. The trust serves as a unifying receptacle for the collection of assets from a variety of sources. This is particularly important if property is owned in more than one state (and it may save heirs a great deal of trouble, aside from avoiding multiple probates).
- There is no publicity, so the amount left, the names of the beneficiaries, and the terms of the gifts are private.
- Setting up a trust during the grantor's lifetime gives him the opportunity to see how well the trustee manages property—and how well the beneficiaries handle the income or other rights. If he doesn't like what happens, there is time for changes.
- A revocable living trust allows the grantor to choose a state where the laws will be most favorable to accomplishing her objectives. It is not necessary to live in that state.
- An RLT reduces the likelihood of an attack on the will—if the trust had been going for some time before death.

- All of the assets in the trust pass directly to the beneficiaries at death, bypassing the probate process.
- An RLT can be used to protect the person who established it if that person becomes incapacitated.

Where Do You Fit In?

If Uncle Stanley (the grantor) had appointed you trustee of his trust during his lifetime, then your duties and obligations are set forth in the trust. For example, your duties might be to invest the trust assets and pay Uncle Stanley the income from these investments during his lifetime. Principal could be paid to him if requested, and income and/or principal could be used for his benefit in the event of his disability. At Uncle Stanley's death the balance after taxes and expenses would be distributed to his nieces and nephews.

Regardless of your duties during the lifetime of the grantor, and the disposition of the assets at death, you have specific obligations to perform at the death of the grantor.

In states that allow this arrangement, revocable living trusts are often set up as follows: An individual names herself as both grantor and trustee. In other words, during the lifetime of that person, she handles all of the trust affairs. At her death a previously named successor trustee settles the trust and distributes the balance to the beneficiaries.

The Trustee's Duties

While many of a trustee's duties in settling a trust are similar to those of an executor, certain formal requirements necessary to probate a will and handle an estate can be avoided. There are three main duties of the trustee:

1. Assembling, protecting, and investing the assets of the trust
2. Paying debts, expenses, and death taxes
3. Distributing the assets to the beneficiaries

Assembling the Trust Assets

In most cases it is easier to assemble the assets of a revocable living trust than an estate, since all property held in trust must be clearly identified as such. For example, a bank account or stock held in trust by the grantor as trustee for himself could be titled: "Stanley Jackson, Trustee, u/d/t dated April 2, 1998, f/b/o Stanley Jackson." If the grantor has named a different trustee, then the asset would be titled: "Sally Johnson, Trustee, u/d/t/ dated April 2, 1998, f/b/o Stanley Jackson."

Some attorneys or institutions use different wording, but the main features are consistent: naming of the trustee, the date of the execution of the trust, and the beneficiary. The designation *f/b/o* means "for the benefit of" (or for and on behalf of) and the *u/d/t* means "under deed of trust" (or "under declaration of trust").

There are trust assets that can be titled in an individual's name during her lifetime and at death are payable to a beneficiary. For example, Uncle Stan might have owned a $100,000 life insurance policy, payable to "Sally Johnson, Trustee, u/d/t of Stanley Jackson, dated April 2, 1998." Other assets paid to beneficiaries at a person's death can include IRAs, pension and profit-sharing plans, and other work-related benefits.

It is possible that the trust records contain no information concerning these assets, so it is necessary for you to have access to the grantor's personal records and to work closely with the executor of the grantor's estate to make certain that the trust receives all of the benefits to which it and its beneficiaries are entitled.

You then file claims for all of the benefits and proceed to collect the other identifiable assets of the trust.

For accounting, and especially for tax purposes, you need a date-of-death balance sheet indicating the value of all trust assets at the grantor's death. You therefore have to contact banks and stockbrokers for a breakdown of the decedent's assets held with their institutions, including date-of-death balances for each bank account and security. (You can adapt the sample Executor's Letter and Information Form in the Appendix.)

If the trust is the owner of real estate, obtain appraisals of any real property as well as any personal property in the trust at the decedent's death.

Also obtain all past checking accounts of the trust and copies of all fiduciary income-tax returns filed by the trust during the grantor's lifetime. If any prior accountings had been made to the beneficiaries, you should have this information as well.

Payments of Debts, Expenses, and Death Taxes

Because the grantor had the right to revoke the trust at any time prior to death, the federal and state governments impose death taxes on the trust assets (see chapters 20 and 21). You must be familiar with the deadlines for filing these returns, and with the death-tax laws of the trust's state (determine whether there are discounts for early payment).

You are also responsible for the payment of any outstanding obligations of the trust, including fees, commissions, and expenses incurred in the administration of the trust assets. It's also possible that trust assets will be needed to satisfy obligations of the decedent's estate. Therefore, coordinate your activities with those of the executor of the estate (of course, the trustee can be named as executor). (Also be aware of the many available options, which are set forth in the Trustee's Checklist in the Appendix.)

Distribution

When you are satisfied that all of the assets of the trust have been identified, assembled, and correctly inventoried, and all outstanding obligations have been satisfied, prepare an accounting of receipts and disbursements and then make distribution to the beneficiaries. This presents you with two major decisions: (1) How formal an account is necessary? and (2) Should you file the account in court in order to be formally (and legally) discharged of your duties and responsibilities?

In a close family situation when the composition of the trust is not complicated, the size of the trust is relatively small, and the relationship between the trustee and beneficiaries is a good one, an informal account and distribution on the signing of a release can be used (see Trust Receipt and Release in the Appendix). This simplifies the distribution process and avoids publicity.

However, if you have any concern about potential outstanding obligations of the trust (such as future income-tax problems, a federal estate-tax audit, or conflict with the trust's beneficiaries), then file a formal court accounting. Send notice of the accounting and the date it will be submitted to the court (registered mail, return receipt requested) to all beneficiaries and other interested parties (according to local court rules), so they will have the opportunity to appear in court and present any objections to the account and proposed distribution. (Some states require a more formal notice called *service*.)

Once the account and schedule of distribution have been approved by the court, you can be formally discharged from your duties. In many instances it is advisable to hold a certain sum in the trust for a period of time after distribution, in the event of any additional claims against the trust following distribution (a future audit of income-tax or estate-tax returns might indicate a deficiency).

Instead of an outright distribution to beneficiaries, the trust may have provided for the trust to continue after the death of the grantor for a certain period of time (for example, until the beneficiaries reach their twenty-first birthday). It is then necessary for you to continue to hold the funds allocated to these trusts in further trust for the beneficiaries and continue to administer the trust until the indicated distribution date. At that time you can make distribution to the beneficiaries in a manner consistent with the above provisions.

A Word of Caution

Since trust assets are only those specifically placed in trust by the grantor, any other assets in the individual name of the grantor/decedent require the appointment of a personal representative (executor or administrator) to pass title to these assets.

Do You Need a Lawyer to Settle a Trust?

Many people establish revocable living trusts to reduce probate costs, and specifically to reduce legal fees. If the trust is small, the duties are routine, and there are no complications, you may be able to do it alone. However, in almost every case, we suggest you consult with an attorney knowledgeable in estate and trust matters.

Consult an attorney (and perhaps a certified public accountant) if it is necessary for the trust to file a federal estate-tax return. Even when no federal estate tax is due because of the way the trust is structured or the size of the estate, allocation of trust assets among different potential trusts can create future problems for the beneficiaries.

Reasonable legal and/or accounting fees are paid from the trust assets, and they are tax-deductible expenses. Consult with an attorney as soon as possible after you assume your duties as trustee.

Trustee's Fees

As trustee you are entitled to a fee for your services. A proper fee should take into consideration your qualifications and expertise, the nature of your duties, and the time and effort expended in performing these duties. You may have no choice: Some states such as New York fix trustees' maximum fees statutorily. If there is more than one trustee, the fee should be allocated according to the duties and responsibilities of each.

If you are also a beneficiary of the trust, it may not be in your best interest to take a fee. Like an executor's fee, a trustee's fee is taxable income. As a beneficiary of the trust, you should receive most of your share of the trust assets free of income tax. By taking a fee, even though it creates a deduction for the trust, your resulting income tax could reduce your after-tax share of the trust.

Another consideration is your relationship to the grantor and to the other beneficiaries. If you charge a high fee for services, it can be questioned as a deduction on the state and federal tax returns, and it can be subject to reduction by the court if objected to by the beneficiaries.

Appendix

EXECUTOR'S CHECKLIST

Stage 1—Preprobate Tasks

	Person responsible	Date accomplished
1. Discuss and make decisions on donation of body organs with close family members.	_____	_____
2. Provide physician with accurate information for death certificate—request 10 copies from funeral director or state Bureau of Vital Statistics.	_____	_____
3. Arrange for security at homes of decedent and close relatives.	_____	_____
4. Meet with decedent's family/heirs; offer assistance, information; obtain psycho-therapeutic aid if needed.	_____	_____

	Person responsible	Date accomplished
5. Ascertain who has right to make funeral arrangements; render assistance (notify clergy if not already informed).	_____	_____
6. Obtain deed to cemetery plot.	_____	_____
7. Help family prepare obituary.	_____	_____
8. Provide care for minors/ family members unable to care for themselves.	_____	_____
9. Provide immediate care/ security for plants/pets/business and personal assets (especially perishables) and documents.	_____	_____
10. Determine cash needs of immediate survivors and adequacy and sources of cash to meet demands.	_____	_____
11. Tell all friends and family members to give you receipts for funeral-related expenditures.	_____	_____
12. Arrange for decedent's mail to be held at post office		

	Person responsible	Date accomplished
until your formal appointment; then arrange for forwarding. Stop newspapers and other deliveries if appropriate.	_____	_____
13. Notify bank—if named as executor or trustee—of death; request immediate appointment of administration officer.	_____	_____

Stage 2—Obtaining "Letters"

1. Locate and examine will.* Advise spouse of right to obtain own attorney and elect against will.	_____	_____
2. Select and meet with attorney to represent estate.	_____	_____
3. Estimate decedent's assets/ liabilities.	_____	_____
4. Prepare petition for "letters" (out-of-state property may require ancillary administration as well).	_____	_____

*If no will can be found after a diligent search, prepare a petition for letters of administration. Then proceed with checklist.

	Person responsible	Date accomplished
5. Probate will at Register of Wills office and order "short certificates."	_____	_____
6. If necessary, arrange for bond with surety. Ascertain if special procedure for small estates is available and/or if estate can be settled by family agreements.	_____	_____

Stage 3—Assembling and Converting Assets

1. Call property casualty insurance agent(s) and have all coverage checked for adequacy. Obtain confirmation in writing.	_____	_____
2. Call life insurance agent: (a) Have health and life insurance on survivors reviewed.	_____	_____
(b) Request claim forms for proceeds on decedent's life (request IRS Form 712) and health/accident claims.	_____	_____
3. Contact bank for opening of safe-deposit box. Open new box for estate.	_____	_____
4. Redraft wills of survivors.	_____	_____

	Person responsible	Date accomplished
5. List all assets/liabilities. Examine checks, tax returns, insurance policies.	_____	_____
6. Locate and take control of all decedent's property.	_____	_____
7. Arrange for appraisal of personal property.	_____	_____
8. Arrange for appraisal of real estate.	_____	_____
9. Sell or dispose of all perishables.	_____	_____
10. Analyze and review securities. Put idle funds into money-market accounts or CDs.	_____	_____
11. Notify Social Security/ Veterans Administration and county and begin to process forms for obtaining benefits.	_____	_____
12. Contact employer and request unpaid salary/ bonus/vacation pay/ pensions/other death-related benefits.	_____	_____
13. Advertise grant of letters.	_____	_____

	Person responsible	Date accomplished
14. Notify local banks of decedent's death. Request information on accounts/ safe-deposit box.	_____	_____
15. Transfer all cash to new checking account in estate's name. Set up accounting and control system and apply for employer identification number from IRS.	_____	_____
16. Obtain all stocks/bonds. Close brokerage accounts. Collect any interest/dividends. Sell securities to extent necessary/appropriate. Place balance in name of executor.	_____	_____
17. Inspect all real estate. Arrange for security, insurance, management/payment of taxes, collection of rents.	_____	_____
18. Put all jewelry/furs/art/ other valuable personal effects into safe-deposit box or similar protected storage.	_____	_____
19. Proceed with, adjust, and settle claims/lawsuits.	_____	_____

	Person responsible	Date accomplished

20. Check will/letter of instructions and consult decedent's heirs and attorney with respect to business continuation. Arrange for immediate supervision and management. Decide on sale/liquidation/continuance.   _____   _____

Stage 4—Filing and Payments of Taxes,* Debts, and Expenses

1. Request family exemption from state death tax if appropriate. Obtain exemption certificates for charitable gifts.   _____   _____

2. File state and federal income-tax returns for (a) period before death and (b) period after death.   _____   _____

3. File federal estate-tax return if necessary and pay tax due.   _____   _____

4. File state death-tax return(s) (including other states) and pay tax due.   _____   _____

*Consider state/federal extension of time to pay taxes and use of code section 303 stock redemption to pay taxes.

	Person responsible	Date accomplished

5. Pay personal or real property taxes due.   _____   _____

6. Pay bills, loans, etc.   _____   _____

7. Pay appraiser's/accountant's/ lawyer's/personal representative's fees and court costs.   _____   _____

Stage 5—Distribution

1. Prepare and file accounting of receipts/disbursements/ schedule of distribution.   _____   _____

2. Notify unpaid creditors and beneficiaries of filing of account and time and date of audit.   _____   _____

3. Notify attorney general of state if charitable gifts are involved.   _____   _____

4. Establish testamentary trusts.   _____   _____

5. Transfer securities and other assets in accordance with court-approved distribution schedule (obtain receipt and release).   _____   _____

	Person responsible	Date accomplished
6. Petition for surety's discharge.	_____	_____

Checklist of Executor's Primary Duties

____ Inventory safe-deposit box.

____ Probate will.

____ Advertise Grant of Letters.

____ Make claim for life insurance benefits—obtain Form 712 from each insurance company:
  Consider mode of payment.

____ Make claim for pension and profit-sharing benefits from decedent's employer:
  (a) Consider mode of payment
  (b) Obtain copies of plan, IRS approval, and beneficiary designation

____ Apply for tax identification number with IRS (Form SS-4) or lump-sum Social Security benefits and VA benefits from Social Security Administration or local VA office.

____ File Form 56—Notice of Fiduciary Relationship—with IRS.

____ Open estate checking and savings accounts.

____ Write to all local banks for date-of-death value of any accounts held by decedent.

____ Value securities.

____ Obtain appraisal of real property and personal property from qualified appraiser.

____ Obtain last three years of individual income-tax returns and last three years of canceled checks.

____ Obtain five years of financial records on business interests plus all relevant agreements.

____ Obtain copies of all U.S. gift-tax returns filed by decedent.

____ Obtain evidence of all debts of decedent and costs of administering estate.

___ Ascertain if any of decedent's medical expenses were unpaid at death.

___ Ascertain if the estate received any income taxable under Section 691 of the Internal Revenue Code.

___ Prepay state inheritance tax to obtain discount if available. Check state law to determine if it is permissible and advantageous, and if so, determine the applicable deadlines.

___ Consider requesting prompt assessment of decedent's U.S. income taxes.

___ File personal property-tax returns—due February 15 of each year estate is in administration.

___ File final U.S. and state individual tax return (IRS Form 1040)—due April 15 of the year after the year in which death occurs—and gift-tax returns—due by time estate-tax return is due.

___ Decide if ancillary (out-of-state) administration is necessary.

___ Decide if administration expenses and losses should be claimed as an income-tax or estate-tax deduction.

___ Obtain alternate-valuation-date values for federal estate-tax return.

___ Consider election of extension of time to pay U.S. estate tax (Section 6161 or 6166)—must be filed on or before due date of U.S. estate-tax returns, including extensions.

___ Consider election to defer payment of inheritance tax on remainder interests—when permitted, determine deadline for election.

___ Consider election for special valuation of farm or business real estate under IRC Section 2032A—must be made with timely filed U.S. estate-tax return.

___ Consider election for family-owned business interest exclusion under IRC Section 2033A—must be made with timely filed U.S. estate-tax return.

___ Elect (or do not elect) to qualify certain terminable interest property (QTIP) for marital deduction.

___ Elect (or do not elect) QDT (qualified domestic trust) treatment if spouse is not a U.S. citizen.

___ Maximize GST (generation-skipping tax) exemptions by making election or redistribute trust assets.

___ Determine the necessity for election on excess retirement accumulations.

___ Ascertain if credit for tax paid on prior transfers is allowable to reduce tax here.

___ File inheritance-tax and federal estate-tax returns—federal due within nine months of death—extensions may be requested. Check state law for due date and possible extensions.

___ File inventory—check state law for requirements and due date.

___ Consider requesting prompt assessment of U.S. income-tax return.

___ Apply for U.S. identification number if estate will file U.S. income-tax returns.

___ File U.S. Fiduciary Income Tax Return (Form 1041)—choice of fiscal year.

___ Consider redemption under IRC Section 303.

___ Apply for tax waivers.

___ File account or prepare informal family agreement.

___ Prepare audit notices and statement of proposed distribution.

___ File schedule of distribution if applicable.

Source: Tools and Techniques of Estate Planning, eleventh ed. National Underwriter Co., Cincinnati, OH 45203 (1–800–543–0874).

POWER OF ATTORNEY

KNOW ALL MEN BY THESE PRESENTS, that I, STANLEY JONES, of Elkins Park, Pennsylvania, hereby revoke any general power of attorney that I have heretofore given to any person, and by these presents do constitute and appoint my niece, SALLY JOHNSON, of Bryn Mawr, Pennsylvania, my true and lawful attorney.

1. To ask, demand, sue for, recover, and receive all sums of money, debts, goods and merchandise, chattels, effects, and things of whatsoever nature or description which are now or hereafter shall be or become owing, due, payable, or belonging to me in or by any right whatsoever, and upon receipt thereof, to make, sign, execute, and deliver such receipts, releases, or other discharges for the same, respectively, as she shall think fit.

2. To deposit any moneys which may come into her hands as such attorney with any banks or bankers, either in my name or her own name, and any of such money or any other money to which I am entitled which now is or shall be so deposited to withdraw as she shall think fit; to sign mutual savings bank and federal savings and loan association withdrawal orders; to sign and endorse checks payable to my order and to draw, accept, make, endorse, discount, or otherwise deal with any bills of exchange, checks, promissory notes, or other commercial or mercantile instruments; to borrow any sum or sums of money on such terms and with such security as she may think fit, and for that purpose, to execute all notes or other instruments which may be necessary or proper; and to have access to any and all safe-deposit boxes registered in my name.

3. To sell, assign, transfer, and dispose of any and all stocks, bonds (including U.S. Savings Bonds), loans, mortgages, or other securities registered in my name; and to collect and receipt for all interest and dividends due and payable to me.

4. To invest in my name in any stock, shares, bonds, securities, or other property, real or personal, and to vary such investments as she, in her sole discretion, may deem best; and to vote at meetings of shareholders or other meetings of any corporation or company and to execute any proxies or other instruments in connection therewith.

5. To enter into and upon my real estate, and to let, manage, and improve the same or any part thereof, and to repair or otherwise improve or alter, and to insure any buildings thereon; to sell, either at public or private sale, or exchange any part or parts of my real estate or personal property for such consideration and upon such terms as she shall think fit, and to execute and deliver good and sufficient deeds or other instruments for the conveyance or transfer of the same, with such covenants of warranty or otherwise as she shall see fit, and to give good and effectual receipts for all or any part of the purchase price or other consideration; and to mortgage my real estate, and in connection therewith, to execute bonds and warrants and all other necessary instruments and documents.

6. To contract with any person for leasing for such periods, at such rents and subject to such conditions as she shall see fit, all or any of my said real estate; to give notice to quit to any tenant or occupier thereof; and to receive and recover from all tenants and occupiers thereof or of any part thereof all rents, arrears

of rent, and sums of money which now are or shall hereafter become due and payable in respect thereof; and also on nonpayment thereof or of any part thereof to take all necessary or proper means and proceedings for determining the tenancy or occupation of such tenants or occupiers, and for ejecting the tenants or occupiers and recovering the possession thereof.

7. To commence, prosecute, discontinue, or defend all actions or other legal proceedings pertaining to me or my estate or any part thereof (to disclaim any part or all of any power or interest in any property to which I or my estate may be entitled); to settle, compromise, or submit to arbitration any debt, demands, or other right or matter due me or concerning my estate as she, in her sole discretion, shall deem best and for such purpose to execute and deliver such releases, discharges, or other instruments as she may deem necessary and advisable; and to satisfy mortgages, including the execution of a good and sufficient release, or other discharge of such mortgage.

8. To execute, acknowledge, and file all federal, state, and local returns of every kind and nature including, without limitation, income, gift, and property tax returns.

9. To engage, employ, and dismiss any agents, clerks, servants, or other persons as she, in her sole discretion, may deem necessary and advisable.

10. To make gifts for and on my behalf to any donees including my said attorney, in such amounts as my said attorney may decide, to create a trust for my benefit, to make additions to an existing trust for my benefit, and

to withdraw and receive the income or corpus of any trust over which I have the power to make withdrawals.

11. To authorize my admission to a medical, nursing, residential, or similar facility and to enter into agreements for my care, and to authorize medical and surgical procedures for me.

12. To nominate any person or institution, including my said attorney, as guardian of my estate or of my person, for consideration by the Court if incompetency proceedings for my estate or person are hereafter commenced.

13. In general, to do all other acts, deeds, and matters whatsoever in or about my estate, property, and affairs as fully and effectually to all intents and purposes as I could do in my own proper person if personally present, giving to my said attorney power to make and substitute under her an attorney or attorneys for all the purposes herein described, hereby ratifying and confirming all that the said attorney or substitute or substitutes shall do therein by virtue of these presents.

14. In addition to the powers and discretions herein specifically given and conferred upon my attorney, and notwithstanding any usage or custom to the contrary, to have the full power, right, and authority to do, perform, and cause to be done and performed, all such acts, deeds, and matters in connection with my property and estate as she, in her sole discretion, shall deem reasonable, necessary, and proper, as fully, effectually, and absolutely as if she were the absolute owner thereof.

15. In the event of my disability or incompetency, from whatever cause, this power of attorney shall not thereby be revoked.

IN WITNESS WHEREOF, I have hereunto set my hand and seal this ____ day of _____ , 19 .

_____
STANLEY JONES

COMMONWEALTH OF PENNSYLVANIA)
_____) SS:
COUNTY OF MONTGOMERY)

Before me, the undersigned, a notary public in and for the Commonwealth of Pennsylvania, personally appeared STANLEY JONES, known to me to be the person whose name is subscribed to the within instrument, and acknowledged that he executed the same for the purposes therein contained.

IN WITNESS WHEREOF, I have hereunto set my hand and official seal this ____ day of _____ , 19 .

_____

LIVING WILL*

DECLARATION MADE THIS _____ DAY OF _____
I,_____ being of sound mind, willfully and voluntarily make known my desire that my dying shall not be artificially prolonged under the circumstances set forth below, do hereby declare:

If at any time I should have an incurable injury, disease, or illness certified to be a terminal condition by two physicians who have personally examined me, one of whom shall

*Also called a Health Care Declaration.
Source: Tools and Techniques of Estate Planning, eleventh ed. National Underwriter Co., Cincinnati, OH 45203 (1-800-543-0874

be my attending physician, and the physicians have determined that my death will occur whether or not life-sustaining procedures are utilized and when application of life-sustaining procedures would serve only to artificially prolong the dying process, I direct that such procedures be withheld or withdrawn and that I be permitted to die naturally with only the administration of medication or the performance of any medical procedures deemed necessary to provide me with comfort care.

In the absence of my ability to give directions regarding the use of such life-sustaining procedures, it is my intention that this declaration shall be honored by my family and physicians as the final expression of my legal right to refuse medical or surgical treatment and accept the consequences from such refusal.

I understand the full import of this declaration and I am emotionally and mentally competent to make this decision.

Signed _____

City, County, State of Residence

_____

The declarant has been personally known to me and I believe him or her to be of sound mind.

Witness _____

Witness _____

INVENTORY AFTER PROBATE

Will No. 481, 1998

REGISTER OF WILLS

INVENTORY

COMMONWEALTH OF PENNSYLVANIA	)
————————————————————	) SS:
COUNTY OF MONTGOMERY	)

JAMES JOHNSON, Executor

of the Estate of WALTER HARRIS, Deceased, being duly sworn according to law, deposes and says that the items appearing in the following inventory include all of the personal assets wherever situate and all of the real estate in the Commonwealth of Pennsylvania of said decedent, that the valuation placed opposite each item of said inventory represents its fair value as of the date of the decedent's death, and that decedent owned no real estate outside of the Commonwealth of Pennsylvania except that which appears in a memorandum at the end of this inventory.

Sworn to and subscribed before me
this 20th day of January, 1998 ————————————————

JAMES JOHNSON, EXECUTOR

ATTORNEY Name   Samuel Smith, Esquire
            Address 7885 Main Street, Norristown, PA 19401

Date of Death	Last Residence	Decedent's Social Security No.
10/28/97	8800 DeKalb Pike Norristown, PA 19401	168–05–4190

1. Real Estate: Premises known as 8800 DeKalb Pike, Norristown, PA 19401. Acquired 6/28/71, Sylvia Lewis to Walter Harris, widower, by deed in Volume 496, Page 267, Recorder of Deeds of Montgomery County, Pennsylvania $ 58,000.00

2. Household furnishings and personal effects at 8800 DeKalb Pike, Norristown, Pennsylvania   3,525.00

3. 1987 Plymouth Horizon   4,000.00

4. Coins—2 U.S. Proof Sets—1984 at $16.25   32.50

5. The Long Life Assurance Society of the U.S., dividend   28.40

6. JFK Industries, Inc., Hourly Pension Trust, period ending 7/31/97   50.12

7. Continental Casualty Co., refund insurance premium on homeowner's policy   40.85

8. Insurance Company of North America, refund of partial premium and cancellation of homeowner's policy   161.22

9. The Norristown Saving Fund Society, Norristown, PA, Savings Account No. 648,281
    balance 10/28/97   10,024.88

10. Fourth Pennsylvania Bank
    Savings Account No. 85–684–3
    balance 10/28/97   1,240.12

Checking Account No. 0841–6214
    balance 10/28/97   425.02

11. Monumental Bank & Trust Co.
    340 shares capital stock at 13$^{3/4}$ 4,675.00
    10/1/97 dividends   77.50
    10/1/97 proceeds from fractional share
        of stock   12.87

12. Morris-Lynch Ready Assets Trust, No.
    487–631–8, balance   <u>22,781.64</u>
    TOTAL $105,075.12

EXECUTOR'S LETTER AND INFORMATION FORM

1924 Old Sage Road
Philadelphia, PA 19100
December 20, 1998

The Philadelphia Bank & Trust Company
1400 Market Street
Philadelphia, PA 19100

Re: Estate of Edward Anderson
    Account Nos. 47651 and 525–314

Dear Sir/Madam:

I am the Executor of the Estate of the late Edward
Anderson, who died on December 10, 1997, and I am
enclosing a short certificate issued by the Register of Wills of
Philadelphia evidencing my appointment as Executor.

The late Mr. Anderson had the above listed accounts
with your bank. Would you therefore please send me written

confirmation of the above and also written confirmation of every asset of the decedent in your institution and every liability owed by the decedent to your institution. Please include in your letter reference to all accounts, including IRAs, business accounts, and all loans or mortgages of the decedent, and the following information, regardless of whether these accounts were in his name alone, or in joint names with other persons:

1. The date-of-death balance in each account, including interest stated to the date of death.

2. The date on which each account was first opened.

3. The exact name or names in which each account is titled on your records. If a change has been made since the account was first established, please include the date that the title of the account was changed.

Would you also advise if Mr. Anderson had, at the date of his death, or ever had, a safe-deposit box at The Philadelphia Bank.

I appreciate the inconvenience of this request, and therefore a form is enclosed to assist you in furnishing this information. If you prefer to use the form, it should be signed by someone on behalf of the bank.

Your cooperation in this matter is sincerely appreciated.

Very truly yours,

JAMES JEFFERSON
Executor of the Estate
of Edward Anderson

Estate of Edward Anderson, Deceased
Date of Death: December 10, 1997

Account #47651

1. Type of account: _____

2. Date opened: _____

3. Titled
   (if changed after opening, date of change): _____

4. Balance as of 12/10/97: $ _____
   Accrued interest to 12/10/97: $ _____

   TOTAL DATE-OF-DEATH VALUE: $ _____

5. Beneficiaries _____
   _____

Account #525–314

1. Type of account: _____

2. Date opened: _____

3. Titled
   (if changed after opening, date of change): _____

4. Balance as of 12/10/97: $ _____
   Accrued interest to 12/10/97: $ _____

   TOTAL DATE-OF-DEATH VALUE: $ _____

5. Beneficiaries: _____
   _____

Safe-deposit box: Yes   No   (Please circle)

   Single title: _____

   Joint title: _____

   THE PHILADELPHIA BANK & TRUST COMPANY

   BY: _____

CHECKLIST TO AVOID FEDERAL ESTATE-TAX AUDIT

General Errors

___ Was the gross estate $600,000 in 1997 [increasing in steps to $1 million in 2006] or less at the date of death? If so, only two of the 17 schedules in IRS Form 706 need to be filed. Did you file the proper schedules?

___ Are all required signatures on the 706?

___ Are all questions answered?

___ Has a *certified* copy of the will (and other required documents) been attached?

___ Does the return take into account prior taxable gifts? (Check gift-tax returns back to 1976.)

___ Did you properly compute the credit for state death taxes? (Be sure to subtract $60,000 from the taxable estate before applying the rates.)

___ Should you request an extension of time to file the return or pay the tax? (This must be done before the return is due.)

Schedule A—Real Estate

___ Was the appraiser qualified and did he list the factors considered in determining value? (List the appraiser's credentials.) The appraiser should discuss:

(a) size of plot	(e) comparable sales, if any
(b) improvements	(f) assessed value
(c) replacement value	(g) actual or potential value
(d) zoning requirements	

___ Was mortgage erroneously deducted from fair-market value of real estate? (See Instruction to Form 706.)

Schedule A-1—Section 2032A "Special Use" Valuation and Section 2033A Business Interest Exclusion

___ Have you filed the appropriate statements? An executor must submit: (1) a notice that special-use valuation of farm or business real estate or exclusion of business interest to extent allowable is desired, and (2) an agreement to the terms of the election signed by all parties who have any interest in the property.

Schedule B—Stocks and Bonds

___ Is stock accurately described (e.g., was common stock described erroneously as preferred)? (Copy description directly from stock certificate.)

___ Were there dividends payable on stock owned by the decedent that are not listed? (Have the decedent's stock-broker confirm this information.)

___ Did you include data to support the valuation you placed on closely held or unlisted stock? (Balance sheets and profit-and-loss statements for the five years preceding death must be attached to the Form 706.)

___ Have you attached to Form 706 any buy/sell agreement affecting closely held stock?

Schedule C—Mortgages, Notes, and Cash

___ Did you fail to list interest on a bank account because it was not credited in the decedent's bankbook? (Obtain and attach written confirmation from bank officer regarding the date-of-death balance and earned interest.)

___ Did you submit data to support the true value of the decedent's interest in a promissory note or mortgage?

Schedule D—Insurance on the Decedent's Life

____ Did you file a Form 712 (Life Insurance Statement) for each policy listed on the return? (This form will be provided free by the insurer upon request of the personal representative. It must be filed even for small estates when Schedule D itself doesn't have to be filed.)

____ Was there a policy on the decedent's life that was not listed? (Include proof that the insured had no incidents of ownership. For example, include copy of the absolute assignment [gift or sale] form or a letter from the insurer.)

Schedule E—Jointly Owned Property

____ Have you reported the form of ownership correctly? (Was the property owned only by husband and wife? Did you submit documents proving the amount or percentage of the surviving tenant's contribution to the purchase price of the asset?)

Schedule F—Other Miscellaneous Property

____ Did you include any state or federal income-tax refunds in the list of assets?

____ Did you submit documents to substantiate a contention that a particular asset should not be included in the gross estate? (For example, certain employer-generated post-death payments to survivors are not includable in the decedent-employee's gross estate.)

Schedule G—Transfers During Decedent's Life

____ Did you include gift taxes paid on gifts made within three years of death? (Examine the last three years' gift-tax returns and separate gift taxes paid on gifts more than three years prior to death from taxes on gifts made within three years of death.)

Schedule H—Powers of Appointment

___ Did you submit a certified copy of any trusts, etc., if you included (or excluded) property subject to a general (or special) power of appointment? You must submit the certified copy even if you feel the property subject to the power is not includable.

Schedule I—Annuities

___ Did you include copies of any annuity contract or a letter from the trustee or insurance company supporting the exclusion of all or a portion of the annuity from the estate tax?

Schedule J—Funeral Expenses and Expenses Incurred in Administering Property Subject to Claims

___ Did you claim an amount of executor's commissions for federal purposes that exceeds the amount that is allowable under state law?

Schedule K—Debts of the Decedent, and Mortgages and Liens

___ Did you enclose photocopies of canceled checks to show payment of debt or documents to show existence and amount of loan(s)?

Schedule L—Net Losses During Administration and Expenses Incurred in Administering Property Not Subject to Claims

___ Have you listed expenses incurred with respect to the transfer of title to life insurance or jointly held real estate?

Schedule M—Bequests, etc., to Surviving Spouse

___ Can ostensibly nonqualified terminable interests be made into QTIP (qualified terminable interest property)? An executor can now elect to qualify property that might otherwise not qualify for the federal marital deduction.

Schedule O—Charitable, Public, and Similar Gifts and Bequests

___ Have you filed a statement—with respect to any charitable gifts for which deductions are claimed—that no suits have been filed or action contemplated that could affect the charitable deduction?

Schedule P—Credit for Foreign Death Taxes

___ Have you attached Form 706CE to support a claim for a credit for death taxes paid to that foreign country? Form 706CE must be attached even for estates of $600,000 (in 1997, increasing in steps to $1 million in 2006) and under, when Schedule P is not required.

Schedule Q—Credit for Tax on Prior Transfers

___ Have you checked your computations?

___ Have you overlooked a tax paid by someone who died within the last 10 years and left property to the present decedent? (Even certain life estates may qualify for the credit, although it technically isn't in the present decedent's estate. Have the estate's attorney check Rev. Rul. 59-9, 1959-1C.B.232.)

___ If you are filing under the "small estate" rules, have you filed a Schedule Q?

Schedule R—Generation-Skipping Transfer Tax

___ Have you completed Schedule A-1 of Form 706?

___ Have you ascertained who the "skip" persons are?

___ Have you determined which skip persons received interests in property?

___ Have you fully utilized and properly allocated the decedent's GST exemption?

___ Did the skip person receive special-use (Section 2032A) property? If so, you may be able to allocate more GST exemption than the direct skip amount.

___ Did you attach a schedule listing all GST transfers and the amount of exemption allocated to each such transfer?

FEDERAL ESTATE-TAX ASSET/DEDUCTION FINDER

Where to List an Asset

Schedule A

Crops
House(s) in sole name of
   decedent
Mineral rights
Oil royalties
Real property in decedent's name
Accrued rents

Schedule A-1

Farm and closely held business
   real property valued at its
   "special-use" value

Schedule B

Bonds
Uncashed bond coupons
Debentures
Stock dividends
Mutual funds
Stocks
Warrants

Schedule C

Bank accounts in sole name of
   decedent
Cash
Checking accounts in sole name
   of decedent
Uncashed checks
Accrued interest
Mortgages (owed to decedent)
Promissory notes owed to
   decedent
Savings accounts in decedent's
   name

Schedule D

Life insurance on decedent's life

Schedule E

Checking accounts owned jointly
House(s) owned jointly

Schedule F

Accounts receivable
Art
Automobiles
Coin collections
Copyrights
Death benefits other than life
   insurance
Equipment
Guns
Household goods
Inventions
Inventories
Leasehold interests
Livestock
Notes receivable
Options
Partnership interests
Patents
Personal property
Refunds
Royalties
Stamp collections
Trademarks

Schedule G

Gifts
Property in trust
Property transferred

Schedule H

Power of appointment
Property interests

Schedule I

Annuities
Pensions

Where to Take a Deduction

Item	Schedule				
	J	K	L	M	O
Abstract fee	X				
Accountant's fee	X				
Ambulance cost		X			
Appraiser's fee	X				
Attorney's fee	X				
Burial expenses	X				
Casualty losses			X		
Charge accounts		X			
Charitable deductions					X
Court costs	X				
Debt of decedent		X			
Doctors' bills		X			
Executor's fee	X				
Filing costs	X				
Flowers for funeral	X				
Funeral expenses	X				
Charitable gifts					X
Hospital bills		X			
Illness, expenses of		X			
Insurance	X				
Leases, unexpired		X			
Loans		X			
Marital deduction				X	
Medical expenses		X			
Mortgages		X			
Notes payable		X			
Personal property taxes		X			
Publication costs	X				

Item	Schedule				
	J	K	L	M	O
Real estate taxes		X			
Repairs	X				
Taxes (unpaid income)		X			
Telephone bills	X	X			
Thefts			X		
Transfer fees	X				
Travel, executor's	X				
Utility bills	X	X			

APPROVAL OF ACCOUNT, RELEASE AND INDEMNIFICATION

RE: ESTATE OF STANLEY JONES, DECEASED

The undersigned is a beneficiary under the Will of Stanley Jones and desires that the Estate be distributed without the formality of a court accounting.

In consideration of the Executrix making distribution without a court accounting, and agreeing to be legally bound hereby, the undersigned does hereby:

1. Waive the filing of an account of the administration of the Estate in any court;

2. Declare that the undersigned has examined the attached informal account of the Executrix, finds it to be true and correct in all particulars; accept and approve it with the same force and effect as if it had been prepared and filed with, audited, adjudicated, and confirmed absolutely by a court of competent jurisdiction;

3. Warrant that the beneficiaries named in the informal account are the sole parties in interest in the Estate and entitled to receive the entire distribution thereof in accordance with the said account, and that the undersigned knows of no outstanding and unsatisfied claims against the Estate;

4. Release and discharge the Executrix, and her heirs and personal representatives, from any and all actions, liabilities, claims, and demands relating in any way to the administration of the Estate and distribution in accordance with the attached accounting;

5. Agree to refund to the Executrix any portion of the distribution of the undersigned which exceeds the amount of the undersigned's share as the Executrix finally determines;

6. Agree to indemnify and hold harmless the Executrix, and her heirs, personal representatives, successors and assigns, from and against any claims or liabilities arising from any cause whatsoever, which the Executrix may incur as a result of the administration of the Estate and its distribution in accordance with this release and indemnification agreement.

IN WITNESS WHEREOF, I have hereunto set my hand and seal this 4th day of January, 1998.

Witnesses:

_____

_____   _____

                                          BARBARA BROWN
                                          Social Security #

(Affidavit Optional)

STATEMENT REGARDING ANATOMICAL GIFTS

I, _____ of _____, _____
make the following statement regarding anatomical gifts
which I have checked and initialed:

SPECIFIC GIFTS

ENTIRE BODY

❏ I give my entire body, for purposes of anatomical study, to
_____.
If, for any reason, _____ does not accept this
gift, I give my body to _____, for purposes of
anatomical study.

GIFTS TO INDIVIDUALS

❏ I give my _____ to _____ if needed
             (part or parts)
by him or her for purposes of transplantation or therapy.
❏ I give my _____ to _____ , if needed
             (part or parts)
by him or her for purposes of transplantation or therapy.

GIFTS TO INSTITUTIONS AND PHYSICIANS

❏ I give my _____ to _____,
         (part or parts)   (name of hospital, bank, storage facility,
                           or physician)
for purposes of research, advancement of science, therapy,
or transplantation.
❏ I give my _____ to_____,
         (part or parts)   (name of hospital, bank, storage
                        facility, or physician)
for purposes of research, advancement of science, therapy,
or transplantation.

PROSTHETIC DEVICES

❏ I give my _____ to _____ for critical
      (type of prosthetic device)   (name of hospital)
evaluation, study, and research.

INTENTION

❏ If any anatomical gift cannot be effectuated because of the donee's nonexistence, inability, or unwillingness to accept it, I request that one of the authorized persons make anatomical donations in a manner consistent with my desires expressed in this statement.

❏ I express my desire not to make anatomical gifts under any circumstances. It is my wish that no part be used for transplantation, therapy, study, or research. I request that my personal representative and next of kin respect my wishes.

THIS STATEMENT INCORPORATES ALL OF THE PROVISIONS ON THE REVERSE OF IT.

Signed this _____ day of _____ , 19 _____ ,

at _____

_____   _____
        Witness   Witness

PRIORITY OF DONATION

A gift of any part to an individual recipient for therapy or transplantation shall take precedence over a gift of that part to any other donee.

INSTRUCTIONS

If I have made any written instructions regarding the burial, cremation, or other disposition of my body, I direct that any donee take possession of my body subject to those instructions, if that donee has actual knowledge of those instructions. If there is any conflict between the statements made in this document and any of those instructions, my wishes regarding anatomical gifts shall be given preference over my instructions regarding the disposition of my body.

COUNTERPARTS

I may be signing more than one statement regarding anatomical gifts. I intend that only signed documents be effective and that no person shall give any effect to any photocopy or other reproduction of a signed document.

DEFINITIONS

The terms "bank or storage facility," "hospital," "part," and "physician" have the same meaning which the Uniform Anatomical Gifts Act accords to them. The term "authorized persons" means the persons authorized to make donations under the Uniform Anatomical Gifts Act in the order or priority provided in that Act.

WARNING

This form is designed to be used with the advice of an attorney. It has been drafted in accordance with the provisions of the Uniform Anatomical Gifts Act. Because the law regarding anatomical gifts may vary in each state, attorneys advising on use of this form should be familiar with the law of the relevant jurisdiction.

Note: This form has been adapted from that of the Real Property, Probate and Trust Law Section of the American Bar Association.

TRUSTEE'S CHECKLIST*

Assembling the Assets

___ File claim for life insurance benefits for which the trust is the beneficiary (obtain Form 712 from each insurance company):
Consider mode of payment.

___ File claim for any pension or profit-sharing benefits from the employer, and for any other work-related benefits payable to the trust:
Consider mode of payment.

___ File Notice of Fiduciary Relationship (Form 56) with IRS. (If the trust does not have a tax identification number, file Form SS-4.)

___ Write to banks for date-of-death value of any trust bank accounts.

___ Analyze and review securities with emphasis on preserving trust assets, and value securities owned by the trust as of the date of death.

___ Obtain appraisal of any real and personal property owned by the trust.

___ Obtain last three years of fiduciary income-tax returns and last three years of canceled checks of the trust.

___ Review all accountings and distributions that have taken place for the last five years (or since the trust was established, if these records are available).

*See *The New Book of Trusts. Trusts After TRA '97* (610-527-5216).

Payment of Taxes, Debts, and Expenses

___ Prepay state inheritance taxes to obtain a discount if available. Check state law to determine if it's permissible and advantageous, and if so, the applicable deadlines.

___ File personal property tax returns, due February 15 of each year of trust.

___ File U.S. Fiduciary Income-Tax Return (IRS Form 1041) and state income-tax returns, due April 15 of each year.

___ Review and coordinate with executor the information necessary to prepare and file the state inheritance-tax return and the federal estate tax. Make certain that items on the Executor's Checklist not the sole responsibility of the trustee are being handled correctly.

___ Obtain alternate-valuation-date values for federal estate-tax return.

___ Consider election of extension of time to pay U.S. estate tax (Section 6161 or 6166), filed on or before due date of U.S. estate-tax returns, including extensions.

___ Consider election to defer payment of inheritance tax on remainder interests; where permitted, determine deadline for election.

___ Consider election for special valuation of farm or business real estate owned by the trust under IRC Section 2032A or election for exclusion of business interest under IRC Section 2033A; must be made with timely filed U.S. estate-tax return.

___ Elect (or determine not to elect) to qualify certain terminable interest property (QTIP) for marital deduction.

___ Elect (or determine not to elect) QDT (qualified domestic trust) treatment if spouse is not a U.S. citizen.

___ Maximize GSTT (generation-skipping transfer tax) exemptions by making election or redistributing trust assets.

Distribution

___ Prepare an accounting of receipts and disbursements.

___ Notify state attorney general if charitable gifts are involved. (Earlier notice may be required; check local requirements.)

___ File accounting in court after proper notices to beneficiaries, *or*

___ If informal distribution, give accounting to beneficiaries and obtain receipt and release from them.

___ Transfer assets in accordance with distribution as indicated in trust.

___ Establish and fund additional trusts if required.

TRUST RECEIPT AND RELEASE

Re: Trust of Stanley Jones

BARBARA BROWN, the undersigned beneficiary of the Trust of Stanley Jones, acknowledges receipt of a distribution in the amount of Twenty-Five Thousand Five Hundred Forty Dollars ($25,540.00) and does hereby:

1. Accept and approve the attached accounting of receipts and disbursements for the Trust with the same force and effect as if it had been duly filed and audited in the Probate Court and had been adjudicated and confirmed absolutely.

2. Agree that if any just and proper claim is hereafter presented to the Trustee of the Trust, to be responsible for her pro rata share of the same, up to the amount of her distribution.

3. Release Sally Smith, Trustee of the Trust of Stanley Jones, of and from any and all claims she has under the law against the said Trust, or the said Sally Smith in her capacity as Trustee.

4. Declare that this instrument shall be legally binding upon her and upon her heirs and personal representatives.

IN WITNESS WHEREOF, I have hereunto set my hand and seal this _____ day of _____ , _____.

Witnesses:

_____

_____   _____
                                         BARBARA BROWN
                                         Social Security #

(Affidavit Optional)

IRS FORMS THAT MAY BE USEFUL IN PLANNING OR ADMINISTERING ESTATES OR TRUSTS*

Form	Title
GPO 3565	Order Blank for Federal Tax Forms and Publications
SS-5	Application for a Social Security Card
W-9	Request for Taxpayer Identification Number and Certification
231	Power of Attorney by Individual for the Collection of Checks Drawn on the United States Treasury
706	United States Estate (and Generation-Skipping Transfer) Tax Return
706-A	United States Additional Estate Tax Return
706CE	Certificate of Payment of Foreign Death Tax
706GS(D)	Generation-Skipping Transfer Tax Return for Distributions
706GS(D1)	Notification of Distribution from a Generation-Skipping Trust
706GS(T)	Generation-Skipping Transfer Tax for Terminations
706NA	United States Estate (and Generation-Skipping Transfer) Tax Return (for nonresident aliens)

*Courtesy *The New Book of Trusts: Trusts After TRA '97*, Leimberg Associates Books, Inc., Bryn Mawr, Pa 19010 (610-527-5216).

Form	Title
709	United States Gift (and Generation-Skipping Transfer) Tax Return
709-A	United States Short Form Gift Tax Return
712	Life Insurance Statement
1040	United States Individual Income Tax Return
1040C	United States Departing Alien Income Tax Return
1041	United States Fiduciary Income Tax Return
2848	Power of Attorney and Declaration of Representative
4421	Declaration—Executor's Commissions and Attorney's Fees
4506	Request for Copy of Tax Form
4768	Application for Extension of Time to File United States Estate (and Generation-Skipping Transfer) Tax(es)
4808	Computation of Credit for Gift Tax
4810	Request for Prompt Assessment Under Internal Revenue Code Section 6501(d)
4972	Tax on Lump-Sum Distributions
5803	Explanation of Tax Return Preparer Penalty Charges

Form	Title
6123	Verification of Fiduciary's Federal Tax Deposit
6166	Certification of Filing a Tax Return
7990	United States Estate Tax Certificate of Discharge from Personal Liability
7990-A	United States Gift Tax Certificate of Discharge from Personal Liability

DEATH TAXES POST TRA '97: HOW MUCH WILL YOUR ESTATE PAY?*

Taxable	1997	1998	1999	2000	2001	2002	2003	2004	2005	2006
$625,000	$9,250	$0	$0	$0	$0	$0	$0	$0	$0	$0
$650,000	$18,500	$9,250	$0	$0	$0	$0	$0	$0	$0	$0
$675,000	$27,750	$18,500	$9,250	$0	$0	$0	$0	$0	$0	$0
$700,000	$37,000	$27,750	$18,500	$9,250	$9,250	$0	$0	$0	$0	$0
$850,000	$94,500	$85,250	$76,000	$66,750	$66,750	$57,500	$57,500	$0	$0	$0
$950,000	$133,500	$124,250	$115,000	$105,750	$105,750	$96,500	$96,500	$39,000	$0	$0
$1,000,000	$153,000	$143,750	$134,500	$125,250	$125,250	$116,000	$116,000	$58,500	$19,500	$0
$2,000,000	$588,000	$578,750	$569,500	$560,250	$560,250	$551,000	$551,000	$493,500	$454,500	$435,000
$5,000,000	$2,198,000	$2,188,750	$2,179,500	$2,170,250	$2,170,250	$2,161,000	$2,161,000	$2,103,500	$2,064,500	$2,045,000
10,000,000	4,948,000	4,938,750	4,929,250	4,920,500	$4,920,250	4,911,000	4,911,000	4,853,500	4,814,500	4,795,000
20,000,000	10,948,000	10,938,750	10,929,500	10,929,250	$10,920,250	10,911,000	10,911,000	10,853,500	10,814,500	10,795,000
50,000,000	27,500,000	27,500,000	27,500,000	27,500,000	27,500,000	27,500,000	$27,500.00	27,500,000	27,500,000	27,500,000

Courtesy: NumberCruncher Estate Planning Software (610-527-5216). Figures include both federal and state death tax.

Warning: Actual cash-need tax total will exceed these amounts in some states. A number of states impose taxes significantly higher than the federal state death tax credit amount assumed! These numbers include only death taxes and do not include debts or administrative costs.

Glossary

Accidental death benefits. The accidental death, or "double indemnity," feature of a life insurance policy provides a larger benefit, often twice the face amount of the policy, if death occurs by accidental means. Insurance policies should be reviewed for this feature when death occurs from other than natural causes.

Accounting. The preparation of financial statements that will give the court, the beneficiaries, and everyone involved in the estate a clear picture of the property in the estate available for distribution, and a history of the transactions dating back to the time the personal representative first took control of the property.

Ademption. The extinction or withdrawal of a legacy by disposing of property or otherwise preventing a beneficiary from receiving a bequest under a will.

Adjudication. The court's formal approval of the estate's accounting and distribution.

Administration. The management of the estate of a deceased person. It includes collecting the assets, paying the debts and taxes, and making distribution to the persons entitled to the decedent's property.

Administrator (*m*); **Administratrix** (*f*). The person appointed to manage an estate if the decedent had no valid will or if the will did not provide for an executor or executrix.

Advancement. Money or property given by a parent to a child or other heir (depending on the state law), or expended by the former for the latter's benefit, by way of anticipation of the share the child will inherit in the parent's estate and intended to be deducted therefrom.

After-born child. A child born after the execution of a parent's will.

Alternate value date. For federal estate-tax purposes, the value of the gross estate six months after the date of death, unless property is distributed, sold, exchanged, or otherwise disposed of within six months. In that case the value of such property is determined as of the date of disposition.

Annual exclusion. For federal gift-tax purposes, an exclusion of $10,000 (indexed annually for inflation after 1998) is allowed the donor each year, provided the gift is a "present interest" in property (the donee must be given the unfettered, ascertainable, and immediate right to use, possession, or enjoyment of the property interest).

Attestation clause. The paragraph at the end of a will indicating by certain persons' signatures that they have heard the testator (testatrix) declare the instrument to be his will and have witnessed the signing of the will.

Audit. The proceeding at which the court approves the executor's account and gives anyone with objections to the account the opportunity to be heard. Tax audits by federal and state authorities are adversarial, with the government attempting to raise the largest tax possible and the taxpayer trying to pay the least allowed by law.

Beneficiary. The person who inherits a share or part of the decedent's estate; one who receives a beneficial interest under a trust or insurance policy.

Bequest. A gift of property by will. *A specific bequest* is a gift of specified property ("my watch" or "automobile"). *A general bequest* is one that may be satisfied from the general assets of the estate ("I give $100 to my brother, Sam"). If the specific bequest (the watch) was sold before the decedent died, the gift will fail.

Buy/sell agreement. Also called business agreement. An arrangement for the disposition of a business interest in the event of the owner's death, disability, or retirement or on the owner's withdrawal from the business at some earlier time. Business purchase agreements take various forms: (1) an agreement between the business itself and the individual owners (a stock redemption agreement); (2) an agreement between the individual owners (cross-purchase agreement); and (3) an agreement between the individual owners and a key person, family member, or outside individual (a third-party business-buyout agreement).

Charitable remainder annuity trust. A trust that permits payment of a fixed amount annually to a noncharitable beneficiary, with the remainder going to charity.

Charitable remainder trust. An irrevocable trust that pays income to one or more noncharitable beneficiaries for a period of years or for life, then pays the remainder over to a designated charity. This trust can take the form of an annuity trust or a unitrust.

Charitable remainder unitrust. A trust designed to permit payment of a variable annuity (i.e., a fixed percentage of the trust's assets as revalued year by year) to a noncharitable beneficiary, with the remainder going to charity.

Codicil. A supplement to an existing will to effect some revision, change, or modification. A codicil must meet the same requirements regarding execution and validity as a will.

Collateral relations. Used primarily in the law of intestacy to designate uncles and aunts, cousins, etc.—relatives not in a direct ascending or descending line, like grandparents or grandchildren, who are designated as lineal relatives.

Common disaster. An accident that results in the death of both the decedent and the intended beneficiary.

Community property. Property acquired during marriage in which both husband and wife have an undivided one-half interest. Not more than half can be disposed of by the will. In some community-property states, the husband can control and dispose of community property during marriage. There are currently eight community-property states: Arizona, California, Idaho, Louisiana, Nevada, New Mexico, Texas, and Washington.

Contingent interest. A future interest in real or personal property that depends on the fulfillment of a stated condition that may never come into existence.

Contingent remainder. A future interest in property dependent on the fulfillment of a stated condition before the termination of a prior estate. For example, a husband leaves property to a bank in trust to pay the income to his wife during her lifetime. After her death the trustee is to transfer the property to the decedent's son if the son is then living—otherwise, it goes to his daughter. The son has a contingent remainder interest—contingent upon his outliving his mother. The daughter has a contingent remainder interest, which she will receive only if the son does not outlive the mother.

Corpus. The principal or trust estate, as distinguished from the income. When we speak of the corpus of a trust, we are talking about the assets in the trust.

Credit estate tax. A tax imposed by a state to take full advantage of the amount allowed as a credit against the federal estate tax.

Curtesy. At common law, the estate by which a man was entitled to a life estate in all lands owned by his wife during marriage, provided lawful issue was born of the union. As with dower, modern-day statutes have in many cases repealed, replaced, or modified common-law curtesy.

Decedent. The person who died (whether man or woman).

Descent. The passing of real estate to the heirs of one who dies without a will.

Devise. A gift of real estate under a will, as distinguished from a gift of personal property.

Devisee. The person to whom lands or other real property are devised or given by will.

Disclaimer. The refusal to accept property that has been devised or bequeathed—a renunciation by the beneficiary of her right to receive the property in question.

Distribution. The passing of personal property to the heirs of one who dies without a will. Also, the formal act of the personal representative disposing of the estate's assets to the designated beneficiaries.

Domicile. An individual's permanent home. The place to which, regardless of where he is living, an individual intends to return.

Donee. The person who receives a gift. Also, one who is the recipient of the power of appointment from another person.

Donor. One who makes a gift. Also, a person who gives a power of appointment to another person.

Dower. The right the law gives a woman to her deceased husband's real estate.

Escheat. In the absence of lawful heirs, and subject to the claims of creditors, the property of a person dying intestate is said to escheat—that is, to "return" to the state.

Estate planning council. In almost every major county of the country there is an estate planning council. This is a professional group consisting of attorneys, CPAs, CLUs and ChFCs, trust officers, and others who specialize in estate planning and administration. An estate planning council is an excellent source for obtaining names of competent advisers, and a directory of members can usually be found in the local phone book.

Estate tax. A tax imposed on the right of a person to transfer property at death. The tax is imposed not only by the federal government but also by various states.

Executor (*m*); **Executrix** (*f*). The person named by the deceased in her will to manage the decedent's affairs; the personal representative of the decedent who stands in the shoes of the decedent, collects the assets of the estate, pays the debts and taxes, and makes distribution of the remaining property to the beneficiaries or heirs.

Fair-market value. The value at which estate property is included in the gross estate for federal estate-tax purposes; the price at which property would change hands between a willing buyer and a willing seller, neither being under compulsion to buy or sell and both having knowledge of the relevant facts.

Family exemption laws. Laws giving surviving family members of a decedent's household specific exemptions from state death taxes.

Federal estate tax. An excise tax levied on the right to transfer property at death, imposed on and measured by the value of the estate left by the deceased.

Fiduciary. One occupying a position of trust. Executors, administrators, trustees, and guardians all stand in a fiduciary relationship to persons whose affairs they are handling.

Generation-skipping transfer tax (GSTT). A flat-rate 55 percent tax imposed in addition to the federal gift or estate tax on transfers to "skip persons" (essentially transfers to grandchildren). The GST tax may be imposed on direct skips (such as when a grandparent writes a check to a grandchild) or when property passes from one generation to another in less obvious ways by trust or otherwise.

Gift tax. A tax imposed on the lifetime gratuitous transfer of property. In addition to the federal gift tax, some states also impose a tax on transfers during lifetime.

Gift-tax exclusion. For federal gift-tax purposes, anyone, married or single, can give up to $10,000 (indexed annually for inflation after 1998) in cash or other property each year to any number of persons (whether or not they are related to the donor) with no gift-tax liability. The exclusion is doubled to $20,000 in the case of a married donor whose spouse consents to "splitting" the gift.

Grace period. A provision in life insurance policies that gives the insured additional time (usually 30 days) in which to pay the premium without losing the benefits of the policy.

Grantor. A person who creates a trust; also called a settlor, creator, donor, or trustor.

Gross estate. An amount determined by totaling the value of all property in which the decedent had an interest, the inclusion of which in the estate is required by the Internal Revenue Code for federal estate-tax purposes.

Guardian. There are two classes of guardians: (1) *A guardian of the person* is appointed by the surviving spouse in her will to take care of the personal affairs of the couple's minor children. Since each parent is the natural guardian of the minor children, only the surviving parent can name the guardian of the person. (2) *A guardian of the property* of a minor or incompetent is a person or institution appointed or named to represent the interests of a minor child or incompetent adult. A guardian of the property can be named in a will or be appointed by a court.

Guardian *ad litem*. A lawyer or other qualified individual appointed by the court to represent the interests of minors or incompetents in a particular matter before the court.

Heir. A person designated by law to succeed to the estate of a person who dies intestate (without a will).

Holographic will. A will entirely in the handwriting of the testator. In many states such a will is not recognized unless it is published, declared, and witnessed as required by statute for other written wills.

Homestead exemption laws. Laws passed in many states allowing the head of a family to designate a house and land as his homestead to exempt it from debts and taxes.

Incompetent. An individual who legally has been found incapable of managing her own affairs.

Incontestable clause. A provision in life insurance policies that prevents the insurance company from denying a claim because of any error, concealment, or misstatement after the contestable period has expired (usually two years).

Inheritance tax. A tax levied on the rights of the heirs to receive property from a deceased person, measured by the share passing to each beneficiary (sometimes called a *succession tax*). The federal death tax is an estate (as opposed to an inheritance) tax. Some states have estate taxes, but most have inheritance taxes.

Installment payments of estate tax under Section 6166. Section 6166 of the Internal Revenue Code provides for the payment of federal estate tax in installments in certain cases in which the deceased had an interest in a closely held business that represented a considerable part of his estate. Under present law, to receive special tax treatment under 6166, the value of the business interest must make up more than 35 percent of the adjusted gross estate.

Insurance trust. A trust composed partly or wholly of life insurance policy contracts.

Intangible property. Property that does not have physical substance. The item itself is only the evidence of value (for example, a certificate of stock or bond, an insurance policy).

Inter vivos **trust.** A trust created during the grantor's lifetime and operative during lifetime, as opposed to a trust under a will, called a *testamentary trust*, which does not go into effect until after the grantor dies.

Intestacy laws. Individual state laws that provide for distribution of property of a person who has died without leaving a valid will.

Intestate. Without a will. A person who dies without a valid will dies intestate.

Inventory. A schedule of all the assets of an estate, to be prepared by the personal representative.

Irrevocable trust. A trust that cannot be revoked or terminated by the grantor. To qualify the trust as irrevocable for tax purposes, the grantor cannot retain any right to alter, amend, revoke, or terminate. The trust can be revoked or terminated by the grantor only with the consent of someone who has an adverse interest in the trust.

Issue. All persons descending from a common ancestor.

Joint tenancy. The holding of property by two persons in such a way that, on the death of either, the property goes to the survivor. If the persons are husband and wife, then the property is said to be held *by the entireties*. This is contrasted to tenancy in common, in which each owner has an undivided interest that upon the death of one is passed by probate.

Joint will. A single instrument that is made the will of two or more persons and is jointly signed by them. This type of will is not recommended.

Lapse. The failure of a testamentary gift due to the death of the recipient during the life of the testator (the person who made the will).

Legacy. Technically, a gift of personal property by will, but in practice including any disposition by will.

Legatee. A person to whom a legacy is given.

Letters of administration. A written document issued by the probate court authorizing the administrator to act on behalf of the estate of a person who died intestate (i.e., without a valid will).

Letters testamentary. A written document issued by the probate court authorizing the executor (person or entity) named in a decedent's will to act on behalf of the estate.

Lien. An encumbrance on property for the payment of a debt.

Life estate. The title of the interest owned by a life tenant; a person whose interest in property terminates at her death.

Life tenant. The person who receives the income from a legal life estate or from a trust fund during his own life. This right terminates at death.

Liquid assets. Cash or assets that can be converted readily into cash without any serious loss (bank accounts, life insurance proceeds, government bonds).

Literary executor. A term sometimes used in the will of an author to authorize a person to assemble unpublished works of the deceased and to try to have published those works the literary executor thinks appropriate, discarding the remainder. Technically, a person designated as literary executor is probably more like the possessor or donee of a power of appointment, and as such should be subordinate to the executor of the estate in any matters not connected directly with the literary material.

Living will. A written expression of an individual's desire that no extraordinary means be employed to prolong her life. Living wills are legal in some states. In other states, whereas the living will itself has no legal effect, it can help physicians by making them aware of a patient's wishes.

Marital deduction. For federal estate-tax purposes, the portion of a decedent's estate that may be passed to the surviving spouse without its becoming subject to the federal estate tax levied against the decedent's estate. Under present federal estate-tax law, the marital deduction is unlimited, provided that the property passes to the surviving spouse in a qualified manner.

Marital deduction trust. A trust set up to take advantage of the marital-deduction provisions of the federal estate tax. It can take the form of a *QTIP trust* or a general *power of appointment* trust. The trust property that passes outside the marital trust is in a "nonmarital" or residual trust. Typically, the beneficiaries of the nonmarital trust are the children of the spouse setting up the trust. Assets in the marital trust are taxed when the surviving spouse dies, while assets in the nonmarital trust are not in the surviving spouse's estate and therefore are not taxed when the spouse dies.

"Ministerial" acts. Acts of an executor or administrator that do not involve major decisions requiring judgment and discretion and whose performance may be delegated to others.

Minor. A person who is under the legal age of majority, which can vary from age 18 to 21, depending on the state law.

Mutual wills. The separate wills of two or more persons, with reciprocal provisions in each will in favor of the other person(s).

Nonliquid assets. Assets that are not readily convertible into cash for at least nine months without a serious loss (such as real estate and business interests).

Nonprobate property. Property that passes outside the

administration of the estate, other than by will or intestacy laws (for example, jointly held property, pension proceeds, and life insurance proceeds paid to a named beneficiary, or property in an *inter vivos* trust).

Nuncupative will. An oral will, declared by the testator in his last illness before a sufficient number of witnesses, and afterward reduced to writing.

Per capita. Equally to each individual. In distribution per capita, the takers share equally without a right of representation. For example, each of five sons would take one-fifth of the estate. In most states, if descendants are related in equal degree to the decedent, they take *per capita*; if descendants are of unequal degree (such as four sons and a child of a deceased son), a *per stirpes* distribution is made.

Per stirpes. "By stock." A distribution *per stirpes* occurs when issue succeed to the shares of their lineal ascendants by representation. For example, if a person dies survived by three children and by two children of a deceased child (the decedent's grandchildren), distribution is per stirpes. The two grandchildren succeed to their deceased parent's share, so that one-quarter of the estate goes to each of the surviving children, and one-eighth to each of the two grandchildren.

Posthumous child. A child born after the death of the father.

Pourover. The transfer of property from an estate or trust to another estate or trust upon the occurrence of an event specified in the instrument. For example, a will can provide that certain property be paid (poured over) to an existing trust. This is called a *pourover will*.

Power of appointment. A right given to a person to dispose of property that she does not fully own. There are two types of powers of appointment. A *general power of appointment* is a power over the distribution of property exercisable in favor of any person the donee of the power may select—including himself, his estate, his creditors, or the creditors of his estate. A *limited power of appointment* is sometimes called a special power. An example of a limited power is giving the donee of the power the right to distribute the property at her death to any of her sister's children that he designates.

Power of attorney. A written document that enables an individual, or "principal," to designate another person or persons as his "attorney in fact"—that is, to act on the principal's behalf. The scope of the power can be severely limited or quite broad. (A "durable power" is one that survives the mental or physical incapacity of the creator of the power.)

Present interest. A present right to use or enjoy property.

Pretermitted heir. A child or other descendant omitted from a testator's will. When a testator fails to make provisions for a child, either living at execution of the will or born thereafter, statutes often provide that such child, or the issue of a deceased child, take an intestate share of the testator's estate.

Principal. The property making up the estate or fund that has been set aside in trust, or from which income has been expected to accrue. The trust principal is also known as the *trust corpus* or *res*.

Probate. The process of proving the validity of the will and executing its provisions under the guidance of the appropriate public official. The title of the official varies from state to state. Wills are probated in the Register of Wills office and in the Probate or Surrogate Court. When a person dies, the will must be filed before the proper officer; this is called *filing the will for probate*. When it has been filed and accepted, it is said to be *admitted to probate*. The process of probating the will involves recognition by the court of the executor named in the will (or appointment of an administrator if none has been named).

Probate property. Property that can be passed under the terms of the will or (if no will) under the intestacy laws of the state. Also, property held in the individual name of the decedent or in which the decedent had a divisible interest.

Prudent man theory. The theory according to which the

duty of an executor is to invest in such assets as an ordinary, prudent man of intelligence and integrity would purchase in the exercise of reasonable care, judgment, and diligence under the circumstances existing at the time of purchase.

Publication. A declaration by the testator to the witnesses that the instrument is her will.

QDT (qualified domestic trust). A trust that can defer the federal estate tax when the surviving spouse is not a U.S. citizen.

QTIP trust (qualified terminable interest property trust). A trust that can qualify for the marital deduction under current tax laws, even though under the trust a spouse is given the income of the trust for life. Assets at death pass to the beneficiaries named by the spouse who set up the trust. Under prior law, only a trust in which the spouse had a general power of appointment over the trust property would have qualified for the marital deduction. This type of trust is called a general power of appointment trust.

Receipt and release. Informal method of settling estates. The executor gives the beneficiaries an informal accounting and obtains a "receipt" from the beneficiaries for their share of the estate and a "release" discharging the executor from any further liability.

Reinstatement. A privilege contained in life insurance policies that enables the insured to reinstate the policy when it has lapsed for nonpayment.

Remainderman. The person(s) or entity(ies) entitled to receive property (usually in trust) after the termination of the prior holder's interest. For example, a mother might set up a trust that pays her income for life, but at her death the principal in the trust would pass to her son (the remainderman).

Renunciation. An unqualified refusal to accept property or an interest in property. It is the abandonment of a right without the direct transfer to someone else of the interest subject to that right.

Residuary estate. The remaining part of the decedent's estate after payment of debts and bequests. Wills usually contain a clause disposing of the residue of the estate that the decedent has not otherwise bequeathed or devised.

Reversionary interest. A right to future enjoyment by the transferor of property that is now in the possession or enjoyment of another party. For example, a son creates a trust under which his father is going to enjoy the income for life, with the principal of the trust to be paid over to the son at his father's death. The son's interest is the reversionary interest.

Revocable trust. A trust that can be changed or terminated during the grantor's lifetime and under which the property in the trust can be recovered.

Rule against perpetuities. A rule of law invalidating interests in property that will vest in the recipient too far in the future, or by which the devisee is restricted in disposing of the property for an inordinate length of time. The common-law rule, which has been changed in many states, holds that "no interest in property is valid unless it must vest, if at all, within a life or lives in being plus twenty-one years."

Rule against unreasonable accumulation of income. A state law that imposes restrictions on trusts or other devices to prevent the withholding of the present enjoyment of income from the life tenant to the enchancement of the trust estate.

Section 303 redemption. Section 303 of the Internal Revenue Code establishes a way for a corporation to make a distribution in redemption of a portion of the stock of a decedent that will not be taxed as a dividend. A Section 303 partial redemption can provide cash and/or other property from the corporation without resulting in dividend treatment; it provides cash for the decedent, shareholders, or executor to use to pay death taxes and other expenses.

Shrinkage. The reduction in the amount of property that passes at death caused by loss of capital and income resulting from the sale of assets to pay death costs.

Sole ownership. The holding of a property by one person in such a manner that upon death it passes either by the terms of the will or (if no will) according to the intestacy law.

Sprinkling or spray trust. A trust under which the trustee is given discretionary power to distribute any part or all of the income among beneficiaries in equal or unequal shares, and authority to accumulate any income not distributed.

Surcharge. The amount awarded by court and payable by an executor, administrator, or trustee who has negligently performed his duty and who has caused a beneficiary any loss due to that negligence.

Tangible property. Property that has physical substance—may be touched, seen, or felt—and itself has value (such as a house, car, or furniture).

Taxable estate. An amount determined by subtracting the allowable deductions from the gross estate.

Tenancy by the entireties. The holding of property by husband and wife in such a manner that, except with the consent of the other, neither party has a disposable interest in the property during the lifetime of the other. Upon the death of either, the property is owned solely by the survivor.

Tenancy in common. The holding of property by two or more persons in such a manner that each has an undivided interest, which, upon the death of one, is passed by probate. It does not pass to the surviving tenant in common.

Testamentary. By will. A testamentary document is an instrument disposing of property at death, being either a will in fact or in the nature of a will.

Testamentary trust. A trust of certain property passing under a will and created by the terms of the will.

Testate. Having left a will or disposed of by will.

Testator. A person who leaves a will in force at death.

Trust. A fiduciary arrangement whereby the legal title of the property is held, and the property managed, by a person or institution for the benefit of another.

Trustee. The holder of legal title to property for the use or benefit of another.

Trustee *ad litem*. Usually an attorney appointed to represent the interest of unascertained persons in a particular matter before the court.

Unfunded insurance trust. An insurance trust that is not provided with cash or securities to pay the life insurance premiums. Such premiums are paid by someone other than the trustee.

Uniform Anatomical Gift Act (UAGA). A broadly adopted law that enables the donation of body parts for the use of science, education, or individuals needing particular organs.

Uniform Gifts to Minors Act (UGMA). A broadly adopted law that enables gifts to be made to minors without the need to create a trust. The law states that an adult, while alive, can make a gift of certain types of property such as securities, money, or a life insurance or annuity contract to a minor by having it registered in the name of the minor or delivering it to an adult person as custodian for the property placed in the minor's account. The fundamental difference between the account and a trust is that legally the child is the owner of the property even though it is held in a UGMA account in his name, whereas in a trust, the legal owner of the property is the trustee (although the trustee must use trust property exclusively for the trust's beneficiaries).

Uniform Transfers to Minors Act (UTMA). This act is similar to the UGMA in purpose but allows any kind of property, real or personal, tangible or intangible, to be the subject of a custodial gift. Most states have replaced their UGMA laws with this much broader and more flexible statute.

Unified credit (for federal gift-tax and estate-tax purposes). A dollar-for-dollar reduction against the federal estate and gift tax. The unified credit was $192,800 as of 1997 and protected an estate of $600,000. The $600,000 applicable exclusion is $625,000 for persons dying and gifts made in 1998, $650,000 in 1999, $675,000 in 2000 and 2001, $700,000 in 2002 and 2003, $850,000 in 2004, $950,000 in 2005, and $1 million in 2006 and later years.

Usufruct. The right to the enjoyment of property owned by another, provided the substance of the property is not changed.

Vested interest. An immediate fixed interest in real or personal property, although the right to possession and enjoyment may be postponed until some future date or until the happening of some event. For example, if a husband leaves real property and securities to a trustee in trust to pay the income to his wife during her lifetime and at her death to transfer the property to his son and his heirs, the wife has a present vested life interest in the right to the income, and the son has a future vested interest in the right to property. If contributions are made to a pension or profit-sharing plan, and the property regardless of any event is going to the employee, then the employee has a vested interest in that property.

Will. Technically, in law, the expression of what you want to happen to your property when you die. Formal requirements vary by states, but usually, at a minimum, a will must be in writing and signed at the end. Requirements for witnesses vary according to states.

Index